South Asian Crisis:
India, Pakistan
and Bangla Desh

Robert Jackson
Fellow of All Souls College
Oxford University

Published for the International
Institute for Strategic Studies

The Praeger Special Studies program—utilizing the most modern and efficient book production techniques and a selective worldwide distribution network—makes available to the academic, government, and business communities significant, timely research in U.S. and international economic, social, and political development.

South Asian Crisis: India, Pakistan and Bangla Desh

A Political and Historical Analysis of the 1971 War

PRAEGER SPECIAL STUDIES IN INTERNATIONAL POLITICS AND GOVERNMENT

Praeger Publishers New York Washington London

Library of Congress Cataloging in Publication Data
Jackson, Robert Victor.
  South Asian crisis.
  (Praeger special studies in international politics and government)
  Bibliography: p.
  1. India-Pakistan Conflict, 1971– 2. South Asia—Politics and government. I. International Institute for Strategic Studies. II. Title.
  DS388.J3   1974   954.9'205   74-8921
  ISBN 0-275-09560-6

PRAEGER PUBLISHERS
111 Fourth Avenue, New York, N.Y. 10003, U.S.A.
5, Cromwell Place, London SW7 2JL, England

Published in the United States of America in 1975
by Praeger Publishers, Inc.

All rights reserved

© 1975 by The International Institute for
Strategic Studies

Printed in Great Britain

CONTENTS

Preface	page	7

Chapter
1 The Division in Pakistan — 9
2 March–June: Action and Reaction — 33
3 July–August: the Indo–Soviet Treaty — 55
4 September–November: the Approach of War — 75
5 December: 'The Fourteen Days' War' — 106
6 Conclusion — 146
Bibliography — 162
Appendixes — 166
 (see list overleaf)
Index — 234

APPENDIXES

		page
1	The Awami League's Six Points	166
2	President Yahya Khan's Broadcast of 26 March 1971	168
3	Resolution of the Indian Parliament, 31 March 1971	171
4	President Nikolai Podgorny's Letter to President Yahya Khan of 2 April 1971	172
5	Mr Chou En-lai's Letter to President Yahya Khan of 13 April 1971	173
6	President Yahya Khan's Broadcast of 28 June 1971	174
7	U Thant's Memorandum to the President of the Security Council, 19 July 1971	184
8	The Indo–Soviet Treaty of Peace, Friendship and Co-operation, 9 August 1971	188
9	Joint Statement by Mr Andrei Gromyko and Mr Swaran Singh in New Delhi, 12 August 1971	192
10	Joint Statement on the Occasion of Mrs Indira Gandhi's Visit to Moscow, 29 September 1971	194
11	President Yahya Khan's Broadcast of 12 October 1971	199
12	Mr Chi Peng-fei's Statement of 7 November 1971	205
13	Dr Henry Kissinger's Press Briefing of 7 December 1971 and Ambassador Kenneth Keating's Comments	207
14	Minutes of the Washington Special Action Group Meetings of December 1971 and Mr Jack Anderson's Article of 10 January 1972	212
15	Diplomatic Cables showing American Attitudes to India as revealed by Mr Jack Anderson, 12 January 1972	232
16	The Instrument of Surrender of Pakistan Eastern Command, 16 December 1971	233

MAPS

| 1 | The Eastern Front | 109–10 |
| 2 | The Western Front | 117–18 |

PREFACE

THIS book is, of course, primarily intended to tell the story of a nine-month episode in the recent history of South Asia. As such it must inevitably have a restricted interest. On the other hand, the events about which I have written coincided with a major shift in the structure of world politics—a reconstruction which both influenced and was in turn influenced by the events described in this book. Whatever wider interest this study may have must lie in what it tells us about this crucial passage in the international politics of our time; and perhaps also in the view which is implicit throughout, that we cannot understand the problems of modern politics without a firm grasp of their historical dimension.

The final chapter, misleadingly called *Conclusion,* is an attempt both to interpret and to summarize the story told in the preceding narrative chapters. Some readers may prefer to read it first, or to read it alone, or not to read it at all.

I would like to thank the Nuffield Foundation for making me a grant to visit India, Pakistan and Bangladesh in March–April 1972; and to thank François Duchêne and the International Institute for Strategic Studies for inviting me to undertake the work and for tolerating its growth beyond the limits which we originally contemplated. Sir Penderel Moon, Peter Lyon, Neville Maxwell and Kenneth Hunt very kindly read the manuscript at an early stage. I am grateful to them, and also to my colleagues of *The Round Table,* who kindled my interest in this subject—especially Sir Olaf Caroe, Michael Howard and Alastair Buchan.

Many people in Britain and in the sub-continent were very helpful to me in my enquiries, most of them in confidence. I should like to thank them all: I hope that each will find in the text a fair reflection of his point of view.

I wish to dedicate this book to the Warden and Fellows of All Souls College, as a first token of my gratitude for what the College has given me—among many other things, the opportunity to undertake this study.

I must also thank Miss Patricia Kerr and Miss Janet Bowling, who turned a wilderness into a typescript, and the publishers, who have turned a typescript into an attractive book.

ROBERT JACKSON

All Souls
1 May 1974

Chapter 1

The Division in Pakistan

THE state of Pakistan that came into existence in 1947 was the expression of a particular historical experience—that of the Indian Muslims. Its disintegration in 1971 was also a product of that experience. Elsewhere in India Islam remained a conqueror's religion. But in the delta lands of eastern Bengal, where Brahminical Hindu culture had never struck deep root, the native inhabitants were peacefully converted to the faith of their Muslim rulers during the first three centuries after the Afghan–Turkish conquerors entered Bengal at the beginning of the thirteenth century. This popular conversion to Islam under a Muslim aristocracy whose origins and affinities lay outside Bengal established the necessary condition of the Muslim civil war in Pakistan in 1971, out of which has now emerged the new state of Bangladesh.[1]

At the end of the period of peaceful religious transformation between the thirteenth and the fifteenth centuries, the Muslim sultanate of Bengal was absorbed during the sixteenth century into the newly established north Indian Mughal empire. Its non-Bengali Muslim rulers were drawn into the ascendant Mughal culture, based on the synthesis of Arabic and Persian influences out of which had sprung the Urdu language. The division already fixed within Muslim Bengal was then consolidated into a division between a native Bengali peasantry, whose version of the Islamic faith was steeped in their local traditions, and a Persianized, Urdu-speaking ruling class which owed its primary allegiance to the wider world of Muslim north India. The higher Bengali culture which had been developing since the tenth century became a mainly Hindu possession, alienated from the Persian civilization of the Muslim ascendancy which in the twentieth century was to provide the cultural basis for the nationality of Pakistan.

In 1764 the English East India Company succeeded the Mughals in the government of Bengal. With the introduction of British

---

[1] S. S. Pirzada (ed.) *The Foundations of Pakistan*; Kamruddin Ahmad, *A Social History of Bengal*. For publication details, see the Bibliography on pp. 162–5.

commerce and administration a social revolution began in Bengal. The Company's rule raised up the Hindu commercial classes at the expense of the local branch of the established Muslim aristocracy; and Cornwallis's Permanent Settlement of 1793 confirmed the reduction of many of the Muslim landowners to the condition of tenants of the Hindu *zamindars*. A renaissance of Bengali culture under Hindu patronage was evoked by the opportunities provided by English rule and by the challenges of English civilization. Although the new Hindu *élites* aroused the antagonism both of the dispossessed Muslim rulers and of the rack-rented peasantry—Muslim and Hindu alike— the culture they were developing was the common inheritance of all Bengalis. And among those who were becoming conscious of this inheritance in the nineteenth century was the emerging native Bengali Muslim middle class, many of whose leaders were educated together with the leaders of Hindu Bengal at the secular University of Calcutta, which was established in 1857.

The social, cultural, and political consequences of British rule continued throughout the nineteenth century to undermine the position of the north Indian Urdu-speaking Muslim ascendancy. Their earliest reaction after the failure of the Mutiny was to establish Urdu-based Islamic institutions of higher education which could provide an alternative to the new Hindu-dominated secular institutions being set up by the British. Out of this Muslim educational movement grew a political movement, inspired by the fear expressed by Sir Syed Ahmed Khan in 1888 that, with the growth of representative institutions, 'the government of the whole country will be in the hands of Bengalis, or other Hindus like Bengalis, and the Muslims will be in a miserable position'.[2] At Dacca in December 1906 the All-India Mohammedan Education Conference established the first modern All-India political movement among the Indian Muslims, calling it the All-India Muslim League.

The native Bengali Muslims had no voice in the establishment of the Muslim League, although one of its original objects was the defence of the 1906 partition of Bengal. This act was an element in Curzon's policy of building up the conservative Muslim upper class as a counterweight to the growing strength of the Hindu nationalists; and in Bengal the chief representative of the Urdu-speaking Muslim *élite* was Nawab Salimullah of Dacca, whose seat was made the capital of the new eastern province. He was the moving spirit behind the establishment of the Muslim League, which he hoped would

[2] Pirzada, vol. 1, p. xxv. Note Sir Syed's failure to observe that the majority of Bengalis were Muslims.

strengthen his position in Bengal. But the partition was fiercely opposed by the Hindus, and, despite the efforts of the Muslim conservatives in 1911, the British government bowed to the Bengali opposition and revoked it. However, the boundaries of the restored province of Bengal were so drawn as to provide a Muslim majority within the new province. With the extension of the franchise and the powers of the representative institutions in Bengal in 1919 and 1935 the Bengali Muslim middle class, whose existence had been ignored by Sir Syed, gained access to power over the whole of the province.

But the tradition upon which the All-India Muslim League drew pointed to separation from Hinduism. The fears out of which the League originated were genuine enough. As India advanced in self-government a separate communal consciousness was increasingly articulated among the Indian Muslims, especially among those who lived in provinces where the Muslims were in a minority. The concept of a sovereign Muslim Indian state of Pakistan did not develop until the 1930s; but already in that decade the development of Muslim nationalism in India gave rise to a tension between the enjoyment of the new representative institutions in Muslim majority provinces, such as Bengal, and the requirements of a Muslim national policy for all the Indian Muslims.

Among the Muslims of Bengal the lines along which this tension worked itself out emerged from the cultural division between the Bengali and non-Bengali Muslims, and the new and corresponding social division between the emerging Bengali middle class and the old Muslim upper class of the province. In the 1937 provincial election there were two Muslim parties in Bengal. A. K. Fazlul Haq's radical, Bengali *Krishak Praja Samiti*—peasants' and tenants' party—represented the most recent line of Bengali Muslim development. The other was represented by the less radical Muslim League—a branch of the All-India League—led by Sir Kwajha Nazimuddin, nephew of Nawab Salimullah, and by the Urdu-speaking barrister H. S. Suhrawardy. After the election, from 1937 until 1941, Bengal was ruled by a Muslim coalition ministry headed by Fazlul Haq, who endorsed the Muslim League's emerging All-India policy in return for its support for his provincial government.[3] In the spirit of this arrangement it was Fazlul Haq who proposed the 'Pakistan resolution' at the March 1940 Lahore session of the League. For all its carefully

---

[3] See K. A. Kamal, *Politicians and Inside Stories: An Intimate Study mainly of Fazlul Haq, Suhrawardy, and Maulana Bashani.*

designed ambiguity, this resolution led to the eventual adoption of Pakistan as the objective of the Muslim League.[4]

After 1939, however, the Second World War and the initiation of the Congress 'Quit India' campaign gave a new urgency to the overriding question of the future of India as a whole. The political focus moved from the provinces to the centre, and the conditions under which the Bengali Muslim coalition had been founded were transformed. Fazlul Haq would not accept the subordination of the policy of his provincial government which was required by Mohammed Ali Jinnah and his colleagues in the leadership of the All-India Muslim League. He was driven to reject Jinnah's policy of co-ordinating and controlling the activities of elected Muslim provincial governments from the All-India Muslim League centre. In December 1941 he was expelled from the League; but he remained provincial Chief Minister until 1943, with the support of a coalition including representatives of the Hindu commercial and land-owning classes.

In the following year Bengal became a war zone, and during 1943 rural society in the province was shaken to its foundations by the great famine in which some two million people died. Adversity heightened the political atmosphere, and the Muslim League, which had gone into opposition to Fazlul Haq in Bengal in 1941, acquired a mass following for the first time. Two years later, in the November 1945 elections, the League captured the Muslim vote everywhere in India; and in the Bengal provincial elections in March 1946 it took 96 per cent of the Muslim seats. With this overwhelming assertion of what was held to be a distinct national consciousness among the Indian Muslims the tensions between national and provincial loyalties were resolved for the time being in favour of the former. The possibility of the revival of such a conflict—which, as we have seen, had already

---

[4] By the Lahore resolution the Muslim League was committed to the principle that 'geographically contiguous units are demarcated into regions which should be so constituted, with such territorial adjustments as may be necessary, that the areas in which the Muslims are numerically in a majority, as in the North-Western and Eastern Zones of India, should be grouped to constitute "Independent States" in which the constituent units shall be autonomous and sovereign'. In 1941 the resolution was amended to the effect that 'the areas in which the Musalmans are numerically in a majority, as in the North-Western and Eastern Zones of India shall be grouped *together* to constitute Independent States as Muslim Free National Homelands in which the constituent units shall be autonomous and sovereign'. There was no mention of 'Pakistan', perhaps because the coinage did not include a reference to Bengal. P stood for Punjab, A for the Afghan province, K for Kashmir, S for Sind and Tan for Baluchistan. See Pirzada, vol. 2, pp. xxii–xxv.

THE DIVISION IN PAKISTAN

appeared as a political factor in 1937 and 1941—disappeared from view in the excitement of victory.

The idea of Pakistan was conceived as an expression of the religious and cultural nationality of the Muslims in India. But, somewhat contradictorily, in the independence negotiations the League attempted to keep its grip on the undivided whole of those provinces where the Muslim population enjoyed a majority—including Bengal. Accordingly, in April 1946 H. S. Suhrawardy played the part performed by Fazlul Haq in 1940. At the Delhi convention of Muslim League legislators, he moved the key resolution demanding a sovereign state of Pakistan comprising Bengal and Assam in the north-east, and the Punjab, North-West Frontier Province, Sind and Baluchistan in the north-west. Only after the failure of the British Cabinet Mission in July 1946 was it finally clear that the creation of a sovereign Pakistan entailed the partition of the historic provinces of Bengal and the Punjab; and by then it was too late to find a basis for the continued unity of Bengal. Calcutta saw the worst of the communal riots which occurred throughout India in August 1946. Suhrawardy and some of the more radical Bengali leaders, both Hindu and Muslim, attempted in vain to find an alternative to the division of the province in the last weeks before the partition was finally decided upon. At the last minute a number of proposals were formulated and discussed for the creation of a sovereign and united Bengal outside both Pakistan and India.[5] But the Congress leaders feared, with reason, that this might be a device to take the whole of Bengal, including Calcutta, into Pakistan; and they were also not prepared to support the aspirations for independence of some radical Hindu Bengali politicians. On 20 June 1947 the members of the provincial Legislative Assembly met together, as provided in the Mountbatten plan which had been announced on 3 June; and the Muslim vote in favour of the entry of a united Bengal into Pakistan was nullified by the Hindu vote in favour of partition. On 14 August 1947 Pakistan came into existence, divided into two parts, separated by a thousand miles of Indian territory. Incorporated in each part was a fragment of a historic province of British India.

It might be said that in 1947 the Hindus of Bengal chose to revoke the revocation of Curzon's partition. Under Muslim provincial government since 1937 they had experienced the consequences of the

[5] H. V. Hodson, *The Great Divide: Britain, India, Pakistan*; Kamruddin Ahmad, pp. 75-86.

existence of a Muslim majority in the population of the undivided province. As for the bourgeois Bengali Muslim politicians of the era of provincial self-government, the renewed division of Bengal led to their temporary eclipse and the restoration of a regime in the same tradition as that which had prevailed in East Bengal in 1906–11. Inside Pakistan the government of East Bengal was inherited by the heirs of the Urdu-speaking Muslim north Indian ascendancy, which in 1947 established itself principally in the western provinces of Pakistan, and which provided the traditions upon which the new state was founded. While Suhrawardy and Fazlul Haq disappeared for a time from public life, the dominant figure in East Bengal politics in the period immediately after independence was Sir Kwajha Nazimuddin, the nephew of the architect of the original Muslim League and the principal beneficiary of the 1906 partition.

But despite its ancient social and cultural superiority among the Muslims of Bengal, under modern conditions the position of the traditional *élite* in Muslim East Bengal could only be maintained with support from the Urdu-speakers who ruled in West Pakistan. Though for two decades Urdu culture and Muslim orthodoxy provided a focus in East Bengal for the idea of Pakistan—reinforced by the Bihari Muslim refugees who came into East Pakistan after Partition—the Urdu-speaking *élite* lacked the capacity to submerge within a wider Islamic loyalty to Pakistan the sense of Bengali identity which had grown up since the nineteenth century.

The pressure of population increase and the process of land reform—including the departure of most of the Hindu *zamindars* of East Bengal after 1947—worked to produce a society in which the average size of land-holding was much smaller and the power of landowners much more fragmented than in West Pakistan. There was consequently a profound difference in social structure and political culture between Bengal and the society of the western provinces, over which a combination of feudalism and plutocracy presided.[6] In the Bengali world of peasants, professional men and traders, the most important social force was not the old Urdu-speaking Muslim upper class, but the Bengali-speaking Muslim middle class—whose political leaders had undergone their formative experiences in the parliamentary government of the former undivided province of Bengal. Alongside their commitment to Islam they possessed a deep loyalty to their Bengali culture, and they were schooled in parliamen-

---

[6] R. S. Wheeler, *The Politics of Pakistan*, pp. 39–41, 64. See also E. Tipper, 'Pakistan in Retrospect', and K. B. Sayeed, 'The Breakdown of Pakistan's Political System', in *International Journal*, Summer 1972.

tary traditions and the practice of the rule of law. In every way except their common faith the attitudes of the East Bengalis differed from those of their fellow-Pakistanis in the western provinces.

These political and social differences between the two parts of Pakistan were underpinned by the facts of geography. The two wings differed greatly in size and density of population—the West Wing being six times as large as the East Wing, while the population of East Pakistan at the time of the 1961 census was 50·8 million as against 42·9 million in the West. Its location on the western seaboard of the sub-continent made West Pakistan a part of the semi-desert world of the Near East, while East Pakistan was climatically and ecologically linked with Burma and the monsoon lands of South-East Asia. By air Baghdad and the oilfields of the Persian Gulf are closer to Karachi than Dacca; and from Dacca, Singapore and Ceylon are closer by air than Karachi. Because of Indo–Pakistani hostilities or suspicions after 1947 it was virtually impossible to maintain land connection between the two wings, and communication had to be by air or by sea—along routes several times longer than the distance by air. Inside West Pakistan, road and rail were the principal means of transport across the plains and into the high mountains of the north. On the other hand, in East Pakistan a great deal of the traffic moved by river craft through a flat watery landscape divided by countless streams and rivers, spanned here and there by the road and rail bridges erected by British engineers. These differences of climate and geography reinforced the differences in mentality and political culture between the two wings and during the quarter-century of East Bengal's history as a component of Pakistan the divergences between the two parts of the country steadily ripened among the Bengalis into a sense of economic subjection, confirming the tendencies to division which we have seen to be latent in the history of Muslim Bengal. As we shall see, these tendencies initially emerged during the constitutional debates which went on in Pakistan between 1947 and 1956. But after the military take-over in 1958 the problem of finding an acceptable framework for Pakistani unity grew into the further problem of dealing with the sense of 'internal colonialism' which the Bengalis increasingly experienced in their relationship with Pakistan.

Although these economic and social issues came to be of crucial importance, we must pay particular attention to the constitutional problem, because it largely determined the lines along which the split eventually developed in 1971. As soon as the bloodshed and confusion of Pakistan's birth had been overcome, the search began for a constitution which would reconcile the different elements in the new state. From the British Raj there came two legacies. One of these was the tradition of strong central government under the Viceroy. This system was enshrined in the parts of the 1919 and 1935 Government of India Acts under which Pakistan continued to be ruled for the time being. The other legacy was the Parliamentary democratic tradition for which the 1935 Act had provided in the provinces of British India—of which Bengal had been politically one of the most advanced. To the problem of reconciling the conflict of these two constitutional inheritances from the immediate past was added that of defining for the new state of Pakistan the contemporary meaning of the Islamic conceptions upon which the theory of Two Nations, Muslim and Hindu, had been erected.

The Islamic question was not merely a problem in political philosophy. It lay at the heart of the debate about the constitutional relationship between the two parts of Pakistan.[7] Although East Bengal had the majority of the population within Pakistan, one-fifth of its people were non-Muslims, and there were more Muslims in the western provinces of Pakistan than in the East. After the Simla agreement of 1905, between the Viceroy's government and the founders of the Muslim League, representative institutions in India under the British Raj had been built around the principle that there should be separate electorates for the members of the main religious communities. But if Pakistan were to continue to sustain the tradition of Islamic exclusiveness in this way, with the East Bengal Hindus being placed on a separate electoral roll, the Bengalis would be deprived of what they conceived to be a natural Bengali majority within the new state. If, on the other hand, Pakistan were to be based on non-communalist principles, a single electorate would need to be set up, and the Bengalis would enjoy the fruits of a permanent majority—which they would owe to their Hindu fellow-countrymen. Consequently for both parts of the new country the Islamic question was from the beginning irretrievably involved with the problems of regional nationalism and the balance of political power between the different social and cultural communities within the state.

To resolve this dilemma the concept of parity of representation between the two wings was eventually worked out to meet West Pakistan's fears of Bengali predominance.[8] This concept, which was embodied in the 1956 constitution, implied the recognition that within the nation of the Indian Muslims there were at least two further communities which must be accorded equal status. There was

[7] Wheeler, pp. 92–106.
[8] Wheeler, pp. 109–116.

another implication : to bring the two parts of Pakistan into parity it was necessary to weld into one unit the three governor's provinces, most of the ten princely states and the one chief commissioner's province which had been taken from British India into what was now called the West Wing of Pakistan. This solution provided a dominant position for the Punjabi majority in the West Wing—for it was they who formed the majority in the unit into which the different communities in West Pakistan were merged to bring about the necessary equipollence between the two wings.

However, this settlement took nearly a decade to devise, and it was never properly applied. During the early 1950s, while protracted debates and negotiations went on in the Constituent Assembly which had been set up in 1947, the sense of the Bengali identity of Muslim Bengal rapidly reasserted itself in East Pakistan. After 1949 the Muslim League in the East decayed. The politicians of the provincial era came out of retirement and rebuilt their organizations with the support of a new generation—among which one of the most notable figures was the General Secretary of H. S. Suhrawardy's Awami League, Sheikh Mujib-ur Rahman.[9] Decisive in the development of Bengali nationalism within Pakistan were the language riots of 1952, which followed Sir Kwajha Nazimuddin's public endorsement of Jinnah's view that Urdu should be the sole state language of Pakistan. Two years later in the provincial elections in East Bengal the Muslim League was swept away by a United Front of the Bengali parties, which brought together Fazlul Haq and H. S. Suhrawardy, the veterans of the 1937 Bengal provincial legislature.

Thus the landmarks of pre-war provincial Bengal began to re-emerge out of the receding Muslim League of 1940–47. In 1954 Pakistan was still without a constitution of her own devising. Nevertheless, the central government in the West responded successfully to the situation created by the provincial elections of 1954, by pursuing much the same policy as that which Yahya Khan attempted with less success in similar circumstances sixteen years later. After the provincial election had taken place in Bengal in March 1954 a split was encouraged within the Bengali United Front Party, and Fazlul Haq was installed as provincial prime minister. Shortly afterwards he visited Calcutta, where he made an emotional speech about the unity of Bengal. The reserve powers of the centre were immediately employed to dismiss the provincial cabinet and impose Governor's rule. The final act of this first major constitutional crisis in Pakistan was the dismissal of the all-Pakistan Constituent Assembly, which had

[9] See K. A. Kamal, *Sheikh Mujibur Rahman and Birth of Bangladesh.*

sat since 1947, and the formation of a 'cabinet of talents' which brought together the representatives of the various leading sections of opinion, under the threat of the imposition of military rule by the army. A commission of experts was then set up to prepare the constitution, which had been delayed seven years in the Constituent Assembly.

Under the chairmanship of H. S. Suhrawardy as Minister of Law, it was this commission which prepared the 1956 constitution on the basis of the concepts of 'parity' and 'one unit'. In spite of what had happened since 1947 these arrangements were able to command the support of most political leaders in East Bengal; and Suhrawardy's principal lieutenant, Sheikh Mujib, stood by him against his opponents within the Awami League and supported him when the radical peasants' leader Maulana Bashani split off to the left in 1957 to form his National Awami Party.[10]

But elections were never held under the 1956 arrangements. After 1956 the intrigues at the centre in Karachi became still more intense. In October 1958 President Iskander Mirza took power and abrogated the constitution. He was promptly deposed by the commander-in-chief, General Ayub Khan, who imposed martial law.[11] Army rule had come at last. Because the politicians had been unable to establish a device for transferring to the people of Pakistan the sovereignty once enjoyed by the King-Emperor in Parliament, that power now devolved upon the strongest force within the state. In 1962 Ayub Khan promulgated a new constitution which proclaimed that sovereignty belonged to Allah, and which created a new basis for Pakistan setting aside the principle of popular sovereignty. In Ayub's 1962 constitution effective electoral power was settled upon an equal number of notabilities in each wing—the Basic Democrats. But although the system of parity was maintained, there was little to satisfy East Pakistan in its new version; and the national and provincial assemblies were reduced to a minor legislative role subordinated to the presidential executive located in the West Wing.[12] This new constitutional structure and political system established by Ayub was a synthesis of the autocratic element in the traditions of the British Raj with the military and aristocratic Islamic traditions of the Urdu-

---

[10] See M. Rashiduzzaman, 'The National Awami Party of Pakistan: Leftist Politics in Crisis'; and 'The Awami League in the Political Development of Pakistan'.

[11] Herbert Feldman, *Revolution in Pakistan; A Study of the Martial Law Administration*, Chapters 1 and 2.

[12] M. Rashiduzzaman, 'The National Assembly of Pakistan under the 1962 Constitution'; Feldman, Chapters 8, 11 and 14.

speaking north Indian Muslim ascendancy. The special character and aspirations of the Bengali Muslims could find little room to express themselves within such a political order.

In his speech promulgating the 1962 constitution President Ayub Khan defined it as 'a blending of democracy with discipline, the true prerequisite to running a free society with stable government and sound administration'.[13] The official justification of Ayub's system was that it provided good government, and that it was associated with a period of rapid economic growth in the 1960s which put Pakistan high in the league table of developing countries.

But in this period of economic expansion in the 1960s, the social and political divergences between the two wings grew into an economic relationship which Bengalis came increasingly to regard as a kind of 'internal colonialism'. A new set of political issues thus emerged, reinforcing the old. For several centuries East Bengal had been a backward region, remote from the main trade routes, lacking in natural resources and hard pressed by the growth of its rice-eating population. On the other hand, it exported two important primary crops—jute and tea—which earned foreign exchange. Before 1947, and for a number of years subsequently, East Bengal had been economically a part of the hinterland of Calcutta, where most of its absentee landowners were settled, and the tea gardens in the north-eastern part of the province around Sylhet continued after 1947 to be owned mainly by British companies and Calcutta-based Hindu firms. At the same time the cheap mass-produced industrial goods consumed in East Bengal had been imported from the western parts of Bengal where eastern Bengal's jute exports were also sent to be processed for onward trade with the rest of the world. After independence, and especially after the acceleration of development in Pakistan from 1958 onwards, this long-established economic dependence of East Bengal upon Calcutta was transferred to the West Wing of Pakistan. The East Bengali market for industrial goods was taken over by West Pakistan suppliers, especially after the India–Pakistan border in Bengal was closed from 1965 onwards. Although jute mills and tea-processing plants were developed in East Bengal, the foreign-exchange earnings from this trade were centrally managed in West Pakistan: for since the values and institutions of the state derived largely from the West Wing, it inevitably supplied the leaders and managers of Pakistan's society and economy.

East Bengal, with its monsoons, its rivers and poor communications,

[13] Wheeler, pp. 158–9.

and the weakness of its commercial and managerial infrastructure, could not offer as favourable an environment for economic development as West Pakistan—with its dry climate, its convenient situation at the point of contact between the Middle East and South Asia, and its access to the skills and resources brought in by the exodus of Muslim refugees from India after August 1947. West Pakistan therefore grew faster than East Pakistan, and for a variety of reasons—not all of them unworthy—it was deliberately favoured in the application of development aid and economic planning. In 1959–60 the *per capita* income in West Pakistan was 32 per cent higher than in the East. Over the next decade the annual rate of growth of income in West Pakistan was 6·2 per cent, while it was no more than 4·2 per cent in East Pakistan. As a result, by 1969–70 the *per capita* income of the West was 61 per cent higher than in the East. The income gap doubled in percentage terms and increased even more in absolute terms.[14]

The East Bengalis were not inclined to see these facts as an ineluctable consequence of an objectively unfavourable situation. They pointed to the concentration in West Pakistan of government and foreign-aid investment, of which East Bengal's share had only risen from 20 per cent in 1950–55 to 36 per cent in 1965–70. And they argued that the central government's powers of economic management had been used to divert East Pakistan's foreign-trade earnings to finance imports into West Pakistan, and to compel East Pakistan to purchase goods and services from the West Wing which might be more cheaply obtained elsewhere. The overwhelming predominance of West Pakistanis in the higher ranks of the bureaucracy and the armed services and in many of the professions was also a source of growing resentment to Bengalis, with their long tradition of Anglicized professional culture.

Meanwhile, the difficult history of Pakistan's constitutional evolution exposed the lack of any bond of solidarity capable of maintaining a sense of common identity between the two parts of Pakistan. As Bengali politics re-emerged in the 1960s after the political freeze imposed by Ayub between 1958 and 1962, the emphasis of previous Bengali leaders on the regional and linguistic nationality of Muslim

[14] Government of Pakistan Planning Commission, *Reports of the Advisory Panels of the Fourth Five Year Plan 1970–75*, vol. 1. These reports are quoted in *Bangla Desh Documents*, which also reprints on pp. 9–15 a report by Edward S. Mason, Robert Dorfman and Stephen A. Marglin, 'Conflict in East Pakistan, Background and Prospects'; and on pp. 15–22, 'Why Bangla Desh?' by 'a group of scholars in Vienna'.

THE DIVISION IN PAKISTAN

Bengal developed increasingly into a further demand for a correction of East Pakistan's relative economic deprivation. Thus in 1966 Sheikh Mujib's Awami League—the heir of the political movements of Suhrawardy and Fazlul Haq—adopted a six-point manifesto which was designed to be a charter for the economic and political autonomy of East Bengal. Under the six points the central government would only be responsible for defence and foreign affairs; it would be deprived of effective control of the economy, and of taxation, trade and aid.[15]

The Awami League's manifesto took shape in the aftermath of the failure of Ayub's war against India in 1965. After the military stalemate of the war and the diplomatic compromise presided over by Mr Kosygin at Tashkent in 1966 the regime began to lose its grasp of events. The war brought home to Bengalis East Pakistan's vulnerability and the impossibility of defending it by military efforts based in the West. Many of them came to see the cause of the war—the Kashmir question—as an exclusively West Pakistan concern; and the complete severance of East Bengal's economic relations with India following the outbreak of hostilities reinforced the sense of economic grievance which was increasingly felt by the East against the West. These developments in East Pakistan were paralleled in the West, when the rapid pace of economic expansion was also fostering radical social tendencies within a society still dominated by the landowning and plutocratic *élites* upon which Ayub's system was based. By the end of the decade 'the common man' had become the cynosure of Pakistani politics in both parts of the country; and in West Pakistan the debilitation of the regime after the 1965 war was ably exploited by Mr Zulfikar Ali Bhutto and his radical Pakistan People's Party. In 1966, after the Tashkent agreements, Mr Bhutto resigned his post as Ayub's Foreign Minister and began to build his popular following on the two themes of social justice for 'the common man' and undying hostility towards India.

At last in 1968 the long-expected succession crisis began. President Ayub fell ill. Student riots and mass demonstrations broke out in West Pakistan; and strong support for Mr Bhutto emerged. The riots spread to East Pakistan, where the Awami League launched a mass campaign for the abandonment of the trial of Sheikh Mujib for an alleged conspiracy with Indian agents.[16] Early in 1969 Ayub called a round-table conference to which Mujib was summoned. But the conference failed to produce a settlement; and on 26 March

---

[15] The Awami League's six points are printed in Appendix 1, p. 166.
[16] For references to the Agartala conspiracy trial, see Wheeler, p. 147.

1969 Ayub Khan resigned his power to General Yahya Khan, the commander-in-chief of the Pakistan army. 'All civilian administration and constitutional authority in the country have become ineffective,' Ayub declared. 'I am left with no option but to step aside and leave it to the defence forces of Pakistan, which today represent the only effective and legal instrument to take over full control of the affairs of this country.'[17]

Ayub Khan's resignation took Pakistan back to the position of October 1958, when martial law had first been proclaimed. His successor did not propose to revert to the 1956 constitution. His policy was to pick up the threads dropped in 1958 and to return more or less to the position which had obtained in 1947 : the election of a new Constituent Assembly, the adoption of a new constitution by the elected representatives of the people, and the transfer of power into their hands. But since two constitutions had supervened since 1947 it was necessary for the President to start with a set of initial definitions embracing many of the points which had been the subject of bitter dispute since independence. It was, of course, inevitable that these definitions should take for granted the continued viability of the concept of the state of Pakistan as it had been established in 1947.

President Yahya's first set of key decisions was announced on 28 November 1969. The elections which were to be held at the end of 1970 were to take place on the basis of universal suffrage with a common vote in both Wings—an arrangement which conceded at a stroke the main political issues in dispute between East Bengal and West Pakistan since 1947. In effect, East Pakistan was to be restored to the majority which it had enjoyed in the Constituent Assembly of 1947–55. At the same time the 'one unit' in the West was to be reconstituted into four constituent provinces—thus conceding the demands of the West Pakistani regional minorities for a stronger position in relation to the Punjab.

Many explanations have been ventured for these decisions. One of the most plausible is that the President hoped that he would be able to re-establish the military regime on a new footing after a period of the same kind of political confusion which had attended the earlier civilian attempts at constitution-making. According to another kind of argument, as the chief executive of Pakistan's 'vested interest', Yahya was planning to establish a Bengali government that would co-operate with the army in protecting the social base of the West

---

[17] Wheeler, pp. 147–8. There is a full account of the 1968–69 political crisis in Pakistan in H. Feldman, *From Crisis to Crisis: Pakistan 1962–1969*.

THE DIVISION IN PAKISTAN

Pakistani 'Establishment'—its industrial and commercial interests and its landed estates in the Punjab which were threatened by Mr Bhutto's militant Pakistan People's Party. There were also those who thought the President genuine in his desire for a peaceful return of political power to representative institutions.

Whatever the reasoning behind his decisions it was natural for him to assume that the achievement of 1947 should remain a settled fact—that after democratic elections he would be able to secure assent to a concept of Pakistan acceptable to all sections of opinion within the state. His Legal Framework Order of 28 March 1970 carried further the set of definitions already made in connection with the election arrangements. The Order laid down the ground rules for the transfer of power, and provided not only that the constitution must be prepared by the Assembly within 120 days on pain of dissolution, but also that it should conform to certain fundamental principles which were set out in the Order.[18] To ensure that this was properly done the constitution was to be submitted to the President for authentication. But this provision was a contradiction of the principles of popular sovereignty which seemed to be endorsed in Yahya's earlier decisions over the election; and a further set of contradictions arose from the nature of the principles which he insisted should govern the making of the constitution. These included a provision that 'the territorial integrity and national solidarity of Pakistan' should be respected; and that there should be established a 'Federation . . . in which the provinces shall have maximum autonomy . . . but the Federal government shall also have adequate powers . . . to discharge its responsibility in relation to external and internal affairs and to preserve the independence and territorial integrity of the country'.

Although general assent was given to these provisions when they were promulgated, it was evident that the difficulty of giving agreed effect to them would remain, unless the outcome of the proposed elections were to be inconclusive. Such a result would of course leave the political initiative and the balance of power within the state in the hands of the martial-law administration. Some such outcome was probably anticipated by the authorities in Islamabad. But although there seem to have been intrigues involving elements of the army leadership with some right-wing sections of the political leadership in West Pakistan, the elections which took place on 7 December 1970

[18] The Text of the Legal Framework Order may be found in the Government of Pakistan's *White Paper*, Appendix B, pp. 18–35. Appendix A, pp. 1–7, contains extracts from policy statements by the President bearing on his decisions about the arrangements for the transfer of power.

were universally regarded at the time as having been impartially conducted.

Nevertheless, whatever hopes there may have been for an inconclusive result were dashed by the effect of the East Pakistan flood and cyclone disasters which occurred at the last stages of the election campaign in November 1970. The incompetence of the administrative response to these events and the apparent lack of West Pakistani interest gave powerful support to Sheikh Mujib's complaints about the effects of rule from Islamabad. At the last moment the Awami League was also favoured by the withdrawal from the election of its principal Bengali political rival—Maulana Bashani's National Awami Party. In the result Sheikh Mujib's Awami League won 167 out of the 313 seats in the National Assembly, taking all but two seats in East Pakistan, but none in the West. And Mr Bhutto's Pakistan People's Party captured 85 seats, all in the West Wing, mostly in the Punjab and Sind.[19]

In this first election ever held by universal suffrage in Pakistan the Islamic parties suffered a severe reverse, winning little more than 10 per cent of the all-Pakistan vote, and less than 7 per cent of the vote in East Pakistan. Mr Bhutto's success reflected a widespread demand for social reforms in each of the Western provinces; and the regional parties in the West, notably Khan Wali Khan's National Awami Party, fared surprisingly badly on their home ground in the North-West Frontier Province and in Baluchistan. On the other hand, in East Pakistan regional nationalism flowed together with the current for social reform; and the Awami League's victory expressed both a long-emerging Bengali nationalism and the growing resentment felt by almost all sections of society in East Bengal against the social and economic dominance of the West Wing.

The Awami League's six points had been adopted four years previously, and before the election it was generally assumed that in the National Assembly Sheikh Mujib would be prepared to regard them as negotiable in detail—for in their full rigour they undoubtedly amounted to the virtual secession of East Pakistan from the West, with almost all the attributes of economic sovereignty being vested in what the Awami League text described as 'the federating units'. But the absolute majority conferred upon Mujib by his election victory

---

[19] There is a full discussion and analysis of the various political parties and the election results in Mushtaq Ahmad, *Politics Without Social Change*, Chapters 3, 4 and 5. The 57 per cent poll in East Pakistan was regarded as a high figure. It must be compared with the 37 per cent poll in the 1954 provincial election. The Awami League won its 167 seats with 72 per cent of the votes cast (*ibid.*, p. 176).

paradoxically reduced his freedom of action. Within the Awami League and among Bengali political opinion outside it there was strong resistance to any retreat from the full realization of the demands expressed in the League's programme, which had now been endorsed by the East Pakistan electorate. This feeling was especially strong in the Awami League student movement, which was very close to Mujib, and which had always been one of his main sources of political support.[20] It was also necessary to take account of the tacit alliance against a strong centre which had been forged between the Awami League in the East and Wali Khan's National Awami Party and other provincial parties in the West. For the existence of such an alliance was the only basis on which the Awami League could form an All-Pakistan movement which could plausibly claim to represent any element of West Wing opinion.

In this complex political situation the dominant force was, of course, the army and the martial-law administration. The political system of military rule was highly centralized, and since 1969 Yahya had reinforced his position at the head of an elaborate system of interdependent civil and military powers.[21] Under his leadership this inter-penetration of authorities had gone further than ever before in Pakistan. At the centre he concentrated in his own hands the offices of Commander-in-Chief—to which Ayub had appointed him in 1968—Chief Martial Law Administrator, President and Supreme Commander. He also held the portfolios of Foreign Affairs and Defence. The parallel civil and military systems of administration flowed together up into the President's office through his Principal Staff Officer, General Pirzada. But within these political and administrative structures opinion was of course not monolithic. The President's authority was not unqualified, and this was reflected in the rivalries of different elements in the administration, some of which were deliberately encouraged so as to strengthen the power of the President. General Pirzada's Staff Office was counter-balanced by the National Security Council under Major-General Umar, who also presided over the two rival intelligence services—the Intelligence Bureau

[20] There is a discussion of opinion among East Pakistan students in T. C. Maniruzzaman, 'Political Activism of University Students in Pakistan'. A striking feature of this article is the survey material, collected in November–December 1968. Only 1 per cent of the East Pakistani students polled at this time favoured the separation of the two wings. Most of the respondents favoured 'the organization of public opinion to restore democracy' as the solution of national problems (*ibid.*, p. 244).

[21] There is an interesting discussion in D. Berindranath, 'Power Politics in Pakistan, One Year of the Yahya Regime'.

under a civilian and the Inter-Services Intelligence under Major-General Akbar. On the other hand, the heads of both Intelligence Services were given the right of direct access to the President. At the provincial level there was a similar system of institutional rivalry. The Governors in each wing—both of whom were officers who had formerly been at the head of their branch of the armed services—were uneasily set off against the local martial-law administrators, who were still serving as military officers, and who held their position by virtue of their military command. At the same time both sets of governors and provincial martial-law administrators enjoyed the right of direct access to the President.

This political system, which endured in essentials from April 1969 until December 1971, was designed more for the political security of its inventors than for administrative convenience or military efficiency. It gave the President great powers of political initiative. But at the same time this centralization of power also gave considerable influence to the *élite* of the Pakistan army, within which, at the beginning of 1971, the President had to reckon with at least three major currents of opinion.

What we might describe as the 'centre' view was that probably held by Yahya himself at this stage. It is likely that he still hoped to effect a successful transfer of power to Sheikh Mujib, by an arrangement in which he would retain the Presidency, with some special provision being made for the position and strength of the defence forces. This was also the policy of the Governor of East Pakistan, Admiral Ahsan, who—like President Yahya—had won the confidence of the Sheikh. If this may be described as the 'centre' position, to the 'right' many senior officers were opposed both to the secessionist tendency of the Awami League and to the populist socialism espoused by Mr Bhutto.[22] Their influence tended to oppose measures which would compromise the central government, the authority of the army and the concept of Pakistan on which they depended. At the same time, to the 'left', particularly among junior officers, there was a strong Pakistani nationalist and radical sentiment which was attracted by Mr Bhutto's rhetoric and which bitterly opposed the weakening of Pakistan which would necessarily follow from the implementation of the Awami League's six points. Within this constellation of 'centre', 'right' and 'left' opinion in the services there consequently grew up a convergence between 'right' and

---

[22] It is rumoured that after the cyclone disaster in East Pakistan in November 1970 an attempt was made by some of these elements in army opinion to prevent the holding of the elections.

THE DIVISION IN PAKISTAN

'left' elements which was opposed to concessions to the Bengalis, and which supported resolute action to restore the authority of the central government.

In the situation after the elections there was of course no lack of opportunity for the assertion of the central power. Sheikh Mujib's parliamentary majority could be of no avail until the President exercised his right to summon the National Assembly into session. Despite his great popular support in East Pakistan and a large majority in the Assembly, Mujib's position was in fact more restricted than that of any other important participant in the negotiations which followed the election. For the parliamentary majority which disposed his followers to reject compromise would be ineffectual without a compromise with the President to bring it into action. Compared with Sheikh Mujib, Mr Bhutto was tactically in a stronger position. By threatening to boycott the Assembly he could make it unworkable unless the President was simply able to disregard him; and in the course of December and January it became apparent that opinion in the army would not permit this. Meanwhile, Mr Bhutto bent his ingenuity to use this position to find some formula by which he could at least share power with Mujib.

His first move was to propose that a consensus should be reached about the outlines of the constitution before the Assembly was summoned into session.[23] This would necessarily involve Mujib in a retreat from his party's six points, to support which he of course possessed a sufficient parliamentary majority—if it could be brought into play. The Awami League refused to co-operate, although its position inevitably involved it in a paradox: asserting its right as the democratically elected majority party to impose a constitution for a radically decentralized Pakistan.[24] On 13–14 January 1971 President Yahya visited Dacca. It is possible that he was still exploring the possibility of reaching an agreement with Mujib which might ensure the future of the defence forces and his own future as President. Yahya's attitude to the six points remained ambiguous, but he seemed to share the view that the Assembly should not meet until some progress in constitutional discussions had taken place between the main parties. On his return to West Pakistan, Yahya referred

[23] Mr Bhutto's statements in *The Pakistan Times*, Dacca, 21 and 22 December 1970; *Dawn*, Karachi, 25 and 28 December 1970; *Bangla Desh Documents*, pp. 132–6.

[24] Mr Tajuddin Ahmed's statement, in *The Pakistan Observer*, 22 December 1970; Sheikh Mujib's statements in *The Pakistan Observer*, 4 January 1971; *Dawn*, 5 and 12 January 1971; *Bangla Desh Documents*, pp. 133, 137–42.

to Mujib as the 'future Prime Minister of Pakistan'.[25] However, there was still no announcement of the date of the Assembly meeting. On 27–30 January Mr Bhutto himself visited Sheikh Mujib, who again refused to accommodate him.[26] Still no date for the Assembly was announced. Two weeks passed. After a number of conversations in West Pakistan between Mr Bhutto and the President, the Assembly was summoned on 13 February to meet on 3 March. But Mr Bhutto immediately announced that his party would not attend the session unless Mujib agreed to take part in discussions beforehand to secure a consensus upon the basis for the constitution.[27] By a number of gestures—including the dismissal of his civilian cabinet on 21 February—President Yahya gave what was regarded as an endorsement of Mr Bhutto's demands. In the last days of February it seems that the secret reinforcement of troops in East Pakistan began. But Mujib was unable and unwilling to respond to these pressures; and on the 28th Mr Bhutto threatened to call a general strike in West Pakistan and to call upon his supporters to prevent West Wing members of the National Assembly from taking part in its deliberations in Dacca. The meeting of the Assembly, he urged, should either be postponed, or the 120 days' time-limit on constitution-making should be abandoned.[28]

A new phase was opened on 1 March, when a message from the President was read out over Pakistan radio, announcing that the National Assembly was postponed *sine die*.[29] At the same time Admiral Ahsan was removed from his post as Governor of East Pakistan and Major-General Yaqub was appointed to act both as Governor and as Martial Law Administrator. Civil disobedience and demonstrations were organized in many centres in East Pakistan, leading to shootings in Dacca and elsewhere. On 3 March Mujib declared the first of the succession of *hartals* (general strikes), which continued until the army forcibly intervened later in the month. Impelled by

[25] *The Pakistan Observer*, 15 January 1971; *Bangla Desh Documents*, pp. 144–5.
[26] *The Pakistan Times*, Lahore, 31 January 1971; *Bangla Desh Documents*, pp. 146–8.
[27] *Dawn*, Karachi, 16 February 1971; *Bangla Desh Documents*, pp. 155–9.
[28] Sheikh Mujib's statement in *The Pakistan Times*, Lahore, 25 February 1971; Mr Bhutto's statement in *The Pakistan Times*, Lahore, 1 March 1971; *Bangla Desh Documents*, pp. 170–9, 184–7.
[29] Text in *The Morning News*, Karachi, 3 March 1971; *Bangla Desh Documents*, pp. 188–9. The fact that Yahya himself did not read the statement, as was his normal practice, gave rise to a rumour that he had been forced into making it against his will.

the pressure for determined action from his followers, his strategy was to call the authorities' bluff by demonstrating the risk that East Bengal might become ungovernable unless the Assembly was called into session. It is also possible that the violence was fed by a decision by the new Martial Law Administrator deliberately to allow the situation to worsen: in the face of the violence, troops in many places were withdrawn to barracks. Also on 3 March Sheikh Mujib refused to attend a round-table conference proposed by the President.[30] It was announced that the Sheikh would speak in a meeting at Dacca racecourse on the 7th, when it was widely expected that he would proclaim the independence of Bangla Desh.

At this point, the day before Sheikh Mujib's rally in Dacca, President Yahya personally announced that he had decided to call the National Assembly into session on 25 March.[31] It is possible that at this stage advocates of a compromise with the Bengalis had regained the initiative in Islamabad. Perhaps, on the other hand, the extent of the disorders in East Pakistan came as a surprise. Perhaps, again, the authorities in East Bengal advised that they had not yet built up sufficient strength to act decisively against the Awami League. The President's statement hinted at each of these possibilities : for, while he proclaimed a new date for the meeting of the Assembly, a further announcement was made—that Major-General Yaqub was to be replaced as Governor and Martial Law Administrator by Lieutenant-General Tikka Khan, who had previously won a reputation in Baluchistan for his toughness in situations of civil disorder.

The leadership of the Awami League was unwilling and unready, psychologically and materially, to carry its programme of civil disobedience through into a full-blooded unilateral declaration of the sovereign independence of Bangla Desh. In his speech at Dacca racecourse on the 7th it became clear that Sheikh Mujib was resisting the call of many sections of his party for such a declaration; and while he formulated a set of conditions for the Awami League's participation in the Assembly, in effect he grasped the olive branch held out to him by the President. At the rally the Sheikh announced a series of 'directives' to Bengalis concerning the conduct of their public business and private affairs. It was intended that the observance of these would demonstrate the strength of Bengali solidarity and give substance to the threat of the emergence of an Awami League

---

[30] *Dawn*, Karachi, 4 March 1971; *Bangla Desh Documents*, pp. 197–8.
[31] The text of his broadcast is in *Dawn*, Karachi, 7 March 1971; *Bangla Desh Documents*, pp. 213–16. Note that the President's statement of 1 March was not delivered by Yahya personally.

administration in East Pakistan. The 'directives' were also a gesture to less moderate opinion in the League. Of greater significance for the constitutional negotiations were the four conditions which Mujib laid down for the attendance of the Awami League at the National Assembly session now planned for the 25th. Their effect was to challenge the legal basis of the President's position as arbiter and 'authenticator' of the constitution. The fourth of these conditions, 'the immediate transference of power to the elected representatives of the people', was not a precise demand, and it left considerable scope for negotiation. But it implied the abandonment by the President of his power under the Legal Framework Order to summon the Assembly at a date of its own choosing, to 'authenticate' the constitution, and to set a time-limit upon the constitutional deliberations of the Assembly.[32]

On 9 March it was announced that the President would visit East Pakistan 'shortly' to prepare for the meeting of the Assembly. Troop reinforcements continued to arrive by air at Dacca, and arms supplies also came by sea to Chalna and Chittagong. Riots and communal violence between Bengalis, Biharis and West Pakistanis continued, as did the shooting of demonstrators.[33] After an interview with President Yahya, the President of the Punjab Awami League, Mohammed Kurshid, flew to see Sheikh Mujib. A series of Martial Law Orders were issued in Islamabad imposing heavy penalties for compliance with some of the Awami League 'directives'. Nevertheless, when the President arrived in Dacca on the 15th he was greeted by the issue of a further thirty-five 'directives'. In this atmosphere of confrontation a new round of talks began.

It seems unlikely that these discussions were conducted in good faith on the President's side. It is possible that Yahya himself hoped to obtain a satisfactory agreement with Mujib. On the other hand because of the pressure which had built up within the Awami League it would have been impossible for Mujib to accept a settlement which fell far short of the six points. By this stage it seems almost certain that the intention of the army leadership was either to bring about a split between the different elements in the Awami League—as had been achieved in 1954 in the case of the Bengal United Front—or to win time to complete the preparations for a military action against Bengali 'secessionism'.

[32] The texts of the various statements are in *Dawn*, Karachi, 7, 8 and 10 March 1971; *Bangla Desh Documents*, pp. 216–27.

[33] In the Pakistan Government's *White Paper*, Ch. 3, pp. 29–43, there are profuse details of the 'Terror in East Pakistan'.

THE DIVISION IN PAKISTAN

Eight days were spent in complicated and increasingly detailed discussions, the main themes of which were (a) the nature of the arrangements by which a complete transfer of power to the Assembly might be effected at the time of its coming into session or before; (b) the more precise definition of the Awami League's position on the constitutional issues embraced by the six points; and (c) the form of the Assembly when it came into session.[34]

Here the key question was whether the Assembly should sit as one body or two. This crucial issue—which eventually provided the official justification for breaking off the talks—was raised by Mr Bhutto on the eve of the President's visit to Dacca. In a speech at Karachi he proposed that if power were to be transferred before the framing of the Constitution, in accordance with the fourth of Mujib's conditions, it should be transferred simultaneously to the two majority parties in each wing.[35] It was not until 22 March that the Awami League accepted this suggestion, which abandoned its West Wing allies to the mercy of Mr Bhutto's majority there,[36] and which could be represented—as it later was—as the final evidence of the League's secessionist intention.

However, the first few days of the talks were largely devoted to a discussion of the issues of principle involved in the implementation of Mujib's condition that power be transferred to the majority party before the coming into session of the Assembly. On the President's side, an elaborate legal argument was constructed to the effect that this would 'create a legal vacuum', since it would involve a gap between the legitimation of the legal succession by the Assembly and the discontinuance of the martial-law powers under which the election had been held—and under which the Assembly had come into being. The importance of this issue was that if it led to the removal of the President's reserve powers it would necessarily involve the abandonment of any constitutional principles other than those

---

[34] The official Pakistani account is contained in the Pakistan Government *White Paper*, 5 June 1971. Rahman Sobham gave the first full account from the Awami League side: *Bangla Desh Documents*, pp. 277–80. There is a colourful account in K. A. Kamal, *Sheikh Mujibur Rahman and Birth of Bangla Desh*, pp. 187–96. Mr Bhutto's version is given in his book *The Great Tragedy*. Another view from the standpoint of the PPP may be found in A. H. Kardar, *People's Commitment: Politics in Pakistan*.

[35] Mr Bhutto's speeches are reported in *Dawn*, 15–16 March 1971; *Bangla Desh Documents*, pp. 234–6, 239–40.

[36] For the reactions of the West Pakistan minority parties to Mr Bhutto's proposal, see *The Pakistan Times*, 16 March 1971; *Dawn*, 16 and 17 March 1971; *Bangla Desh Documents*, pp. 241–6, 249–50.

adopted by the elected politicians. This was a proposition which—if it were accepted—would resolve at a stroke the dilemma upon which all previous attempts at constitution-making had failed: for as we have seen, the constitutional history of Pakistan since 1947 had always been bedevilled by the failure to establish a legitimate sovereign power, whether 'Allah', or the peoples of Pakistan acting through their representatives.

For all that, there was more jubilation than surprise in the Awami League camp when Yahya's team of negotiators indicated, after much argument, that a formula for the immediate transfer of power by proclamation would be acceptable to the President. On 22 March it was agreed that the National Assembly session should be postponed yet again to give time for the proclamation to be prepared; and the Awami League at last embraced Mr Bhutto's proposal for the transfer of power to be accomplished separately in the two wings.[37] In their draft of the proclamation to be issued by the President, the Awami League negotiators thus suggested that the National Assembly should meet from the beginning in two constitutional committees, one for each wing. As the Pakistan government's *White Paper* pointed out, this proposal differed from the earlier suggestion that *after* the Assembly had met it should divide into committees made up of members from each wing. The Awami League's proposal was later represented by the authorities as 'virtually a constitutional formula for secession'.

Meanwhile, on 23 March, which since 1947 had been celebrated in both wings as 'Pakistan Day', Bangla Desh militants demonstrated in the streets of East Pakistan. Bangla Desh flags were hoisted on buildings everywhere, and 'Independence Day' was proclaimed. Members of the Awami League Women's Section were photographed on parade with rifles. In Dacca the West Wing minority-party leaders made a last attempt to persuade the Awami League leaders to return to the concept of a single Assembly in which Mr Bhutto's supporters could be outvoted. They failed: their alliance with the Awami League had now been ruptured by the Bengalis. On the 24th they began to pack their bags.[38] In Dacca discussions about the details of the draft proclamation continued between the Awami League spokesmen and the President's aides throughout the day. Elsewhere in East Pakistan the disturbances which had been going on since 1 March continued.

[37] Various Press reports on this stage of the negotiations are collected in *Bangla Desh Documents*, pp. 258–75.
[38] A statement of their attitude is given in *The Morning News*, 25 March 1971; *Bangla Desh Documents*, pp. 264–5.

Chapter 2

March–June: Action and Reaction

ON the late afternoon of 25 March the political confusion was ended abruptly when the President suddenly flew home to West Pakistan. His departure was not anticipated among political leaders in Dacca; nor was any public announcement made beforehand. That morning Sheikh Mujib denounced the 'reign of terror' at Chittagong and Rangpur, where a 24-hour curfew had been imposed after shooting incidents the previous evening.[39] On the afternoon of the 25th more barricades were set up by rioters in Dacca, between the cantonment and the centre of the town.

That evening the 35 foreign journalists in Dacca were confined to the Intercontinental Hotel. They were deported on the 27th. West Pakistan units of the army—which had been brought up to a strength of about 40,000 men scattered throughout East Bengal—moved up against the 5,000 Bengali police with their headquarters at Raja Bagh in Dacca. At the same time they attacked the detachments—about 1,000 men—of the East Pakistan Rifles at Pielkhana; and several units were sent to take over the student halls in the university area. The offices of opposition newspapers were seized, and the homes of Awami League supporters were raided. Most of the Bengali leaders were already in hiding. But shortly after 1.00 a.m. on the 26th, Sheikh Mujib was arrested at his house in Dhanmandi. Several hours later the army cleared the remaining barricades in the older parts of the city, where many civilians were killed.[40]

[39] Text in *Bangla Desh Documents*, pp. 272–5.

[40] There are full accounts, written from the Bengali point of view, in A. Mascarenhas, *The Rape of Bangla Desh*, pp. 110–120 and D. Loshak, *Pakistan Crisis*, pp. 78–88. A selection of contemporary newspaper 'descriptions' of the Pakistani actions in Bengal during March and subsequently are reprinted in *Bangla Desh Documents*, pp. 345–434. L. Rushbrook-Williams, *The East Pakistan Tragedy*, pp. 66–76, gives an account very similar to that set out in the Government of Pakistan *White Paper*. My own view is closer to Mascarenhas and Loshak than to Rushbrook-Williams. I do not believe any serious attempts were made by the Awami League to organize a revolution, a *coup d'état*, or a Bengali military uprising before 25 March, though it is clear some of its leaders contemplated a uni-multilateral declaration of independence.

Outside Dacca the West Pakistan forces also attended first to the Bengali officers and men in the army, then to other possible centres of organized opposition among the East Pakistan Rifles, the police, and the para-military *ansars*. Since the end of February, the four-and-a-half battalions of the East Pakistan Rifles left in the East had been divided into many small units, mostly dispersed towards the borders. These units found themselves cut off from radio communication with their headquarters late in the evening of the 25th, and West Pakistani detachments were later sent out to destroy them. In some places, as at Dacca, they were immediately overwhelmed, along with the Bengali para-military forces and police. Elsewhere, notably at Jessore, Rajshahi, Saidpur, Khulna, Comilla and Chittagong, there were struggles which sometimes lasted several days. Nearly everywhere there was widespread destruction and heavy casualties; and in most places outside Dacca the Pakistani army did not immediately establish its mastery. In the tumult which followed, the Pakistani army directed its fire against the Bengalis, and in turn the Bengalis wherever they could murdered members of the Urdu-speaking minorities, including both West Pakistanis and Biharis.[41]

On 26 March President Yahya Khan made a broadcast statement. At this stage he did not accuse the Awami League of planning a military uprising—this charge was not made until 6 May. Rather Sheikh Mujib's crime was said to be an attempt to lay the legal foundations for 'doing everything with impunity'. Sheikh Mujib, he argued, had suggested that Martial Law should be withdrawn and that the National Assembly should meet from the beginning in two committees because he was deliberately seeking to create 'a legal vacuum'. 'The proclamation that he proposed was nothing but a trap.' The President declared that, speaking for himself, he had not found Mujib's scheme unacceptable. But 'the political leaders were very much perturbed over Sheikh Mujib's idea of dividing the National Assembly into two parts right from the start'. This convinced Yahya that he should reject the plan: Mujib's 'obstinacy, obduracy and absolute refusal to talk sense' had left no alternative to action by the army to 'fully restore the authority of the government'. For the time being, all political activities were banned, Press censorship was imposed and the Awami League was proscribed. Nevertheless, the President would reveal of his plans for dealing with the imprisoned Sheikh only that his 'crime [would] not go unpunished'.[42]

---

[41] There is a list of alleged atrocities of this latter kind in Appendix G of the Government of Pakistan *White Paper*, pp. 64–9.

[42] See Appendix 2, p. 168.

MARCH–JUNE: ACTION AND REACTION

Scattered, separated from one another, and led by relatively junior officers, the surviving Bengali military and para-military units responded in many different ways to the various situations in which they found themselves. Those attacked tried to resist; and here and there units which had got away set themselves to march on Dacca. A number of them fought costly textbook engagements before they began to withdraw towards the borders. In Chittagong Major Zia broadcast a Declaration of Independence over the radio on 27 March. Withdrawing northwards to Belonia, in early April his forces blew up the important Feni road bridge and the Muhuri rail bridge, which connected Dacca and the tea gardens of the north-west with the port of Chittagong.

Meanwhile, Pakistani reinforcements were not able to leave Dacca until 28 March. Resistance at Jessore and Saidpur was not overcome until the first week in April. Pabna and Kushtia were reached on 10 April, and Rajshahi was only taken on the 16th. There is no evidence that Indians played any part in this stout resistance. But for the first two weeks after the 25th the Indian and world Press was filled with wild reports of Bengali successes. This optimism collapsed abruptly early in April; and the fall, on the 18th, of Chuadanga, the 'provisional capital' of Bangla Desh, was generally reported to the outside world as marking the end of formal resistance inside East Pakistan.

Nevertheless, in the confused conditions which prevailed outside the main centres of population, the nucleus of a future Bangla Desh army was able to cross over into India. In some places these Bengali units also established themselves in enclaves straddling the border— where they were welcomed by the Indian border security forces. These centres of resistance were strongest on the eastern side, where Majors Shaffiullah and Khalid Musharraff took up positions opposite Brahmanbaria; and where Major Zia's group made its way to the Belonia salient. In the north-west the Bhurungamari, Patgra and Pachagarh salients remained under the control of Bengali forces. Around the borders of East Pakistan the Pakistan army was able to re-establish fewer than a quarter of the 370 border posts which had existed before 25 March.

In India the general election had been completed less than a week before the Pakistan army began its action in East Bengal. There had been little public news of the progress of the talks in Dacca, and the news that was available had been optimistic in tone. But immediately after the crisis broke rumours both terrifying and exultant began to flourish in the absence of authentic reports. The first Indian reaction came on 26 March, when Foreign Minister Swaran Singh expressed his government's concern.[43] Responding to pressure for intervention on the following day, Mrs Gandhi told the Rajya Sabha that 'one wrong step or wrong word may have an effect entirely different to the one which we all intend'.[44] Two days later a more defiant Indian view was set out in a resolution unanimously adopted by both Houses of the Indian Parliament on 31 March. According to this resolution, the origin of the 'macabre tragedy' in East Bengal—'amounting to genocide'—lay in the refusal of the government of Pakistan 'to transfer power to the legally-elected representatives of the people of East Bengal . . . The historic upsurge of the 75 million people of East Bengal will triumph. The House wishes to assure them that their struggles and sacrifices will receive the wholehearted sympathy and support of the people of India.'[45]

These first Indian responses to the crisis in Pakistan were hesitant and cautious—designed to head off mounting public pressure for immediate intervention.[46] The resolution of 31 March was not a call to action. Rather, the Indian government expressed faith in the working out of what it described as an inevitable historical development. This analysis had a twofold significance. It implied a reversal of the doctrine upon which Indian policy towards East Pakistan had been based since partition: that the defence of Indian unity against fissiparousness implied that India should herself respect the unity of Pakistan. By arguing that the secession of East Bengal was now inevitable the Indian government was by implication asserting that whatever the possible consequences for the unity of India, her efforts to respect Pakistani unity could no longer be sustained. At the same time the Lok Sabha's resolution provided a rationale for delay. If it was implied that India should align herself with the forces of history, it was also implied that she had only to wait upon their pre-ordained development. This was the basis upon which Mrs Gandhi took her first steps towards a new East Bengal policy. It was decided to assist the voluntary organization of efforts in India to help the Bengali cause, and to encourage the escaped deputy-leader of the Awami League,

---

[43] *Bangla Desh Documents*, p. 671.

[44] The important section of this speech of 27 March is reprinted in Indira Gandhi, *India and Bangla Desh: Selected Speeches and Statements*, pp. 11–13; *Bangla Desh Documents*, pp. 671–6.

[45] See Appendix 3, p. 171.

[46] The strength of Indian public opinion after 25 March, and the verbal lengths to which the Indian government had to go to appease it, are documented in *India's Two Faces: A Study in Contrast* (no place, no date), a publication of the Government of Pakistan issued *c*. July 1972.

MARCH–JUNE: ACTION AND REACTION

Mr Tajuddin Ahmed, in his endeavour to form a provisional government-in-exile of Bangla Desh, early in April. However, when the independence of Bangla Desh was proclaimed, on 10 April,[47] the Indian government refused to yield to demands for the recognition of the provisional government which she had helped into existence.

It seems likely that the Indian government, as well as the Indian people, were taken by surprise at the sudden turn of events in East Pakistan. As we have already remarked, throughout February and March their attention had been almost exclusively occupied by their own general election;[48] and it is certainly in the context of the election and of Indian domestic politics that we must view the hard anti-Pakistani line that was taken by Mrs Gandhi's government during the curious episode of the hi-jacking of an Indian airliner to Lahore, allegedly by 'Kashmiri freedom-fighters', at the end of January.[49] The army and intelligence services were watching the development of the constitutional crisis in Pakistan with close attention. But their advice to the Cabinet at the end of March 1971 appears to have been that India was not ready for immediate intervention in East Bengal, and

[47] Text in *Bangla Desh Documents*, pp. 281–2; related statements by Mr Tajuddin Ahmed, pp. 282–98.

[48] Some idea of the flavour of sophisticated unofficial Indian opinion in this earlier period can be gathered from the texts of contemporary broadcast discussions and articles of December 1970–February 1971, published in K. Subrahmanyam, *Bangla Desh and India's Security*, pp. 24–36.

[49] On 30 January 1971 the airliner was flown at gun-point to Lahore. Mr Bhutto was among the Pakistanis who took part in the jubilant celebrations with which the two hi-jackers were greeted. They declared that they were members of the Kashmir NLF, and they demanded the release of thirty-six members of the Front detained in (Indian) Kashmir. On 31 January it was announced in Islamabad that the two 'freedom fighters' had been granted political asylum. The Indian Government retaliated on 4 February by cancelling the facilities for Pakistani military and civil overflights across Indian territory until compensation for the wrecked aircraft had been paid. The effect was to add some 2,400 miles to the length of the air route between the two wings of Pakistan, via Ceylon. In East Bengal Sheikh Mujib denounced the Punjab authorities for furnishing a possible pretext for the postponement of the transfer of power — which was at that stage the main issue in Pakistani politics. Nevertheless, after the events of March it was alleged by the Pakistani authorities that the hi-jacking had been arranged by the Indian intelligence services with the intention of encouraging separatism in East Pakistan (report of a judicial enquiry commission headed by Mr Justice Noorul Arfin, 15 April 1971). This allegation became an important element in the Pakistani 'evidence' that 'Indian agents' were to blame for the trouble in East Pakistan.

that any military action to help the Bengalis would have to wait until after the mid-year monsoon.

Meanwhile from 25 March onwards Islamabad called down a hail of protests against Indian 'interference' in Pakistan's 'internal affairs'. The main purpose of Yahya's diplomacy at this stage was to remove any possible ground for Indian intervention by securing international recognition that what was happening in East Pakistan was exclusively a matter of Pakistan's domestic jurisdiction.[50] Terminology became especially important. References to 'East Pakistan' were approved in Islamabad: 'East Bengal' won praise from Delhi.

Britain was the first major power to express a view, in statements by the Prime Minister on the 27th and by the Foreign Secretary on the 29th. The British government's determination to resist pressure from parliamentary and public opinion for a British or Commonwealth effort at mediation led it to adopt a position very close to that desired by Pakistan.[51] Similarly, at the end of April President Pompidou told Yahya's special envoy that France desired that everything should end 'for the best on the human, moral and political levels under President Yahya's leadership'.[52]

The non-Arab Muslim powers were among the first to give public support to Pakistan—Indonesia and Iran on 28 March, Turkey and Malaysia on 3 April.[53] At the end of April Turkey and Iran helped her to secure a declaration from the Central Treaty Organization (CENTO) Ministerial Council calling for the principle of non-interference in the affairs of sovereign states to be respected. The Arab–Muslim powers came forward more slowly.[54] But three months later, at the end of June, a twenty-two-nation conference of Muslim countries in Jiddah adopted the diplomatic formula advanced by Islamabad in expressing its support for 'Pakistan's national unity and territorial integrity'.[55] More practically, in the course of the year, a

[50] See, for example, the Pakistan government's note to the Indian government, 27 March 1971, and its note to the Secretary-General of the United Nations, 8 April 1971. Pakistan's case is outlined in *Pakistan Horizon*, XXIV, No. 2, pp. 18–30. For United Nations texts see *ibid.*, pp. 93–101.

[51] British policy is discussed from a Pakistani viewpoint *ibid.*, pp. 48–53 (texts pp. 141–5), and with less moderation in *Pakistan Horizon*, XXIV, No. 3, pp. 3–9.

[52] Text in *Pakistan Horizon*, XXIV, No. 2, pp. 154–5.

[53] Texts, *ibid.*, pp. 155–7.

[54] Texts, *ibid.*, pp. 159–63.

[55] *The Times of India*, 27 June 1971.

MARCH–JUNE: ACTION AND REACTION

variety of trade and financial support agreements were discussed between Pakistan and some of the richer Arab states—notably Saudi Arabia.[56] The only significant Muslim voice not wholly sympathetic to Pakistan was Egypt; and although in June President Sadat referred to Egypt's support for Pakistan's integrity, his government continued to express its sympathy towards its Indian partner in non-alignment and friendship with the Soviet Union.[57]

The Soviet Union was the first super-power to state her position. Since the Tashkent agreements of 1966 Russia's hopes of a steady improvement in her relations with Pakistan had been disappointed. The Soviet Union's Tashkent policy was essentially an attempt to bring about 'good neighbourly relations' by impartial mediation between the major sub-continental powers. But this policy had so far failed to bear fruit.[58] Although Mr Kosygin was the first major international figure to visit President Yahya—shortly after he came to power in 1969—he failed to bring about a restoration of the 'Tashkent spirit'. Despite inducements afforded by Soviet economic and military aid, Indo–Pakistani relations had not improved; and, while Pakistan's friendly attitude to Russia continued, her relationship with China had become increasingly intimate. In November 1970 President Yahya visited Peking and returned with a large aid agreement. The crisis in East Pakistan placed the Russians in a quandary, to which their first response was cautious, hesitating and not wholly coherent. Throughout the year the Soviet Press was always more critical of Pakistan than was the government; and, as we shall see, the interventions of Mr Kosygin—architect of the Tashkent settlement—were generally more favourable to Pakistan than those of his colleagues.

The first Soviet action appears to have been a private approach on 28 March to President Yahya through the Russian consul-general in Karachi. This included a request for information about the intentions of the Pakistan authorities in East Bengal. On 2 April, in a letter unilaterally published in Moscow, the Russians took a bolder stand.[59]

[56] *The Statesman* (Calcutta), 22 May 1971; *The Times of India*, 22 May 1971; *Dawn*, 20 and 23 September, 9 October 1971.

[57] *Indian Express*, 9 June 1971; *Dawn*, 16 June 1971; *The Statesman*, 4 August 1971; *The Times of India*, 19 June 1971. The reactions of the Muslim states are discussed in *Pakistan Horizon*, XXIV, No. 2, pp. 56–8.

[58] Soviet policy towards Pakistan after Tashkent is discussed in Zubieda Hassan, 'Pakistan's Relations with the U.S.S.R. in the 1960s', *The World Today*, January 1969; and in Zubieda Hassan, 'Soviet Arms aid to Pakistan and India', *Pakistan Horizon*, 4th quarter 1968, pp. 344–55.

[59] See Appendix 4, p. 172.

President Podgorny addressed an 'urgent appeal' to Yahya to take 'most immediate measures so as to put an end to bloodshed and repressions against the population of East Pakistan'. By referring to the Declaration of Human Rights the Russians held out the possibility that Soviet support might be extended to Indian diplomacy at the United Nations. On the other hand, President Podgorny was careful to reiterate his references to 'East Pakistan' and the 'whole Pakistani people'. He described his letter as 'a kind word, a word of friends'. When he went on to declare that 'the solution to the complicated problems which have recently arisen in Pakistan can and must be reached by political means without applying force' his comment was clearly intended to be noted as much in Delhi as in Islamabad; and his plea for a 'peaceful political settlement' in East Pakistan was carefully balanced by a reference to 'the cause of maintaining peace in this region'.

In his response to this first statement of the Russian position Yahya maintained an unyielding attitude. His reply to President Podgorny's letter revealed the earlier contact through the Soviet consul-general in Karachi, and baldly declared that 'the situation in East Pakistan is well under control and normal life is being gradually restored'. For the rest, he repeated his attacks on 'India's interference in Pakistan's internal affairs', and his letter concluded with an implicit reference to China which must have made an impression in Moscow. 'For any power to support such interfering moves or to condone them,' he concluded, 'would be a negation of the UN Charter as well as the Bandung principles.'[60]

This sharp retort, together with the overcoming of organized resistance in East Pakistan during April, induced a diplomatic withdrawal by the Soviet government later in the month. At the end of April an apparently more complaisant, unpublished letter was addressed by Mr Kosygin to President Yahya; and, as we shall see later, between April and August the Russians made a number of gestures in the field of economic relations to indicate their continuing interest in close co-operation between Pakistan and the Soviet Union.

This shift in Soviet policy after their first reaction to the crisis may well have been influenced by China's formal definition, on 13 April, of her view of the situation in Pakistan. The caution of the Chinese statement may have been taken by the Russians to hold out some

---

[60] The text of Yahya's reply, 5 April 1971, is reprinted in *Pakistan Horizon*, XXIV, No. 2, pp. 150–1. The Soviet Union's first reactions to the crisis after 25 March are discussed in *ibid.*, pp. 53–5.

MARCH–JUNE: ACTION AND REACTION

hope of an extension of their influence in Pakistan.[61] For China's commitment was very slow in coming; and although it was as firm as it was delicately phrased, the phrasing did not fully measure up to Pakistan's expectations. There was no direct comment from Peking until 6 April, when the Chinese government gave an indirect indication of its support for Pakistan by protesting to India against a demonstration outside the Chinese mission in Delhi. Although this note contained a reference to India's 'flagrant interference in the internal affairs of Pakistan', it was not until a week later that Pakistan received her first public official communication from China since the events of 25 March. In a letter of 13 April, the Chinese Prime Minister, Chou En-lai, supported President Yahya's efforts 'to uphold the unification of Pakistan and to prevent it from moving towards a split'. In the next sentence he remarked—in a comment which must have pleased Mr Bhutto, who had long been the leading advocate of Pakistan's China policy—that 'the situation in Pakistan will certainly be restored to normal by the wide consultations and efforts of your Excellency and leaders of various quarters in Pakistan'. But the key passage in Chou En-lai's letter was that containing the formula which China consistently maintained thereafter : 'should the Indian expansionists dare to launch aggression against Pakistan, the Chinese government and people will as always fully support the Pakistan government and people in their just struggle to safeguard State Sovereignty and national independence'.[62]

Although the tone of this and later Chinese interventions was not unsatisfactory to Pakistan, over the succeeding months the exactness of the phrase setting out China's position was a cause for growing concern in Islamabad. The formula preferred by the Pakistanis was that which, as we have seen, was accepted in June by the Conference of Muslim Foreign Ministers, and which was reaffirmed by President Yahya in his speech of 28 June, when he referred to 'our friends abroad' who 'have given complete support to the action taken by the government to maintain the *unity and integrity of Pakistan*'. But in spite of pressure from Pakistan for a broadening of the terms of their commitment, the Chinese refused to be drawn. Although from April onwards there was an increasing flow of Chinese military and

---

[61] Some elements of the background of Chinese relations with Pakistan can be found in S. P. Seth, 'China as a Factor in Indo–Pakistani Politics', and in A. Syed, 'The Politics of Sino–Pakistan Agreements'.

[62] See Appendix 6, pp. 174–83. The texts of the Chinese notes are printed in *Pakistan Horizon*, XXIV, No. 2, pp. 153–4. See also discussions on China's role in *ibid.*, pp. 39–42.

economic assistance to Pakistan, it was always subject to this scrupulously limited guarantee.[63] Thus in November 1971, eight months after the crisis broke, one of the main purposes of Mr Bhutto's visit to Peking was to obtain an extension of the Chinese formula to include a reference to the unity as well as to the independence of Pakistan. But in his speech at the banquet concluding the visit, the Chinese acting Foreign Minister, Mr Chi Peng-fei, would do no more than repeat China's 'resolute support' for Pakistan's 'State Sovereignty and national independence'. Her struggle for 'territorial integrity' and 'national unity' was merely noted and commended in another part of the speech. This was naturally interpreted in India as an indication that, while China would lend general diplomatic and material support to Pakistan's efforts in the East, her 'resolute support' would only be given if the very existence of Pakistan—in the West—was at stake.

Washington was equally slow to take up a public position on the merits of Pakistan's action in the East; and the first American reaction was that Pakistan must be persuaded to accept humanitarian support, as far as possible through multilateral international agencies —despite her insistence on her exclusive jurisdiction in her own domestic affairs. The emphasis in the first American statement, on 2 April, therefore fell on 'the loss of life, hardship and damage, suffered by the people of Pakistan', and on the need for international assistance to relieve the suffering. On the 7th, the State Department spokesman further developed this position—'we continue to believe it important that every feasible step be taken to end the conflict and achieve a peaceful accommodation'.[64]

The White House's main concern was that the civil strife in East Pakistan should not develop into an international crisis in the subcontinent which would threaten the balance of power in Asia. In the year when President Nixon's approach to Communist China was to be consummated he was most anxious to avoid developments—such as a war in the sub-continent—which might jeopardize his diplo-

[63] There are references to Chinese economic and military assistance to Pakistan during 1971 in *Dawn*, 21 May, 12 and 25 August, 29–30 September; *Financial Times*, 29 April; *The Times of India*, 16 May, 28 June, 9 July, 22 September; *Hindustan Standard*, 17 June 1971; *International Herald Tribune*, 14–15 August 1971.

[64] The statements are printed in *Pakistan Horizon*, XXIV, No. 2, pp. 145–7. On pp. 41–8 there is a hostile assessment of American policy in these first stages of the crisis, reflecting the pressure brought to bear on Pakistan by the United States in April–May 1971 to accept United Nations relief support in East Pakistan.

MARCH–JUNE: ACTION AND REACTION

macy. The particular importance that China attached to her friendship with Pakistan was also appreciated by the United States.[65] Nevertheless, the American government seems to have understood quite early that West Pakistan's domination of East Bengal could not be maintained indefinitely, and that as time passed the movement of American public opinion was likely to restrict the scope for support for Pakistan. These considerations perhaps reinforced humanitarian concerns in inducing Washington to press the Pakistani authorities to accept a role for United Nations relief efforts in East Pakistan. With American encouragement, on 22 April U Thant wrote to President Yahya, reaffirming his statement of 5 April, that he recognized that the events in East Pakistan fell strictly within the domestic jurisdiction of Pakistan under Article 2 (7) of the UN Charter. But 'prompted purely by humanitarian considerations', the Secretary-General declared his belief that 'the United Nations and its specialized agencies have a most useful role to play, with the consent of your government, in providing emergency assistance'.[66]

But despite these pressures Islamabad was still at this stage firmly resisting any form of outside intervention in Pakistan's internal affairs. Yahya's reply to U Thant came on 29 April, welcoming the offer, but affirming that the gravity of the situation in East Pakistan had been greatly exaggerated. He declared that, after the Pakistan government had completed its assessment of its requirements, 'international assistance, if and when required, will be administered by Pakistani relief agencies. . . .' In the face of this refusal of United Nations offers of assistance, dramatic predictions of impending famine in East Pakistan began to be disseminated from Washington and New York. Over the next two months the United States worked closely with the British government and the United Nations to overcome Pakistan's resistance to a role for the UN and other international agencies in providing relief in East Pakistan.

Meanwhile, by the middle of April 1971, the first and, as it seemed to many at the time, the decisive phase of the crisis in East Pakistan had been completed. On the military level, on 18 April Pakistani forces took Brahmanbaria and Akhnur in Comilla and entered the

[65] In President Nixon's Report to the Congress, *US Foreign Policy for the 1970s*, pp. 48–51, the rationale of American policy towards the sub-continent in 1971 is, however, defined almost exclusively in terms of the defence of United Nations principles. See Chapter 6: *Conclusion*, p. 146.

[66] Text in *Pakistan Horizon*, XXIV, No. 2, p. 140. Yahya Khan's reply of 29 April is on p. 41.

erstwhile provisional capital of Bangla Desh at Chuadanga in Kushtia. On the diplomatic level, most governments had already publicly or privately expressed the view that the situation in East Pakistan must be regarded as the internal affair of Pakistan. The Indian government had been forced back on to the defensive—its position being, as Mrs Gandhi put it on 4 April, that it was 'neither proper nor possible' for India to remain silent over the situation in East Pakistan. A peevish and protracted wrangle between the Indian and Pakistani governments now began over the control of the Pakistan Deputy High Commission premises in Calcutta, which had been taken over by the so-called Provisional Government of Bangla Desh.[67] Meanwhile the dissensions among the East Bengali exiles were already coming to the surface and embittering their mutual relations and their relations with the Indians.

By the middle of April it was clear, therefore, that after some unexpected initial difficulties the Pakistani authorities had prevailed in the first round of the East Bengal crisis. The Indian government had found itself unable to act upon the strong demand of many sections of Indian public opinion for immediate intervention to assist the Bengalis. Subsequently, when it was seen that the government would not undertake military action, there was powerful pressure during April and May for Indian diplomatic recognition of the Bangla Desh provisional government, culminating in a debate in the Indian Parliament at the end of May. While the most powerful consideration influencing Indian public opinion was the conviction that India must necessarily be on the side of a people 'struggling to be free', it was also argued that it was in India's national interest that Pakistan should break up; and the failure of the government to act decisively against Pakistan was attributed by some to a combination of softness and an excess of moralism inherited from a bankrupt philosophy of interna-

---

[67] The texts of some of the Pakistani notes and statements in the controversy over the diplomatic missions are reprinted in *Pakistan Horizon*, XXIV, No. 2, pp. 129–35. On 18 April Pakistan's Deputy High Commissioner in Calcutta and other Bengali members of the mission staff announced their allegiance to Bangla Desh and took over the Pakistani mission building. A new Deputy High Commissioner was immediately appointed by the Pakistan government; but he was unable to take over the premises. Pakistan then decided to close her office in Calcutta, and on 24 April requested the Indian government to close her equivalent mission in Dacca. However, it was not until August that agreement was reached on the repatriation of the staffs from both missions – Pakistan being concerned to assert her jurisdiction over defecting East Bengali diplomats.

tional relations.[68] The Bangla Desh crisis deepened and extended the radical reappraisal of the premises of Nehru's foreign policy that had been going on in India since the Sino–Indian border war of 1962.

Nevertheless, the Indian government still refused to recognize Mr Tajuddin Ahmed's cabinet in Calcutta as the provisional government of Bangla Desh.[69] After it was recognized in Delhi at the beginning of the crisis that India's diplomatic and military unpreparedness made it impossible for her to intervene immediately in East Pakistan there followed several weeks of intense analysis and debate at the highest levels of military and diplomatic policy-making. By the end of April the Indian government had made the key decisions which were to govern its support for the Bangla Desh movement—a policy which was of course implicit in the resolution of 31 March. As we shall see below, from about the beginning of May the formation, training, and arming of Bangla Desh forces began inside India, and covert official support was extended to the efforts of the Bangla Desh provisional government to organize a guerrilla war in East Pakistan. Meanwhile the Indians consolidated their plans for a long-drawn-out confrontation with Pakistan, which it was clearly understood was likely to end in a third Indo–Pakistani war.

In the first phase of the crisis, during April, India concentrated on bringing diplomatic pressure to bear on Pakistan through the influence of international opinion. Although the main Indian argument was that the international community was bound to intervene because the policy being carried out in East Pakistan was a violation of human rights, it was also argued that Pakistan's actions were a danger to peace in the sub-continent. Accordingly the Indians seized every occasion to dramatize the deterioration in Indo–Pakistani relations and to find issues to support an intensification of the long-established quarrel between the two countries. This theme in Indian policy matched Pakistan's desire to blame the crisis on Indian interference. While the Pakistani army was re-establishing control in East Bengal exchanges of notes between the two governments set the stage for a renewed confrontation on the diplomatic level—a conflict in which the quarrel over the Deputy High Commissions was one of the initial episodes.

[68] See, for example, K. Subrahmanyam, pp. 40–45.
[69] The statement by Mr Swaran Singh, the Indian Foreign Minister, before the Rajya Sabha on 25 May 1971 is reprinted in *Bangla Desh Documents*, pp. 676–8. On recognition he remarks, 'We are clarifying our position. Our position in a nutshell is that the situation does continue to be fluid . . .' For Mrs Gandih's more elegant formulation see *ibid.*, pp. 680–82.

SOUTH ASIAN CRISIS

However, among the decisions made by the Indian government at this stage of events early in April the most fateful were those connected with the reception of refugees from East Bengal. It is uncertain how far the Indians then understood the possible implications of these decisions. They might have appreciated how difficult it would be for the Pakistanis to regain control of the border areas and to restrict the outflow of refugees. But the scale of the refugee problem and its eventual significance does not seem to have been anticipated either by India or by Pakistan. In the first five weeks after 25 March the number of refugees entering India was on a small scale, set against the experience of India and Pakistan since 1947. On 21 April it was announced in Delhi that no more than a quarter of a million people had crossed over into India by that date. But very early in April the Indian government decided that these refugees should not be treated as just another instalment of the exchange of populations implied in the 1947 partition: for one thing, many were Muslims. Mrs Gandhi put the distinction to the Lok Sabha on 24 May: 'they are not refugees in the sense we have understood this word since the partition. They are victims of war who have sought refuge from the military terror across our frontier'.[70] From the beginning of April, as they crossed the border, the refugees were registered as foreigners. Those who did not register failed to receive a ration card.[71]

From the third week of April onwards, not long after the Indians adopted this policy, the number of refugees—'displaced persons' in Pakistani terminology—began to mount dramatically. Most of the refugees in the first waves were Muslims. Hindus did not begin to preponderate until June. On 6 May, the Indian Minister of Labour, Mr R. K. Khadilkar, declared that the total had reached 1,480,000. Of these about 1,200,000 were in West Bengal, 142,000 in Assam and Meghalaya, and 137,000 in Tripura, where they already amounted to 30 per cent of the local population by the middle of May. The Indian government, he declared, had already spent Rs 100 million (about £5½ million) on shelter, food and clothing for the refugees; and the rate of influx was 60,000 per day.[72] Ten days after these

---

[70] *Bangla Desh Documents*, pp. 671–5.

[71] In June the Pakistani authorities made a statement disputing the Indian claims about the size of the refugee problem, and issuing detailed figures very substantially lower than the Indian estimate. Most independent observers now agree that the Indian figures were much nearer the truth than those submitted by Pakistan.

[72] Further details from the Indian side are given in *Bangla Desh Documents*, pp. 675–6.

MARCH–JUNE: ACTION AND REACTION

figures were announced Mrs Gandhi toured the refugee reception camps in West Bengal, Tripura and Assam.

Throughout April and May the Indian official and unofficial agencies along the East Bengal borders were preoccupied in the main with the reception and settlement of the refugees. Meanwhile, although Indian support for the organization of Bangla Desh armed resistance forces among refugees probably began early in April, the political importance of the refugee inflow was immediately recognized to lie not in the provision of manpower for the guerrilla struggle, but in the reinforcement for Indian diplomacy. International concern for the plight of the refugees led in almost every country to the growth of sympathy towards India and hostility towards Pakistan. As the exodus grew India was able to assert with increasing conviction that, whether or not the East Pakistan crisis was an internal problem of Pakistan, it had come to have a deep impact upon India's domestic affairs. Referring to the refugees in her speech of 24 May, Mrs Gandhi declared that 'what was claimed to be an internal problem of Pakistan has also become an internal problem of India'. The central theme of Indian diplomacy in the crisis now became the insistence that 'Pakistan was fully responsible for creating such conditions forthwith as would facilitate the return of the refugees to their own homes'. The precise definition of what Mrs Gandhi described as 'credible guarantees for the future safety and well-being of the refugees' was a political instrument of great potency. For the problem was, how were those guarantees to be defined?

In the face of these developments in the Indian position, early in May the Pakistani diplomatic line began to shift, helped on by the consolidation of the army's control in East Bengal after the struggles of late March and April. The authorities in Islamabad now began to revise their view of the possibilities of co-operation with the international agencies. The adoption of a new attitude in Pakistan was also influenced by the pressure which the United States and other Western powers brought to bear to persuade Yahya to reverse his rejection of U Thant's proposals in April for a United Nations role in East Pakistan. For although during April and early May Islamabad was able to insist on excluding any kind of international intervention in East Bengal, Pakistan was vulnerable to Western pressure because of her very weak economic position.

Her vulnerability stemmed essentially from her shortage of foreign exchange, which was growing worse because of the increase in military imports and food purchases from abroad—especially after the bad harvests of 1971. Between July 1970 and February 1971 reserves fell by Rs 575·8 million, as compared with a decline of Rs 144·8 million over the same period in the previous year. While West Pakistani exports had risen by 24 per cent over 1969–70, export earnings from East Pakistan had fallen by a quarter.

The difficulties were immediate. Pakistan was entering a period when she would be obliged to repay a heavy load of foreign debt, covering the cost of Ayub Khan's 'decade of development'. Repayments had risen from an annual average of $138 million during the Third Plan period (1965–9) to a level of $185 million in 1969–70.[73] One-fifth of Pakistan's normal export earnings were committed to these charges; and the possibility of some relief or restructuring of the debt before the next payment fell due in June was due to be discussed at the end of April at a meeting of the eleven-nation Pakistan Aid consortium of the World Bank in Paris.

At this meeting the Pakistani representatives continued to pursue the line they had been taking since 25 March, and when the conference failed to give satisfaction, Pakistan unilaterally announced that she was imposing a six-month moratorium on the repayment of her debt. This was perforce accepted by the members of the consortium; but it was agreed that another meeting should be held at the end of June, and that Mr P. M. Cargill of the World Bank's South Asia Department should draw up a report on Pakistan's economic prospects.

At the same time, Pakistan followed up her declaration of the moratorium by a series of initiatives to gain economic and financial support from friendly countries. Talks began with Saudi Arabia, Libya and a number of other Arab states. At the end of April, the Soviet Union signed an agreement to double the export to Russia of Pakistani leather for footwear manufacture. The prospective foreign-exchange earnings for Pakistan were not significant—more important were the hopes the agreement raised that the trade route via Afghanistan to Russia would be opened up at last.[74] Two weeks after this agreement it was announced that the Russians had finally approved the blueprint for a steel mill to be set up with Soviet help near Karachi. It was reported that in the previous August the Soviet Union had rejected the feasibility report on the same project

[73] *Financial Times*, 1 May 1971; *The Statesman*, 9 May; *Pakistan Times*, 14 May.

[74] This route had not been used by Pakistan since its completion in November 1969, and it had been a major objective of Soviet diplomacy towards Pakistan in the period after Tashkent to secure her participation in the operation of the new overland trading system – which might eventually be extended to India. See Chapter 6: *Conclusions*, p. 146.

MARCH–JUNE: ACTION AND REACTION

and had virtually withdrawn her offer to help in setting up the mill.[75]

At the same time as Pakistan was improving her relations with the Soviet Union, she concluded an agreement with China for a further Chinese interest-free loan—said to amount to another Rs 100 crores ($200m) in addition to the Rs 100 crores already agreed in November 1970. On 16 February, the all-weather Karakoram highway between Kashgar and Gilgit had been formally opened. Over it was carried some of the military aid which China had agreed to provide for the enlargement of the Pakistan army. Early in May China also began to supply newsprint to Pakistan to replace the disrupted supplies from Khulna in East Pakistan. Various other forms of commodity aid came under discussion; and at Taxila work on the Chinese-built heavy engineering complex was accelerated towards its completion in November.[76]

However, Pakistan still required Western assistance, especially in connection with her debt repayments. The position taken up by the Western powers rested upon a distinction between relief and development aid. The United States government announced that it would continue with its existing development projects, but that future development assistance depended upon Pakistan's co-operation with internationally supervised relief efforts in East Pakistan. On 11 May, after consultation with the Americans, the British government declared that it took the same view and that the appropriate international agency for organizing relief to East Pakistan was the United Nations. On 13 May the British position was defined in the House of Commons by Mr Richard Wood : 'we are ready ... to resume aid for development, but we can clearly do so only if conditions are restored in which that aid could be effectively deployed ... a political solution in East Pakistan is necessary, and that must be a matter for the Pakistan government and people to achieve'.

Nevertheless, the Americans, in particular, were anxious not to jeopardize their influence in Islamabad. Although American military assistance to Pakistan was ended immediately after 25 March, licences for the export of arms continued to be granted for several months, and the flow continued until November.[77] However, at the beginning of May a Senate Foreign Affairs sub-committee began hearings on United States economic and military assistance to Pakistan; and on 7

[75] Radio Pakistan, 26 April; *Motherland*, 8 May.

[76] *Dawn*, 21 and 22 May; *Financial Times*, 29 April; *The Statesman*, 4 May; *The Times of India*, 16 May.

[77] *US Foreign Policy for the 1970's, A Report to Congress*, February 1972, p. 48.

May it voted for the suspension of American arms sales to Pakistan. Ten prominent Republican and Democratic Senators sent a telegram to the Secretary of State, Mr William Rogers, calling for the suspension of aid unless Pakistan allowed Red Cross officials to co-ordinate relief measures in East Pakistan.

This demonstration was the preliminary to the first breakthrough for American policy. When Yahya Khan's economic adviser, M. M. Ahmed, visited the United States in the middle of May, he informed U Thant on the 17th that Pakistan would now be willing to accept United Nations aid in East Pakistan, provided it was 'co-ordinated' by Pakistani officials. On the 21st, an American government spokesman, after noting this first step forward, declared that, contrary to 'misleading reports', United States economic assistance to Pakistan was continuing. 'We are now reaching the point, thanks to the Secretary-General's efforts, at which longer term and more substantial assistance under the United Nations can be decided upon.'[78]

The decision to accept a United Nations relief presence in East Pakistan was evidently made in Islamabad early in May. At the same time it was decided that the military 'crack-down' in the East should be followed by efforts at conciliation which would bring the refugees back and make possible a return to normality in Pakistan's international relations. This policy was in line with the American attitude; and on 28 May President Nixon wrote to Yahya encouraging him in his new course of 'political accommodation' in East Pakistan. On the same day he also wrote to Mrs Gandhi, stating: 'We have been discussing with the Government of Pakistan the importance of achieving a peaceful political accommodation under which the refugee flow would stop and the refugees would be able to return to their homes. . . . As one of Asia's major powers,' he went on, 'India has a special responsibility for maintaining the peace and stability of the region.'[79]

[78] Texts in *Pakistan Horizon*, XXIV, No. 2, pp. 148–9. This development in American policy brought to a head the disagreements which had been brewing since March between the staff of the American mission in Dacca and the higher authorities in the embassy in Islamabad and in Washington. At the beginning of June the United States Consul-General in Dacca, Mr Archibald Blood, was recalled. He was later replaced by Mr Herbert Spivack. Britain's Deputy High Commissioner, Mr Frank Sargent, was also recalled at the same time. Both officials had been publicly critical of the policy being pursued by the government of Pakistan in East Bengal. *Times of India*, 7 June; *Guardian*, 8 June.

[79] *US Foreign Policy in the 1970's, A Report to Congress*, February 1972, p. 49.

MARCH–JUNE: ACTION AND REACTION

On 21 May, President Yahya made the first of a series of conciliatory public declarations—an appeal to 'law-abiding' citizens of East Pakistan to return to their homes. On 24 May he announced that he would shortly reveal a revised plan for a return to the orderly progress towards a transfer of power to 'the representatives of the people' which he had been pursuing up till 25 March. Nevertheless, Yahya still refused to commit himself on the question of what was to be done with Sheikh Mujib. He declared that only those Awami League elected members who had revolted or were guilty of crimes would be disqualified from taking up their seats in the assemblies. By-elections would be held to fill the vacancies. He did not find the Awami League oath itself incompatible with the concept of a united Pakistan. In his view it was merely a commitment to the perfectly legitimate objectives of maximum autonomy and the end of exploitation.[80]

Subsequently, from mid-May until mid-June, a period of intense political activity followed both outside and inside Pakistan, directed to reversing the growth of the refugee outflow into India and to laying the foundations for a political settlement in East Pakistan. On the international front, on 19 May U Thant had followed up the first indications of Pakistan's new attitude by an appeal for a programme of international assistance to support the refugees in India until their 'voluntary repatriation' could be brought about.[81] Within three weeks, some $38m was collected through the United Nations. Early in June, it was announced that a United Nations group and a Pakistani inter-governmental committee would work 'very closely together in planning and organizing' relief work in East Pakistan. Mr Ismat T. Kittani, the Iraqi United Nations Assistant Secretary-General for inter-agency affairs, visited both parts of Pakistan to prepare a report on the rehabilitation needs of East Bengal.[82] Meanwhile, on 30 May it was announced in Dacca that the Pakistan government was setting up reception camps near Jessore, Kushtia, Rajshahi, Dinajpur, Mymensingh, Sylhet, Rangpur, Comilla and Chittagong. Early in June, the United Nations High Commissioner for Refugees, Prince Sadruddin Aga Khan, visited Islamabad and Delhi to discuss the problem of the repatriation of the refugees. On 10 June Lt.-Gen. Tikka Khan reiterated President Yahya's appeal to the refugees to return. He went on to declare a general amnesty for 'all classes of people' who had fled to India, including political workers and leaders, and members of the armed forces and other law-enforcing agencies.[83]

[80] *Dawn*, 25 May.
[81] *Bangla Desh Documents*, p. 626.
[82] Texts in *ibid.*, pp. 628–92; and *Pakistan Horizon*, XXIV, No. 3, p. 123.
[83] *Dawn*, 11 June 1971.

The shift to this more moderate policy indicates that within Pakistan President Yahya Khan still retained the political initiative, in the face of the resistance from 'hard-line' army opinion to measures which they felt might jeopardize Pakistan's permanent hold on the East, and despite Mr Bhutto's calls for the immediate creation of a civilian government. It was rumoured that there were bitter struggles within the leadership in Islamabad and Dacca relating to the adoption of the new policy. But reliable information was and is impossible to secure. Meanwhile Mr Bhutto's case for the return of power to civilian hands — 'it is not the function of bureaucracy to overcome a political crisis' — was opposed by both the military leadership and the minority parties, arguing that the transition to civilian rule should be made simultaneously in both wings, lest allegations of the colonial status of East Pakistan be confirmed. On the other hand, the right-wing parties in the East — the Muslim Leagues, the Jamaat-i-Islami, Nezam-i-Islami, and the People's Democratic Party — announced that they were preparing to fight the by-elections announced in the President's statement of 24 May. Perhaps after all a right-wing parliamentary majority might emerge, based in East Pakistan?

Early in June, Begum Akhtar Suleman, the daughter of H. S. Suhrawardy, a friend of Sheikh Mujib, visited Dacca and held a series of meetings with some of the Awami League members of the National Assembly who had remained in East Pakistan. Subsequently it was reported that 109 Awami League members of the National Provincial Assembly had signed a declaration upholding the ideology of Pakistan and accepting the reintroduction of separate electorates for Hindus in East Bengal.[84] On 12 June the Begum spoke over Dacca radio, urging East Pakistan political figures to take advantage of General Tikka Khan's amnesty; and on the 17th she told reporters in Rawalpindi that she felt it would be unwise at that time to yield to Mr Bhutto's demands for the transfer of power. The next day Nurul Amin, the only Bengali member of the National Assembly from East Pakistan not to be elected on the Awami League ticket, declared that the co-operation of the Awami League members of the National Assembly would be required if any political solution was to be found to the problems of East Pakistan.[85]

The climax of these efforts came on 28 June, when Yahya Khan made a broadcast statement sketching out his scheme for political

---

[84] These reports were followed by a call from Yahya Khan on 18 June for Hindu refugees to return to their home – they were 'Pakistani citizens and the question of discriminatory treatment against them does not arise'.

[85] *Financial Times*, 8 June. *The Hindu*, 7 and 9 June. *Dawn*, 18 June. *Hindustan Standard*, 22 June.

MARCH–JUNE: ACTION AND REACTION

reconciliation and for a resumption of progress towards the adoption of a constitution and the transfer of power to a civilian government.[86] Yahya's new proposals were designed to bring about the co-operation of the army regime with a combination of rightist forces including those Awami League elected members willing to respect the unity of Pakistan in the form laid down in the new constitution. This was now to be promulgated by the President—a logical, if familiar, resolution of the fundamental dilemma which we have diagnosed in Pakistan's constitution-making. This new proposal for the framing of the constitution was the main feature of the speech. The task was to be removed from the National Assembly and transferred to a group of experts, as after the 1954 constitutional crisis. When the draft came to the Assembly, it was only to be subject to amendment according to procedures which were to be laid down in the constitution itself. According to Yahya the committee had also been asked to consider whether it would be possible to ban any party 'which is confined to a specific region and is not national in the practical sense'.

The President followed this thinly-veiled threat to Mr Bhutto with the comment that 'a reasonable amount of normalcy' must have returned before the transfer could be effected. He anticipated that this could be accomplished within 'a matter of four months or so'. Although he again denounced the Awami League leadership and Mujib by name, Yahya still did not reveal what he proposed to do with the Sheikh. He carefully avoided any blanket denunciation of the League, and he appealed to those of its members 'who had nothing to do with the secessionist policies of the ruling clique' to 'come forward and play their part in rebuilding the political structure in East Pakistan'. He added that a list of members of the National and Provincial Assemblies who were to be disqualified was being prepared but was not yet complete. While these preparations for a return to normal politics were going ahead, the President hoped that the 'displaced persons' would return to their homes. 'We shall gladly and gratefully accept any assistance that the United Nations can extend in facilitating the move of these displaced persons back to Pakistan.'

Yahya Khan's rambling but apparently purposeful oration of 28 June was the high-water mark of his policy after the action of 25 March. In the preceding months the army had re-established control in all the major centres of population in the East, and during late May and June groups of foreign journalists and parliamentarians had been

---

[86] Text in *Pakistan Horizon*, XXIV, No. 3, pp. 111–23. See Appendix 6, p. 174.

allowed to visit them. In West Pakistan, despite the conflicting pressures within the army, Yahya had remained on top of the situation; and there seemed to be a growing prospect of a political settlement based on a dictated constitution. An alliance between the army regime in Islamabad and a selection of right-wing politicians from both parts of Pakistan offered the hope of maintaining the unity of the country and of overriding Mr Bhutto in the West.

Externally also, by the end of June Pakistan seemed to have recovered her balance. Although China's diplomatic commitments had not gone as far as Pakistan had wanted, her material support had been both practical and extensive. In the United States the administration was successfully resisting criticism from within the Congress of the continuance of American economic aid to Pakistan.[87] American arms sales to Pakistan were still going on. Within the United Nations the groundwork was being laid for an extensive relief programme in East Pakistan; and this increasingly active international presence in East Bengal was taking place on terms acceptable to the authorities in Islamabad. In India, after a brief scare about the possibility of a cholera epidemic, the inflow of refugees had fallen sharply in mid-June. Delhi was coming under increasing pressure from 'world opinion' to permit internationally supervised repatriation of the refugees. In the Soviet Union the Indians had been disappointed to find that Mr Kosygin's carefully balanced approach to Pakistan's problems was to the fore during Mr Swaran Singh's visit to Moscow in early June. Although in Washington and London the Indian Foreign Minister had obtained statements reiterating the importance of a peaceful political settlement, it was clear that when the Aid Pakistan consortium met again at the end of June the support of the United States would be given to Islamabad's request for a renewal of Western aid to Pakistan.[88]

[87] See, for example, *Bangla Desh Documents*, pp. 520–61.
[88] Texts relating to Mr Swaran Singh's visits are in *Bangla Desh Documents*, pp. 686–96, 697–8.

Chapter 3

July–August: the Indo–Soviet Treaty

DESPITE these successes at the diplomatic level, in East Bengal itself the military and political situation facing the Pakistani authorities after the end of June became increasingly difficult. There was a continuing outflow of refugees; and although there was a lull in the second and third weeks of June, it proved to be temporary.[89] The refugee figures again began to mount steadily from the approximately six millions reported by the Indian government in mid-June. Very few of those who had crossed the border earlier seemed to be willing or able to make use of the facilities provided for their repatriation. Inside East Pakistan the widespread damage done to property and communications during the military operations still had to be repaired. Amost everywhere those Bengalis who had stayed at their posts maintained a sullen and uncooperative passivity which delayed the work of reconstruction.

In East Pakistan and in India the leaders of the Bangla Desh movement and their official and unofficial supporters had spent the months of May and June in preparing for a terrorist and guerrilla campaign against the Pakistani 'occupation forces'.[90] As we have seen, by the end of April the establishment of control by the Pakistan army over the main centres of population in East Bengal had been followed by the withdrawal of a nucleus of organized Bengali resistance forces with the other refugees over the borders into India. Groups of 'freedom fighters' were also beginning to form in the interior, among the swamps of the Sundarbans in the south-west, in the Noakhali area (where there had been a small-scale revolutionary peasant 'Naxalite' movement before 25 March), and especially in the forested hilly areas in the centre of East Pakistan, south of Mymensingh.

The entry on to Indian soil of these armed groups of former members of the East Bengal Rifles, the East Pakistan Rifles, the Bengali

---

[89] On pp. 75–6 there is a discussion of the possibility that the renewal of the exodus—in which Hindus had now become the largest elements was deliberately fostered by the military administration in East Pakistan, notwithstanding Islamabad's official policy of reconciliation.

[90] Their problems are discussed in K. Subrahmanyam, pp. 54–67, 77–9.

Police and other paramilitary forces—perhaps some 20,000 men in all—provided a means for the extension of Indian support for Bangla Desh. The provision of assistance for the *Mukti Fauj* (people's army), followed logically from the earlier Indian decision, made at the end of March, that there could be no immediate direct intervention. As soon as it had become apparent by the end of April that a nucleus for a Bangla Desh military effort existed, the support already given to the Bangla Desh political forces was extended to it. When the straggling and dishevelled groups which had taken part in the Bengali resistance after 25 March arrived at the Indian borders they were greeted by the Indian Border Security Force and by representatives of the Bangla Desh Awami League provisional government, which had been proclaimed by Mr Tajuddin Ahmed earlier in the month. In mid-April the rudiments of a military structure was set up across the Indian borders under a former regular officer in the Pakistan army, Colonel A. G. Osmani, who was appointed to serve as a member of the Bangla Desh cabinet and as the commander of the *Mukti Fauj*. In later months his preoccupation with the preparation of a regular war on conventional lines came under heavy criticism from those who envisaged a long-drawn-out partisan war. But the authority he carried over from his former rank provided a valuable link between those Bengalis who, like himself, had been regulars in the Pakistan army and their new leaders in the complicated and fractious world of the exiled Bengali politicians.

Early in May Osmani's forces were already beginning to think out their strategy while they were being regrouped in camps provided for them by India. As well as the regulars from the former Pakistan military and paramilitary units, there were among the floods of refugees who were beginning to pour across the border many young men anxious to volunteer for the fight against Pakistan. Some were recruited into the regular formations under Osmani's command, but for most of them a brief spell of training as 'freedom fighters' was all that could be arranged. Much of this effort at military training arose spontaneously among young Bengali refugees; but instruction, arms, and other facilities were increasingly provided by the Border Security Forces and the Indian army. As the months passed after the beginning of May the Bangla Desh government-in-exile was also more and more active in mobilizing financial support in India and elsewhere for the purchase of arms.

Although the political world of Bangla Desh in exile was deeply divided by factional disputes, its almost complete dependence upon Indian support nevertheless held it together. Within the Awami League provisional government the most important of these divisions

JULY–AUGUST: THE INDO-SOVIET TREATY

centred on Mr Tajuddin Ahmed's position as acting leader. Personal rivalries and long-standing ideological differences now shaded into disagreements over policy—notably, from mid-May onwards, over the proper response to President Yahya's overtures and the accompanying blandishments of the Americans.

The possibility that Sheikh Mujib might be dead was one source of conflict. Another was the possibility that if he were still alive he might be persuaded to co-operate with President Yahya. In that event, what future could there be for the Bangla Desh movement in exile in India?

In this situation the exiled leaders of the Awami League faced a strong challenge from the left. The most important of the leftist groups were Maulana Bashani's wing of the National Awami Party, the less radical 'pro-Moscow' Muzaffar group of the NAP, and a number of organizations describing themselves as 'Communist'. Their strength lay in their freedom from the taint of compromise with the oppressor which clung to some sections of the Awami League, and also in the widely held conviction that, as the terrorist movement and guerrilla campaign developed into peasant insurgency, the revolutionary forces of the left would inevitably take over the lead from the bourgeois constitutionalists dominating the Awami League. On the other hand, the Awami League claimed that it alone was competent to form a provisional government, by virtue of its victory in the 1970 general election. Members of the groups outside the Awami League were therefore jealously excluded from the government-in-exile; and during the early period of the formation of the *Mukti Fauj* the League leadership also sought to 'screen' volunteers for the 'freedom struggle' in an attempt to exclude the supporters of their leftist opponents. But as well as eroding the fragile political unity of the liberation movement, this endeavour to maintain political control over the armed struggle put a further strain on relations between the politicians in Calcutta and the emerging groups of militants in the refugee camps. Until it was abandoned it helped to foster the growth of a variety of guerrilla bands outside the regular organization of the *Mukti Fauj*.

These disagreements of course gave rise to a long-drawn-out argument in Calcutta and Delhi about what should be the official relationship between the Awami League and the other political forces. As we shall see, this argument was not resolved until late August, and then only imperfectly.

Apart from these factional disputes, during May and June two main questions dominated the thinking of the exiles—how should they prepare for war, and what, if any, should be the terms of peace?

Early in April, as they withdrew towards the Indian borders, the Bengali regulars had destroyed a number of important communication links along this line of retreat. Major Zia's destruction of the Feni and Muhuri bridges had cut most of the country off from its main port at Chittagong. In many places—especially on the eastern side of the province—important roads and railways lay conveniently close to the Indian border and the guerrilla-held enclaves. It was clear that, with its wide rivers, the East Pakistani terrain lent itself to attacks on the system of communications.

It was necessary to move rapidly to take advantage of the opportunities presented by these circumstances, because during the monsoon period between June and September the conditions for a campaign directed against the Pakistani communications would be at their best. Two-thirds of the country was waterlogged; and while the mobility of the Pakistani forces was severely reduced by seasonal flooding, most of the interior could be reached rapidly and surreptitiously by water routes from the border zones. At the same time, the monsoon months were the period in which the key export crops of jute and tea were assembled and marketed;[91] and these activities depended upon a complex and fragile network of communications by river and rail. By the destruction of river craft, bridges and rolling stock the export sector of the East Pakistani economy could be brought to a halt. The guerrillas therefore planned to achieve the greatest possible disruption by attacking these targets with a combination of deep, small-scale raids over the border and sabotage and terrorism carried out from within. Directions and encouragement were transmitted to every part of East Bengal by sound broadcasting from 'Radio Bangla Desh', which began to operate almost immediately after 25 March—after the defection of the staff of Chittagong Radio. There was also a network of couriers, who were able to move almost without hindrance through the by-ways of the flooded province.

The prospect of strengthening their position in this 'monsoon offensive' was one of the factors which helped to discourage the waverers in Calcutta from compromise with President Yahya when he began to make his first tentative gestures of conciliation at the end of May. The language of his appeals and promises did not inspire confidence, especially when compared with the statements he had made between 25 March and 21 May. There were also reports of continuing brutalities in East Pakistan. While the President still kept

---

[91] There are accounts of tea and jute marketing in M. Habibullah, *The Tea Industry of Pakistan*; and in a Dacca University report on *The Marketing of Jute in East Pakistan*.

JULY–AUGUST: THE INDO–SOVIET TREATY

silent about his plans for Sheikh Mujib, he continued to attack him in his broadcasts and public statements and to denounce the Awami League leadership and other 'miscreants' and 'Indian agents' who had fled across the border. Heavy penal sentences were imposed upon the members of the Bangla Desh government-in-exile at the beginning of June after they had been tried *in absentia* by Pakistani military courts.[92]

Although, as we have seen, some Awami League legislators had come forward in Dacca early in June in response to Begum Akhtar Suleman's initiatives, the gestures made by the authorities failed to have an effect on the majority of nationalist East Bengali political leaders, many of whom had fled to India. While the Indian government continued to refuse to accord official recognition to Mr Tajuddin Ahmed's government, it encouraged the refugees in their refusal to respond to Yahya's overtures, at the same time pressing for integration of non-Awami League elements into the leadership of the government-in-exile. At the beginning of June Mr Tajuddin Ahmed assured an interviewer: 'there is no room for compromise within the framework of Pakistan. Bangla Desh is sovereign and independent, and we shall defend its separate and free identity at any cost.' When the climax of President Yahya's first set of initiatives for a settlement came in his broadcast at the end of the month, this commitment among the exiles remained unbroken; and, most significantly, it was upheld by the more moderate sections of the Awami League in exile. Their view was expressed on 29 June by A. H. M. Kamurazzaman, the 'Home Minister of Bangla Desh', when he declared: 'Bangla Desh is an independent nation with Bangabandu Sheikh Mujibur Rahman as President. If there are any persons competent to speak about Bangla Desh they are the people elected by the people of Bangla Desh —that is the government of Sheikh Mujib.'[93]

As we have seen, during May the Indian government had been preoccupied with the consequences of the decision it had taken early in April not to restrict the inflow of refugees from East Bengal. Unofficially, during this period it also began to support and encourage the consolidation of the Bangla Desh government-in-exile. Meanwhile the Indian armed forces began to lay the groundwork of military assistance to the Bengali resistance movement.[94] But on the

[92] *Radio Pakistan,* 8 June 1971.
[93] Text in *Bangla Desh Documents,* pp. 324–45.
[94] *The Times of India,* 13 July, carries a report of a speech by the Indian Defence Minister, Mr Jagjivan Ram, declaring that the Bangla Desh freedom fighters had 'all our sympathy and support'.

official level India continued to express her reliance on the force of world opinion and the intercession of the great powers—a hope expressed in Mrs Gandhi's statement in the Lok Sabha on 24 May, when she declared that 'a political solution must be brought about by those who have the power to do so. World opinion is a great force. The great powers have special responsibility.'[95]

While preparing to bring military pressure to bear both through the guerrilla movement and by conventional means, the primary purpose of Indian diplomacy in the first two months after the events of March was to promote intervention by the United Nations to create political conditions in East Pakistan which would 'stop any further influx of refugees and ensure their early return under credible guarantees for their future safety and well-being'. But, as Mrs Gandhi pointed out, 'if the world does not take heed, we shall be constrained to take all measures as may be necessary to ensure our own security and the preservation and development of the structure of our social and economic life'. The Indian government knew that, as the exodus of refugees continued, it was acquiring a powerful hold over Pakistan by becoming a necessary party to any settlement: for the definition of 'credible guarantees' lay very largely in Indian hands. At first India had attempted to use the refugee issue primarily as a means of supporting her pleas for international pressure on Pakistan, arguing that the refugees had created an internal problem for her. This was the basis for her call for United Nations action against Pakistan at the meeting of the United Nations Economic and Social Council (ECOSOC) early in May 1971. At this stage, as we have seen, the Pakistanis had not yet begun their shift of policy towards the admission of an international presence into East Pakistan. Pakistan's representative therefore tried to have the discussion ruled out of order, on the ground that it was an interference in the internal affairs of his country.[96] But immediately after the May meeting of the ECOSOC the Pakistani position on international intervention began to change; and the Indians saw that the kind of settlement they thought appropriate could not be obtained through the United Nations. Early in June Mr Swaran Singh made a tour of the capitals of the great powers. Although his visits led to an increase in the provision of international assistance for the refugees in India, and had some effect on the attitude of the Western powers to the continued grant of economic assistance to Pakistan, it also became quite plain to the Indians that international pressure alone could not be relied

[95] The text of this speech is in *Bangla Desh Documents*, pp. 672–5.

[96] In the event the meeting could only reach agreement on the basis of a resolution concerning the internal affairs of South Africa.

JULY–AUGUST: THE INDO-SOVIET TREATY

upon to produce a result which would satisfy Indian opinion. A dramatic deterioration in the relations between India and the United States began when this fact became apparent. Shortly after the Foreign Minister's return to Delhi in mid-June it was revealed that, despite what were regarded in India as their firm denials, the Americans were continuing to deliver arms bought under licence by Pakistan. The next few months were punctuated by news of these continued arms shipments, which Washington seemed unable—or unwilling—to stop.[97]

At the same time, India's suspicions of the political implications of a United Nations role in East Pakistan grew as plans for co-operation in relief operations inside East Pakistan were elaborated between the Pakistani authorities and the United Nations agencies. The efforts of the United Nations' High Commission for Refugees to achieve the repatriation of the East Bengali refugees were viewed with increasing distrust in Delhi; and there was a public outcry when it was reported in the Indian Press at the end of June that the High Commissioner, Prince Sadruddin, had allegedly blamed the liberation movement for giving rise to a 'gigantic problem' of displaced persons.

Thus, in the course of May and June the Indians and the Pakistanis both simultaneously changed the attitude they had previously taken up towards the United Nations. While at first India had been pressing for international intervention and Pakistan had opposed it, from June onwards these positions were reversed. Pakistan became more and more anxious to secure the active presence of sympathetic outside powers and agencies, while India became more and more concerned to prevent it. When the ECOSOC met again in July Pakistan did not repeat her previous opposition to the discussion of her 'internal affairs'; and when a proposal emerged for the posting of United Nations observers at the borders, Islamabad accepted it with alacrity and Delhi rejected it. By the end of June India had fully occupied the diplomatic positions abandoned with such suspicious alacrity by President Yahya in May, when he had himself changed direction and commenced the long march towards the 'internationalization' of the East Pakistan problem.[98]

---

[97] See footnote [103] on p. 64, for references to Mr Swaran Singh's discussions in Washington. The deterioration in relations between India and the United States is illustrated in Mr Swaran Singh's speeches of 12, 19 and 20 July, reprinted in *Bangla Desh Documents*, pp. 699, 702–3, and 703–11.

[98] For further references to the ECOSOC meeting see pp. 66–7. The statement made to the ECOSOC by Mr Samas Sen, India's permanent representative at the UN, on 12 May 1971, is printed in *Bangla*

A new phase of the crisis began early in July, when the Bengali 'monsoon offensive' began to get under way and when Yahya Khan's political initiatives in East Pakistan failed to evoke a significant response among the refugees in India. President Yahya's conciliatory gestures after the middle of May had perhaps in any case been designed mainly to encourage Western support and to impress the next meeting of the World Bank's Pakistan aid consortium, which was due to meet in Paris in the third week of June. But on 21 June his diplomacy suffered a major reverse when the consortium adjourned *sine die* without reaching agreement on the future of multilateral Western economic aid to Pakistan—although it recommended the continuation of humanitarian relief assistance.

This decision to terminate World Bank development aid was influenced by the strenuous diplomatic efforts which India had made since April, including Mr Swaran Singh's world tour early in June. But probably even more important was the highly critical oral report made by Mr Peter Cargill, the head of the ten-man team of World Bank officials which had been established in May to study economic prospects in both West and East Pakistan on behalf of the Bank. Early in July, two weeks after the adjournment of the consortium, Mr Cargill's written report was leaked to the world's Press. It described widespread and heavy damage to property in East Pakistan, the destruction of communications facilities, and the disruption of the economy by repressive military action and by continuing punitive measures against the civilian population. One of the members of the team reported, perhaps a little imaginatively, that the town of Kushtia looked like 'the morning after a nuclear attack'. The report concluded that administration and commercial and industrial life had virtually come to a halt. Renewed international development assistance 'would serve little purpose now'.[99]

[99] *The Times*, London, 12 July; *The Times of India*, 13 and 17 July. Some extracts from the report are printed in *Bangla Desh Documents*, pp. 515–19. The statement of the World Bank Aid-to-Pakistan Consortium is printed in *Pakistan Horizon*, XXIV, No. 3, pp. 142–3.

Desh Documents, op. cit., pp. 618–23. The contrast between India's position at this time and her view by the end of May can be traced in *ibid.*, pp. 660–63, where the Indian reply on 2 August to U Thant's initiative arising from the July meeting of ECOSOC is reprinted. The parallel evolution of Pakistan's position may be followed in the comparison between President Yahya's letter to U Thant on 29 April and the *aide-mémoire* submitted by Pakistan to the Secretary General on 13 August 1971. See *Pakistan Horizon*, XXIV, No. 2, p. 141, and XXIV, No. 3, pp. 131–9.

JULY–AUGUST: THE INDO–SOVIET TREATY

The bilateral assistance programmes of the Western powers were immediately affected in their turn by the report of the Cargill team and by the World Bank's decision, which followed hard upon Mr Swaran Singh's visit to the Western capitals. On 23 June Sir Alec Douglas-Home told the House of Commons that Britain would not resume her development aid programme in Pakistan until there was firm evidence of progress towards a political solution in the East Wing.[100] A series of Pakistani protests against British policy followed, and it was reported that a study-group had been set up in the Ministry of Foreign Affairs to consider the future of Pakistan's links with the Commonwealth.[101] The Swedish, Dutch and West German aid schemes were also suspended early in July;[102] and in the United States opinion in Congress and among the wider public—already disturbed by the revelations of continuing American arms exports to Pakistan —moved more and more sharply against the continuance of support for Yahya's regime. On 15 July the House of Representatives' Foreign Affairs Committee voted by seventeen votes to six to suspend economic as well as military aid to Pakistan until the situation had returned to normal in the East.

However, the American government was moving in a different direction. On the 14th the Administration announced that United States economic and technical assistance would be withheld from Pakistan—but only till a fresh list of development projects was submitted, 'taking into account the present situation' in East Pakistan. At the same time the official spokesman declared that the Administration's previously announced request for an appropriation of

[100] Sir Alec's statement of 23 June, and the text of the agreed statement issued by Mr Swaran Singh and Sir Alec Douglas-Home on 21 June, are printed in *Bangla Desh Documents*, pp. 508–10.

[101] *Dawn*, 16 July. There was, however, a temporary improvement in relations between Britain and Pakistan during July, when Sir Alec gave his support to the proposals made at ECOSOC and endorsed by U Thant, for the sending of United Nations 'observers' or 'representatives' to the East Pakistan borders. On 27 July a Foreign Office spokesman declared that in the British view the achievement of a political settlement in East Pakistan was 'the exclusive responsibility of the Pakistan government'; and on 7 August it was announced in London that Britain would send two landing-craft to East Pakistan to assist relief operations. Two days later President Yahya declared that he would welcome British or Commonwealth mediation between India and Pakistan. British policy during the last months of 1971 is discussed from a Pakistan standpoint in Khalida Qureshi, 'Britain and the Indo–Pakistan conflict over East Pakistan', *Pakistan Horizon*, XXV, No. 1, pp. 32–44.

[102] *The Times of India*, 9 July.

$188 million for economic assistance for Pakistan in 1972 would still be pressed and that humanitarian relief to East Pakistan—including help with the restoration of communications—would be increased.[103]

One element in the reasoning behind the position taken up by the American government was probably the view expressed by the Cargill team:

> Just as at the time of the mission's visit all the major elements in the situation appeared to reinforce each other in making early normalization impossible to envisage, it is conceivable that a major improvement in one of them may have a snow-ball effect. Thus it is possible that the railways will function better than the mission thought likely, and that, if in addition the carrying capacity of the coastal fleet is increased considerably and the country-boats reappear, the physical constraints to recovery could be reduced considerably, and thus incentives for renewed economic activity will be strengthened to the point where the psychological constraints lose some of their power.

On the other hand, the strategy of the *Mukti Bahini* 'monsoon offensive' was based on the same reasoning but directed to a different end—strengthening the 'psychological constraints' on immediate recovery by reducing incentives and capacity for economic activity in

---

[103] *The Times of India*, 15 July. The American government's policy was extensively discussed in the Foreign Assistance Appropriations Sub-Committee during the first two weeks of July. Mr William Rogers' testimony of 1 July was published on 8 September. He stated that Mr Swaran Singh had been told that the United States 'would not condition future economic assistance to Pakistan on a political settlement in East Pakistan'. He explained that 'the decisions to provide developmental assistance would be made on the basis of development criteria'. The two foreign ministers had also 'spoken briefly' about military sales by the United States to Pakistan. Mr Rogers remarked that 'resumption of military sales on a normal basis would naturally increase our influence with the martial-law administration in Pakistan'; and that while 'economic' aid would not be extended to acquire leverage, it was a fact that:

> by not suspending aid for political reasons we stand to retain influence whereby we should be able to continue the dialogue we have had with the Pakistanis—expressing our concern over developments in East Pakistan, counselling restraint, recommending a genuine political settlement reflecting the sentiments of the people and urging the co-operative implementation of an international relief programme.

Indian Express, 9 September.

JULY–AUGUST: THE INDO–SOVIET TREATY

East Pakistan. A fundamental divergence of view accordingly began to emerge, between what we might call the 'United Nations approach', which put social and economic recovery first—although it could have had the effect of strengthening the Pakistani authorities—and the 'Indian approach', which insisted upon a political solution founded upon the principle of self-determination and independence for Bangla Desh.

However, the support given by the White House to the 'United Nations approach' was not determined solely by the desire that America should contribute to the restoration of normality in East Pakistan. Other factors came into play. On 6 July Dr Henry Kissinger visited Delhi on his way to Islamabad. He explained that the continuing flow of arms to Pakistan was nothing more sinister than a case of 'bureaucratic muddle'.[104] It was widely believed in India that the purpose of his visit to Pakistan was to assist the effort to bring President Yahya closer to a compromise with the Awami League, along the lines which President Yahya had opened up during the previous month. On 9 July Dr Kissinger was reported ill with 'stomach-ache', and it was rumoured that he was secretly trying to win over Sheikh Mujib's legal adviser, Dr Kamal Hussain, imprisoned with the Sheikh in West Pakistan.

In fact, Dr Kissinger was talking with the Chinese Prime Minister in Peking; and on 15 July President Nixon announced on American television that it had been agreed that he should visit China at some date before May 1972.

This dramatic development was regarded in Islamabad as a major diplomatic success for Pakistan. For his part in bringing it about, Yahya had increased his store of goodwill in Washington; and he knew that he could count upon Chinese co-operation in helping to induce the Americans to continue their support for Pakistan.[105] The Sino–American rapprochement which now seemed likely would unite Pakistan's principal friends, for so long at loggerheads. This coming together was regarded as a decisive deterrent to any Indian adventures in East Bengal. It also opened up the possibility of the entry of Pakistan's most vehement supporter into the United Nations Security Council before the end of the year.

---

[104] *The Times of India*, 8 July.

[105] The delicacy of relations with Islamabad was reflected in the fact that in Washington more stress was laid upon Rumania as the main channel of communication with Peking. But Pakistan's part was obviously more important.

President Yahya immediately pressed his advantage. The policy which he had been developing since mid-May—in line with American advice—was to act through the United Nations to compel India to give up her support for the Bangla Desh forces and to reduce the border tensions which impeded the return of the refugees. Since the beginning of the crisis in March, the situation in East Pakistan had been represented by Pakistan as yet another round in the perennial quarrel between the two sub-continental states. In accordance with this concept Yahya stated on 12 July that he was willing to meet Mrs Gandhi anywhere and at any time, and that he would welcome United Nations representatives at all refugee repatriation centres in East Pakistan.[106] But 'the lady said no', he told Neville Maxwell in an interview published on the 18th.[107] And he added that if any attempt was made to seize an area of East Pakistan as a rebel base 'I shall declare a general war—and let the world take note of it'. Reports began to circulate of military preparations along the West Pakistan border with India.[108]

By mid-July the reversal of Pakistan's previous attitude to the introduction of the United Nations into East Pakistan was complete. On 17 July, U Thant's special representative Mr Ismat T. Kittani—an Iraqi—submitted a report on East Pakistan's relief needs. On the basis of his consultations with Pakistani officials he recommended the immediate raising by the United Nations of a sum of $28 million for the first phase of rehabilitation—including help with the reconstruction of road and rail transport.[109] He calculated that some 450,000 tons of food grains, 15 coastal vessels, 25 river boats, and 1,000 trucks were needed. Such was the scale of the relief aid needed to provide the foundation for a return to normality in East Pakistan. But, as we have seen, such a relief effort would necessarily involve the reinstatement by international action of destruction being deliberately carried out in East Bengal by the Bengali liberation movement. Mr Kittani's report was therefore as welcome in Islamabad as it was unwelcome in Calcutta—and Delhi.

Throughout July the activities of the United Nations in East Pakistan continued to expand. At the ECOSOC meeting which began in Geneva on 5 July Pakistan no longer blocked the discussion of her 'internal problems', and a special report on the refugee situa-

[106] *Indian Express*, 14 July; *The Times of India*, 15 July.
[107] *Financial Times*, 18 July.
[108] *The Times of India*, 23 July.
[109] A similar, American, report was released by the American government on 17 July, emphasizing the need for immediate help for East Pakistan with food supplies—and transport equipment.

JULY–AUGUST: THE INDO–SOVIET TREATY

tion was submitted by the High Commissioner for Refugees.[110] On the 9th, the Pakistani representative, Mr Agha Shahi, advanced a mild and conciliatory defence of the actions of his government. In his speech he described the refugees as 'undoubtedly a burden on India'.[111] On 19 July, it was announced that Mr John Kelly was to represent the High Commissioner for Refugees in Dacca—a new role for the United Nations in addition to its recently acquired functions as a relief agency in East Pakistan. Meanwhile, earlier in the month—with American encouragement—the Pakistanis had begun to urge that United Nations 'observers' or 'representatives' should be sent to the East Pakistan border to help to create favourable conditions for the return of the refugees.[112] This suggestion was discussed at the ECOSOC meeting; and it was reported on 12 July that President Yahya himself had endorsed it. These pressures reached a peak on the 19th—the same day as Mr Kelly was appointed to Dacca—when U Thant sent an *aide-mémoire* to the two governments, suggesting that UNHCR 'representatives' be stationed along both sides of the border.[113] This proposal did not involve 'humanitarian peace-keeping' or the placing of 'observers'—which would require a positive initiative of the Security Council. The suggestion was immediately welcomed by the Pakistanis and by the American and British governments.

But on 27 July Mr Hossain Ali, the head of the Bangla Desh mission in Calcutta, declared that U Thant's scheme 'should be viewed with the utmost contempt' and that, although United Nations personnel were 'honoured people', their safety against the *Mukti Fauj* could not be guaranteed.[114] On 18 August a senior *Mukti Fauj* commander was reported as saying: 'we have no other recourse but to give the United Nations observers the same treatment as is meted out to the Pakistani supporters and collaborators in Bangla Desh'.[115] On 3 August, two weeks after U Thant's initiative, the Indian Foreign Minister officially rejected his proposal on the ground that it could not by itself create 'the necessary feeling of confidence' among the

---

[110] The texts of many of the important statements at the July session of the ECOSOC are reprinted in *Bangla Desh Documents*, pp. 642–55.

[111] *The Times of India*, 13 July.

[112] *The Times of India*, 22 July.

[113] The *aide-mémoire* is reprinted in *Bangla Desh Documents*, pp. 657–8. On 24 August the United Nations presence in East Pakistan was reinforced by the appointment of M. Paul-Marc Henri to represent the Secretary-General in Dacca.

[114] *The Statesman*, 27 July.

[115] *Hindustan Times*, 18 August.

refugees—whose numbers were by now in excess of seven million. 'What is needed is an immediate stoppage of military atrocities . . . and a political solution acceptable to the people of Bangla Desh through their already elected representatives.' India, he declared, particularly objected to any United Nations action which might allow Pakistan to shuffle off her responsibility for the crisis by making the issue one between herself and India—the 'mere posting of observers will only create a façade of action as a cover for the continuation of the present policies of the military rulers of Pakistan, and further aggravate the suffering of the people of Bangla Desh'.[116]

Nevertheless, the United Nations was not without influence. A decision by the Security Council to endorse the Secretary-General's plan for the stationing of observers would at the very least be profoundly embarrassing for India. On 20 July, the day after he had addressed his *aide-mémoire* to the governments of India and Pakistan, U Thant took the unusual step of presenting a memorandum to the President and members of the Security Council describing the dangers of the situation in East Pakistan and recommending the stationing of UNHCR representatives on the border . 'Border clashes, clandestine raids, and acts of sabotage appear to be becoming more frequent, and this is all the more serious since the refugees must cross this disturbed border if repatriation is to become a reality.' The Secretary-General wished the members of the Security Council to consider the situation, and to attempt to reach 'agreed conclusions as to measures which might be taken. . . . Naturally it is for the members of the Security Council themselves to decide whether such consideration should take place formally or informally, in public or in private.'[117]

The prospects of great-power pressure on India which these proposals opened up, and the negative Indian reaction to U Thant's suggestions, placed Pakistan in an increasingly favourable position for securing an increase in relief aid and a restoration of economic assistance, and for acting through the United Nations to restrain the guerrilla operations being conducted across the Indian border. At the same time the dramatic developments in Sino–American relations during July brought home to India the difficulty of pursuing her policy of assisting the Bangla Desh liberation movement without the support of one of the great powers. There was a danger that if she

[116] The Indian reply of 2 August to U Thant's *aide-mémoire* is printed in *Bangla Desh Documents*, pp. 660–63.
[117] *Bangla Desh Documents*, pp. 658–60. See Appendix 7, p. 184.

JULY-AUGUST: THE INDO-SOVIET TREATY

could find no backing in the Security Council, her rival might be successful in her efforts to invoke United Nations assistance.

For India in this situation there were only two possible courses. She could give up her commitment to support 'the elected representatives of the people of Bangla Desh', in the hope that world opinion as expressed in the United Nations would succeed in inducing President Yahya to give substance to his promises of a 'transfer of power'. That is, she could accept U Thant's proposals, and co-operate with the United Nations in securing the 'voluntary repatriation' of the refugees. Or, on the other hand, she could remain adamant against the growing pressure from Pakistan's friends and continue to give the 'wholehearted sympathy and support' she had pledged to the Bangla Desh government—in the hope that sustained and increasing military activity across the borders would eventually lead to an acceptable settlement. The prospect of direct Indian involvement in the war in East Pakistan was implied in such a strategy: for India could not continue indefinitely to support the burden of the refugees, and neither could she live with a protracted and perhaps increasingly extreme state of tension in East Bengal. In making its choice the Indian government was obliged to take into account the fact that within India—and particularly in the troubled state of West Bengal—there was very strong opposition to any slackening in the pursuit of self-determination in Bangla Desh. Many influential voices had declared themselves in favour of a war with Pakistan over East Bengal. Most Indians believed that to accept U Thant's suggestions would be to abandon Bangla Desh to many more years of continuing savage repression; and they held that the consequences of submitting to United Nations pressure would be humiliation for India and the collapse of confidence in Mrs Gandhi's government, followed by endemic bloodshed and instability in East Bengal—until in the end the position became untenable for Pakistan. But how were these prospects to be avoided? And how, in particular, was India to prevent the United Nations from providing a shield for Pakistan?

As we have already remarked, after President Podgorny's letter of 3 April to President Yahya, the Soviet Union had returned to a balancing attitude calculated to strengthen her influence in both India and Pakistan. Mr Kosygin's correspondence at the end of April with President Yahya had softened the impression created in Pakistan by the Soviet letter earlier in the month. In May a number of agreements for Soviet-Pakistani economic co-operation were announced; early in June it was revealed that Pakistani visas were being reissued to the Russian technical advisers who had been withdrawn from East

Pakistan after 25 March.[118] On 8 June, in a joint statement at the end of Mr Swaran Singh's visit to Moscow, the Russians expressed an identity of views with India concerning the 'creation of conditions for the return of refugees to their homes, the granting of guarantees of their personal safety, and a possibility to live calmly and work in East Pakistan'. But they refused to be drawn into an endorsement of the Indian emphasis on the need for a specifically political settlement to make it possible for the refugees to return.[119] Later in the month, Mr Kosygin was reported as having again affirmed to the Pakistani ambassador that the Soviet Union held to its view that the situation in East Pakistan was an internal affair of Pakistan.[120] In July, as the Western powers moved one by one to suspend economic assistance to Pakistan, Russian aid continued. On the other hand, Moscow took great pains to reassure Delhi that arms supplies to Pakistan had been discontinued a year previously.[121]

The indications in the Soviet Press were equally ambivalent. At the beginning of July, a Moscow Radio commentary declared that Soviet policy was still guided by the Tashkent spirit of 'peace and good neighbourly co-operation between the Hindustan countries', and attacked 'the Peking leadership' for 'seeking to create a favourable situation for implementing its hegemonistic policies in South Asia'. But only a week later *Izvestia* listed 'Acting President of the Democratic Republic of Bangla Desh, Syed Nazrul Islam' among those leaders who had sent condolences on the death of the Soviet cosmonauts.[122]

This ambivalence concealed a genuine hesitation. Since 1965 Soviet policy had aspired to even-handedness between the two sub-continental powers, in the hope that out of a new South Asian balance a spirit of reconciliation and restraint would grow up between them. But, on the other hand, it was becoming increasingly evident that if the mounting difficulties in which India found herself—or had deliberately placed herself—were not satisfactorily resolved she would be gravely weakened and embittered. The domestic prospects and the international alignment of Mrs Gandhi's government could now be seen to turn upon her success in handling the Bangla Desh issue. The Russians also recognized that they would be compelled to take sides if the situation drifted towards war, and that war would inevitably

---

[118] *Hindustan Standard*, 5 June.
[119] The text of the statement is reprinted in *Bangla Desh Documents*, pp. 511–12.
[120] *Dawn*, 25 June.
[121] *The Statesman*, 5 July; *The Times of India*, 6, 7, 8 July.
[122] *Hindu*, 16 July.

JULY–AUGUST: THE INDO–SOVIET TREATY

strengthen Pakistan's relations with China—who did not find herself in any difficulty in siding against India.

Until July the Russians balanced these various considerations uneasily one against the other. In the hope that war might be held off, they strove to sustain the impression that they were genuinely concerned for both sides; and in both Islamabad and Delhi they urged caution and restraint. But President Nixon's announcement of 15 July created a new situation, even if merely by dramatizing a development which had been inevitable for several years. Chinese and American influence would henceforth be more deeply entrenched in Islamabad than ever before. And the way had been opened for redoubled pressure on India through the United Nations, which threatened to force Delhi either into reluctant and recalcitrant abdication or into a desperate and dangerous war. President Nixon's statement thus clarified the issues for both India and the Soviet Union. In the new circumstances, the South Asian implications of Mr Brezhnev's call in 1969 for a 'collective security system in Asia' required urgent re-examination.[123]

The immediate background to the Indo–Soviet Treaty of Peace, Friendship and Co-operation, which was signed in Delhi on 9 August by Mr Gromyko and Mr Swaran Singh, was supplied by these reflections, prompted in Moscow and Delhi by the sudden improvement of Soviet–American relations, as well as by India's anxious consideration of how to respond to U Thant's initiatives for extension of the United Nations role in East Pakistan.[124] Since March 1971 Indian foreign policy had in any case been undergoing a reappraisal. Mrs Gandhi's success in the 1971 elections had given her the authority to map out a new foreign policy for India, and the improvement of relations with the Soviet Union was always bound to be an important element in Indian policy whatever the state of India–Pakistan relations. It was later reported that the draft of the Indo–Soviet Treaty had been prepared by the Soviet Union in September 1969, three months after Mr Brezhnev had referred to an Asian collective security arrangement at the World Congress of Communist Parties. We do not know who took the model draft of the treaty from his drawer in 1971 and dusted it down—although according to the Joint Statement issued on the 9th by Mr Gromyko and Mr Swaran Singh it was the Indians who had issued the invitation to Mr Gromyko to visit Delhi.[125]

[123] See Chapter 6: *Conclusion*, for a further discussion of the thinking which underlay Soviet policy in the crisis.
[124] J. A. Naik, in *India, Russia, China and Bangla Desh*, discusses the background to the treaty, and its character and implications.
[125] See Appendix 9, p. 192.

But whoever took the initiative, the treaty was completed and agreed with extraordinary speed, and ratified in Moscow within 24 hours of signature.

The text of the treaty was modelled on the earlier agreement between the Soviet Union and Egypt in May 1971.[126] But, unlike the Soviet–Egyptian treaty, the Indo–Soviet agreement contains a clause safeguarding the established policy of non-alignment. It does not provide for a Russian military presence, and it does not embody a commitment by India to 'socialist reconstruction'. The central Article IX of the Indo–Soviet treaty is stronger than its equivalent article VII of the Egyptian treaty. In the Indian agreement, immediate 'mutual consultations' upon an attack or threat of attack on either party are provided for, 'in order to remove such threats and to take appropriate effective measures to ensure peace and the security of [both] countries'. The Egyptian equivalent indicates that when, 'in the opinion of both sides', a danger to peace arises, both parties 'will contact each other without delay in order to agree their positions with a view to removing the threat. . . .' The Indo–Soviet treaty also provides that neither party will give 'any assistance to any third party that engages in armed conflict with the other party'; and in Article X it states that both sides will refrain from undertaking any obligation 'which might cause military damage to the other party'.

Nevertheless, in the joint statement which followed the signing of the treaty the Russians were at pains to declare to Pakistan and to the world that 'the treaty is not directed against anyone'.[127] Although it was remarked that 'both sides noted with satisfaction that their positions on the various problems discussed were identical or very close', this statement was immediately followed by a double-edged assertion that in respect of East Pakistan 'there can be no military solution'. A political settlement was needed—'which alone would answer the interests of the entire people of Pakistan and the cause of the preservation of peace in the area'.

Although the Russians thus indicated that they now accepted the Indian view that the crisis in Pakistan could not be resolved without a political settlement in East Bengal, the signing of the Indo–Soviet treaty did not mean a total commitment by the Soviet Union to the Indian position, or the end of Russian attempts to bring about a peaceful solution. As we shall see, sympathetic Soviet gestures to Pakistan continued until mid-October. And while rumours in Islama-

---

[126] Naik, pp. 66–83. The text of the treaty is reprinted in Appendix 8, p. 188.
[127] Naik, pp. 147–9. See Appendix 9, on p. 192.

JULY–AUGUST: THE INDO–SOVIET TREATY

bad about the possibility of a Pakistani–Soviet non-aggression pact were scotched by the Russians in the middle of August, less than a week after the signing of the Indo–Soviet treaty, it was again confirmed that Soviet economic aid to Pakistan would continue.[128]

In Pakistan the most optimistic interpretation was naturally put upon these hints of continuing Russian sympathy. But despite these gestures Russian backing for India in the five months after the signing of the treaty was steadily available in the place where it was most immediately wanted—in the United Nations. After August the Soviet Union conscientiously supported India in opposing every proposal for any kind of United Nations intervention which might allow President Yahya to secure a political settlement unacceptable to India.

This new Soviet line became apparent immediately after the signing of the treaty. We have already remarked how, during July, President Yahya's well-publicized efforts to arrange a meeting with Mrs Gandhi through the good offices of the Shah and other intermediaries had petered out in the face of India's insistence that the crisis could only be resolved by a political accommodation between Islamabad and the representatives of the Awami League. U Thant's *aide-mémoire* of 19 July and his letter of the 20th to the President of the Security Council had opened a new phase; and for several weeks Pakistan had attempted to keep alive the Secretary-General's project for the establishment of a United Nations presence at the East Bengal borders. These attempts were now abruptly put down by the Russians. On 11 August—two days after the Indo–Soviet treaty—the Pakistani ambassador at the United Nations, Mr Agha Shahi, wrote to the President of the Security Council proposing that a 'good offices' team of the Council should visit the border areas of India and Pakistan to 'defuse the tense situation' there. Shortly afterwards it was revealed that the Pakistani Foreign Secretary's proposed visit to Moscow had been postponed.[129] On the 17th an acrimonious meeting is reported to have taken place between President Yahya and the Soviet ambassador in Pakistan, Mr A. A. Rodionov;[130] and on the 20th it was revealed that the Soviet ambassador to the United Nations had informed the Secretary-General that his country was opposed to the holding of a Security Council meeting to discuss the East Pakistan problem.[131] On 18 August, when India once again rejected the notion

[128] *The Pakistan Times*, 16 August; *Dawn*, 19 August; *The Times of India*, 10, 17, 19, 21, 25 August.
[129] *Pakistan Times*, 16 August; *The Times of India*, 25 August.
[130] *The Statesman*, 19 August.
[131] *The Statesman*, 20 August. Despite – perhaps because of – this deterioration in Pakistan–Soviet relations, economic discussions between

of United Nations 'observers' or 'good offices' teams being sent to the borders, her action took place in a very different international atmosphere from that in which she had rejected U Thant's similar proposals only two weeks previously.

Pakistan and the Soviet Union continued throughout August and September. On 23 August Pakistan took a step towards fulfilling the Russian plan for open overland transit across Afghanistan into the subcontinent. For the first time since the route was completed in November 1969 it was made use of by Pakistan—a consignment of chrome leather in ten trucks was exported through Chaman to the Soviet Union.

Chapter 4

September–November: the Approach of War

AFTER the signing of the Indo–Soviet treaty and the Soviet moves in support of India's efforts to obstruct the resolution of the crisis through the United Nations, the focus of events shifted for a time away from the diplomatic level. There was a brief lull until the next opportunity for international pressure to bring about a settlement, which would arise during the meetings of the 26th Session of the United Nations, due to begin in New York on 21 September. Over the remaining weeks of August and early September, India and Pakistan concentrated on strengthening their positions in preparation for the next round of the diplomatic contest; and the military operations being carried out by the *Mukti Fauj* across the border into East Pakistan began to mount in intensity.

In Pakistan, Yahya's attempts since June to encourage some of the moderate elements in the Awami League to co-operate with the authorities were still not making a serious impression on opinion either in the East or among the exiles. The growing military efforts of the *Mukti Fauj* after the beginning of the monsoon in June strengthened Bengali solidarity and provoked intensification of the repressive reaction of the Pakistani forces in the East under the command of Lt.-Gen. Tikka Khan. The amnesty which he announced on 10 June failed to produce a significant response. The widespread absenteeism and non-co-operation noted by the Cargill mission dragged on despite the pleas and threats of the military government. As we have seen, during the first two weeks of June the refugee outflow had fallen sharply when cholera made a brief appearance in the Indian refugee camps. But after the middle of the month the exodus began to mount again, with a growing proportion of Hindus in the total outflow. In India there was a growing belief—which was probably justified—that the army in East Bengal was deliberately seeking to expel the Hindu community in the hope of redressing the balance of population and ideology between the two wings of Pakistan. By the end of June it was reported that the exodus had reached a total of seven million.

Whether or not he encouraged the expulsion of Hindus, General Tikka Khan's policy in the East was certainly designed to purge Pakistan of Hindu influences.[132] On the other hand, it was also in part a natural response to the tactics adopted by the *Mukti Fauj*. Weak in numbers and partially immobilized by the monsoon, the Pakistani troops were compelled to use counter-terrorist tactics against the civilian population to counter the small-scale but pervasive and damaging activities of the Bangla Desh militants. Paramilitary and police forces were imported from West Pakistan, and East Pakistan *razakars* were recruited from the Bihari community and from among the Bengali supporters of the traditionalist Islamic movements. But until September the monsoon made it impossible for the Pakistani forces even to attempt to cover the borders and to prevent movement across them in both directions. The countryside lay wide open to raids and infiltration directed against Tikka Khan's forces and against the communications network supporting the economy of East Bengal. In this situation, there was almost an element of substance in the claim of the Bangla Desh spokesman during the monsoon period that 90 per cent of the province had been 'liberated'.[133] A very large part of East Pakistan was indeed not under the army's control during this period.

President Yahya's first set of political initiatives in June had been answered by a gathering of exiled Awami League leaders in the second week of July, at which some 110 members of the National Assembly and 200 members of the East Pakistan Provincial Assembly took an 'oath of all-out war till victory'. It was also decided that the guerrilla forces hitherto known as the *Mukti Fauj* were to be renamed the *Mukti Bahini* to mark the 'advent of the Air Force and the Navy'.[134] From July onwards the widely dispersed attacks on the

[132] *The Pakistan Economist*, 5, 11 June, and *The Weekly Mail*, 4, 10 June, are quoted in the *Hindustan Standard*, 17 June, as advocating the replacement of the Bengali script by Arabic or Persian script. *Dawn*, 28 May, reports a statement by the Secretary-General of the Jamaat-i-Islami, on the need for Islamic education in East Pakistan. *Dawn*, 18 July, also reports the establishment of an academy for Pakistan Affairs in East Pakistan by an ordinance of the Governor; and *The Statesman*, 28 July, discusses a number of educational measures in support of Pakistani ideology. See also *The Times of India*, 9 July, on the renaming of streets in Dacca. A Press note issued by the Dacca Municipal Corporation gave the new Islamic names which were to replace the un-Islamic ones. Chittarajan Avenue became Nazimuddin Avenue, and one street was renamed after the General himself: Shankari Bazar Road became Tikka Khan Road.

[133] *The Statesman*, 9 September.
[134] *The Statesman*, 16 July.

SEPTEMBER–NOVEMBER: THE APPROACH OF WAR

communications system and on the export crops of jute and tea developed into a co-ordinated series of attacks upon East Pakistan's communications with the outside world. The guerrilla training being provided in India began to bear fruit in the second week of August when a series of 'naval' attacks on supply ships began. On 23 August two vessels were sunk in Chittagong Harbour by limpet mines. Over the next few days several more coastal vessels and river boats were destroyed.[135] Although river craft and trucks were being provided for Pakistan in increasing numbers by friendly powers, the movement of supplies and soldiers by sea to East Pakistan and by water and land around the interior of the province was now increasingly restricted by sabotage. As its success in these efforts gained momentum, the *Mukti Bahini* grew in self-confidence; and, as we have seen, by the end of the month its spokesmen were warning that the lives of any United Nations personnel who impeded their operations would not be respected.

Internationally, the cause of Bangla Desh was also gaining in strength during this period. In August many of the Bengali officials remaining in Pakistani missions in the West defected, and the network of Bangla Desh political connections around the world became increasingly elaborate. An overseas mission was set up in London on 27 August, and an office was opened in Delhi on the 30th.[136] The flow of funds and arms to Calcutta grew in proportion to this expanding diplomatic effort.

At the same time the pressures upon the Awami League government-in-exile from the political forces of the right and left were becoming more and more clearly defined. To the right we may identify those among the refugee leaders who were not prepared to rule out the possibility of coming to terms with Pakistan and Yahya Khan, either with or without the consent or participation of Sheikh Mujib. But most of these doubters had already defected by early July, when the Awami League oath of 'war till victory' was sworn. The so-called 'Mujibists' remained more or less unreconciled to the leadership of Mr Tajuddin Ahmed and its leftward political tendency, and fearful of what would happen if Sheikh Mujib were eliminated by the Pakistani authorities. After it was announced on 9 August that Mujib was to be put on trial in Pakistan this element in opinion among the exiles—which was especially strong in the Awami League Student Movement—was compelled to accept an increasing dilution of the loyalty of the Bangla Desh government to the leadership of the

---

[135] *The Times of India*, 21 August; *India Express*, 12 August.
[136] *The Times of India*, 28 and 30 August; *Hindustan Times*, 3 August.

Sheikh. As we have seen, in the initial stages of the organization of the *Mukti Fauj,* attempts had been made to exclude members of the various political movements outside the League—just as their representatives were excluded from the government-in-exile. But during July and August the recruitment of non-members of the Awami League began. On the political level, on 15 July the leftist groups had formed a Bangla Desh National Liberation Struggle Co-ordination Committee, pledged to 'carry on armed struggle relentlessly' and to resist any compromise in their pursuit of a peasants' war.[137] This move was denounced by the Mujibists and other moderates in the Awami League government.[138] But the left-wing groups continued to press for the formation of a broad-based united-front government in which they would be included; and during August they were increasingly supported in these efforts by the Indians.

In the eyes of the Indian government these dissensions within the political leadership of the Bangla Desh movement threatened both to lead to the uncontrolled proliferation of armed leftist groups in the neighbouring Indian states, and perhaps also to the breakdown of the government-in-exile in Calcutta and the defection of the right-wing elements of the Awami League. It was also increasingly widely believed that the League alone could not represent and co-ordinate the different forces within the Bangla Desh movement and ensure their co-operation with Indian policy. Consequently, after the announcement of Mujib's trial and the signing of the Indo–Soviet Treaty, the weight of Indian influence was added to the pressure to broaden the Bangla Desh government and to widen the gap between the Bengalis and the Pakistanis.

At the end of the month Mr D. P. Dhar—the chairman of the Policy Planning Directorate of the Indian Ministry of External Affairs—held a series of meetings with representatives of the East Bengali leadership. In an interview on 30 August, he repeated that India's attitude to the recognition of Bangla Desh was still unchanged; but he went on to say that India's general commitment to a 'political solution' in East Bengal was now specifically related to the resolution calling for 'complete independence' which had been adopted at a recent meeting of the elected legislators from Bangla Desh.[139] 'When there is such intensity of faith and determination of the people for independence, the struggle is bound to succeed.' A week later, on 8 September, it was announced that a 'Five Party Consultative Com-

---

[137] *Indian Express,* 16 July.
[138] *Ananda Bazar Patrika,* 16 July.
[139] *The Statesman,* 31 August.

SEPTEMBER–NOVEMBER: THE APPROACH OF WAR

mittee' had been formed with eight members, drawn from the Awami League, the National Awami Party (Bashani), the National Awami Party (Muzaffar), the Communist Party of Bangla Desh, and the Bangla Desh National Congress.[140] Its function was to 'advise the Bangla Desh government in matters affecting the liberation struggle. Although it fell a long way short of satisfying the demand for a united-front government-in-exile, its effect was to strengthen the commitment of the Bangla Desh political and military leadership in their demand for complete independence and to reinforce their resistance to any suggestion of compromise with Yahya Khan.

While India directed herself to consolidating her diplomatic defences against United Nations intervention and to stiffening the will of the Bangla Desh exiles, in Pakistan the division of opinion between the exponents of the hard line and the supporters of the 'United Nations approach' was resolved for the time being in favour of the latter. Against the opposition of those who favoured a tough military regime in East Pakistan and the reduction of its Hindu population, Yahya Khan kept alive the project of a United Nations political role in East Pakistan. To support this policy he moved some distance farther along the road he had marked out in June, towards an official transfer of power into the hands of an administration which it was hoped would appeal to international opinion and attract Bengali political support.

After the failure of his initiatives in June, and the set-back represented by the Cargill mission's report at the end of that month, there was a round of consultations between the President and the Pakistani political leaders during the second half of July. The central political problem was once again that of the constitution, a question revived by the concern of the United States and other powers for some visible signs of constitutional advance in East Pakistan. Since March the authorities in Islamabad had been arguing that no transfer of power in either wing could take place until the situation in East Pakistan had been normalized. Now a new question presented itself: how to satisfy international opinion by accomplishing some formal devolution in East Pakistan before the coming into session of the National Assembly —that is, before the promulgation of the new constitution and the establishment of a new, civilian government for the whole country. After everything that had happened since March, Mr Bhutto had now to be obliged to accept a more rapid advance to civilian rule in the East than was to be permitted in the West. It was also necessary to

[140] *Hindustan Standard*, 10 September.

persuade the hard-liners in the armed services that this process would not culminate in the secession of the Eastern Province.

The solution of these difficult political equations was preceded by several weeks of intense political debate inside Pakistan. The first move was made by the President on 11 July, when he announced the appointment of Dr A. M. Malik, a Bengali and a former cabinet minister, to be his Special Assistant in Dacca, with special responsibility for displaced persons and for relief and rehabilitation work in East Pakistan.[141] Throughout July there were rumours of bitter disagreement between Lt.-Gen. Tikka Khan and his fellow advocates of a strong line in East Pakistan, and the supporters of the more moderate approach favoured by the President. It was reported in the Indian Press that a proposed visit by President Yahya to the East in July had been postponed because of these differences.[142]

Early in August the Pakistani regular and para-military forces in East Bengal were substantially reinforced.[143] On 5 August the Pakistan government published a white paper giving its fullest account to date of the origins of the crisis.[144] At the same time the names were announced of 88 out of a total of 167 Awami League Members of the National Assembly who would be permitted to take their seats in the Assembly.[145] Four days later on the 9th—fortuitously the day of the signing of the Indo–Soviet treaty—it was officially revealed in Islamabad that Sheikh Mujib would be tried *in camera* before a military court on a charge of 'waging war against Pakistan'. This decision, and the further decision to make it public, was the key to the compromise which Yahya was seeking between the various political forces in Islamabad. Civilianization in East Pakistan was to go forward, but its limits were to be both restricted and clearly defined by eliminating the possibility of an agreement with Mujib.

There was of course, a sharp and immediate international reaction to this drawing of a firm line beyond which it was now made clear that Pakistan would not be pressed in its search for a political solution. U Thant and the Pakistan government exchanged notes, and many countries also protested. But over the remaining weeks of August and during September the more positive elements in Yahya's programme emerged. On 3 September General Tikka Khan was replaced as

[141] *Dawn*, 15 July.

[142] *Hindustan Standard*, 9 August; *The Statesman*, 9 August; *The Times of India*, 20 July; *Patriot*, 14 August.

[143] *Hindustan Standard*, 17 August.

[144] Government of Pakistan, *White Paper on the Crisis in East Pakistan*, 5 August 1971.

[145] *Dawn*, 8 August.

SEPTEMBER–NOVEMBER: THE APPROACH OF WAR

Governor of East Pakistan by Dr Malik, and Lt.-Gen. Amir Abdullah Khan Niazi was appointed Chief Martial Law Administrator in East Pakistan. Maj.-Gen. Farman Ali remained in Dacca as military affairs adviser to the Governor. On 2 September Press censorship in Pakistan was officially lifted. An official government statement on refugees in India was issued on the same day, giving a total of only 2,002,623, allegedly assessed on the basis of a district-by-district count.[146] On the 5th an amnesty was granted to all civilians and members of the armed forces alleged to have committed offences in East Pakistan since 1 March—save those 'already charged with specific criminal acts'. It was also stated that a number of detainees had been released.[147] On 8 September the membership of Pakistan's delegation to the 26th session of the United Nations was announced. It was to be headed by Mr Mahmud Ali, an East Bengali leader of the People's Democratic Party.[148] Ten days later, on the 18th, ten civilians were sworn in as members of Dr Malik's Council of Ministers for East Pakistan. They included two former members of the Awami League, a Buddhist, and members of the Krishak Shramik party, the People's Democratic Party, the Jamaat-i-Islami, and the Council Muslim League.[149]

On 20 September, the Election Commission announced that National Assembly by-elections for the 79 vacant seats in East Pakistan would be held between 25 November and 9 December. Two days later came the perhaps fateful decision to put them back 21 days until 12–23 December—to ensure the fullest participation, it was said, of all intending candidates. Finally, on the 18th, President Yahya issued an amendment to his constitutional statement of 28 June. He now promised that a simplified procedure would be provided by which the draft constitution prepared by the experts could be amended by the National Assembly. While the President still reserved the right to give or withhold assent to any amendments after full consideration in the national interest, Yahya's statement of 18 September nevertheless restored a constitution-making function to the Assembly.[150]

The reports of these developments in Islamabad coincided with the opening of the United Nations Session in New York. The Bangla Desh government-in-exile had also prepared for this event. On 18 September it issued the first of a series of *Mukti Bahini* 'war bulletins';

[146] *Dawn*, 2 September.
[147] *Dawn*, 10 September.
[148] *Dawn*, 9 September.
[149] *Dawn*, 19 September.
[150] *Dawn*, 19 September.

and it announced that guerrilla attacks on bridges, trains and power plants in East Pakistan were to be intensified. The next day, 19 September, U Thant's annual report on the work of the United Nations was published. 'While the civil strife in itself is an internal affair of Pakistan,' he declared in the section on the East Pakistan crisis, 'some of the problems generated by it are necessarily of concern to the international community.' There had been, he said, 'a lack of substantial progress towards a political reconciliation'.

> The situation on the borders of East Pakistan is particularly disturbing . . . Border clashes, clandestine raids, and acts of sabotage appear to be becoming more frequent, and this is all the more serious since the refugees must cross this disturbed border if repatriation is to become a reality.[151]

Between September and December the United Nations was the principal scene of the next round of intense diplomatic activity, in which both sides tried to mobilize 'world opinion' in their favour, and Pakistan sought to bring the Secretary-General and the Security Council into action to restrain India from continuing her support for 'secessionism' in East Pakistan. Islamabad's argument against India was that 'in violation of its solemn obligations under the Charter of the United Nations India not only refuses to honour its commitments with regard to the peaceful settlement of outstanding disputes between Pakistan and itself, but is also openly interfering in the internal affairs of Pakistan'.[152] In reply, the Indian Foreign Minister insisted before the General Assembly on 28 September: 'I must firmly and categorically state that this is not an India–Pakistan problem and we have no intention of turning it into one.' The Indians argued that there was consequently no scope either for action by the United Nations or for the kind of bilateral discussions between India and Pakistan which President Yahya had publicly sought in July and August.[153] Meanwhile, behind the scenes, the Soviet Union continued to fulfil her commitment to India to prevent Pakistan from securing protection through the United Nations. In September, the newly elected President of the General Assembly, Adam Malik of Indonesia, declared that although India and Pakistan should be pressed

---

[151] *Hindustan Standard*, 20 September.

[152] Letter of the Pakistan Foreign Secretary to the United Nations Secretary-General, published on 25 September.

[153] On 28 September, the Shah publicly declared that he had abandoned his attempts at mediation, because the Indian government had spurned his efforts. He added that he was 'one hundred per cent behind Pakistan'. *Pakistan Horizon*, XXIV, No. 4, p. 98.

SEPTEMBER–NOVEMBER: THE APPROACH OF WAR

to come together in bilateral negotiations, he was not in favour of a General Assembly debate on the East Pakistan problem 'because there would be no end to it'.[154]

But despite the Russian refusal to countenance United Nations intervention, both the Russians and the Americans were agreed that a war in the sub-continent should be avoided—not least because of the damage it might do to Soviet–American relations on the eve of the 'era of negotiations' which it was hoped that President Nixon's visit to Moscow in 1972 would consolidate. The date of his visit had not yet been fixed, although the Americans intended that it should take place after Mr Nixon's visit to Peking. With these considerations in mind the Russians sought to restrain India from open attack on Pakistan; and to this end they pressed the Indians not to make specific commitments in advance of any negotiations which might be brought about between Yahya Khan and the Bengali leaders. From the Soviet point of view the Indian commitment to the independence of Bangla Desh should therefore be dropped. For their part, the Americans attempted to induce Pakistan to move further still in the direction of conciliation and compromise with the Bengalis. In New York on 30 September the American Secretary of State, Mr William Rogers, discussed the situation in South Asia with Mr Gromyko, the Soviet Foreign Minister. The Pakistani Press reported a United States official as stating:

> both the United States and the Soviet Union recognize that there is a dangerous and complex situation in the sub-continent and believe that war is not a solution. Both of the big powers, therefore, are going to continue to urge restraint by India and Pakistan and counsel them to have discussions to see if some solutions can be worked out. The Soviets advised the Americans that they have already been urging restraint.[155]

[154] *The Times of India*, 23 September.
[155] *Dawn*, 2 October. The Chinese attitude of implicit support for these efforts is discussed in a *Times of India* editorial of 9 October. France, too, took a hand. On 6 October the French Foreign Minister, M. Schumann, was quoted in *Le Monde* as saying: '[While] our attitude regarding this crisis is inspired by general principles which determine our attitude in the international field, that is, non-interference in internal affairs,' nevertheless, 'it is up to the Government of Pakistan to find a political and constitutional solution based on the consent of the people of Pakistan' (*Dawn*, 8 October). By the end of the month, however, the French position had changed under Russian influence. France's ambiguous concern for a solution 'based on the consent of the people of Pakistan'—including those of West Pakistan?—was abandoned by President Pompidou

However, this late exercise in Soviet-American joint management of the sub-continental balance was a failure, mainly because the Americans were unable or unwilling to persuade President Yahya to accept the revised position which India was to concede under Russian pressure early in October. Among the instruments the United States tried to use to secure Pakistan's co-operation was the promise of increased aid for relief in East Pakistan. Although the 1972 appropriation for development aid to Pakistan had been defeated in the House Foreign Affairs Committee on 15 July, on 3 August the House of Representatives had voted to provide $100 million for humanitarian relief. Now, on 1 October, President Nixon issued a statement urging that 'in addition to completing action on the House initiative, the Congress [should] authorize and appropriate an additional sum of $150 millions for the relief and rehabilitation of refugees from East Pakistan and for humanitarian relief in East Pakistan'. This provision was to be supplemented by food provided under Public Law 480.

Russia adopted more conventionally diplomatic means of influencing Indian policy. During the first ten days of October a substantial Soviet diplomatic effort was made to bring the Indians to blur the definition of the 'political solution' which they would regard as an acceptable outcome in East Pakistan. The Soviet theme was that the conclusion of any discussions between President Yahya and the Bengalis should not be prejudged and it was implied that Yahya should settle with Mujib. When Mrs Gandhi visited Moscow on 28–29 September, the statement issued after her talks with Soviet leaders was distinctly unsatisfactory from the Indian viewpoint. Their differences were dramatized in the statement by the contrast between the Indian (English) version, which referred throughout to 'East Bengal', and the Russian version, which spoke only of 'East Pakistan'. It was recorded that 'the Soviet side reaffirmed its position . . . as laid down in President Podgorny's appeal to President Yahya on 2 April'. This was of course an appeal which had been made four months before the Indo–Soviet treaty was signed, and which had confined itself to calling for 'a peaceful political settlement'—without attempting a definition of what would be appropriate. In his speech

---

in the joint statement issued at the conclusion of his visit to the Soviet Union on 30 October. Mr Brezhnev and M. Pompidou 'expressed their understanding of the difficulties confronting the Government of India as a result of the mass influx of refugees. Both sides expressed the hope that a political settlement of the problems of East Pakistan that would make it possible, in particular, for the refugees to return home would be reached with utmost speed.' *Pakistan Horizon*, XXIV, No. 4, p. 170.

SEPTEMBER–NOVEMBER: THE APPROACH OF WAR

welcoming Mrs Gandhi to Moscow on the 28th Mr Kosygin publicly departed even further from the Indian view when he described the Russian idea of what would be a satisfactory settlement in East Pakistan— 'it is necessary above all to provide the refugees with the opportunity to return home, and to give them a full guarantee on the part of the Pakistani authorities that they will not be persecuted and will have the opportunity of living and working in tranquillity in East Pakistan'. This scheme of things did not in fact differ in principle from the purposes which President Yahya's policy and his appeals to the refugees were designed to effect. 'Peace-loving opinion,' Mr Kosygin went on, 'expects of the Pakistani authorities an early political settlement in East Pakistan, which will *take into consideration* [author's italics] the legitimate interests of the population, safeguard its normal development, and remove the danger of a further worsening of Pakistan–Indian relations'. It was left to Mrs Gandhi to insist in her reply that 'the situation in East Bengal is not an Indo–Pakistani dispute', that 'the growing agony of the people of East Bengal does not seem to have moved many governments', and that 'what has happened in East Bengal, or Bangla Desh as the world has begun to call it, can no longer be regarded as Pakistan's domestic affair'.[156]

Although Mrs Gandhi's visit to Moscow was followed by a number of semi-official Soviet statements insisting upon Russia's sympathy with India's plight, when President Podgorny accompanied the Indian Prime Minister back to Delhi for a return visit, he repeated that Soviet concern was limited to what he referred to as the legitimate rights and interests of the East Bengalis. 'We consider,' he declared at a banquet in Delhi, 'that any further sliding towards a military conflict must be prevented'.[157] A week later, on 8 October, Mr Kosygin agreed to a joint communiqué with President Boumedienne of Algeria, referring to Pakistan in the terms preferred by Islamabad —'respect for the national unity and territorial integrity of Pakistan' —and appealing to India and Pakistan 'to find ... a peaceful solution according with the principles of non-interference, mutual respect, good-neighbour relations and the spirit of the Tashkent meeting'.[158]

---

[156] See Appendix 10, p. 194, for the text of the Joint Statement. Mrs Gandhi's comments are printed in Indira Gandhi, *India and Bangla Desh*, pp. 42–3. On 30 September Radio Pakistan announced that Russia would help Pakistan in laying a 5 kW transmission line connecting Lyallpur with Gudu. *The Statesman*, 1 October.

[157] *Hindustan Standard*, 2 October; *Dawn*, 20 October.

[158] *Dawn*, 10 October; *The Times of India*, 10 October, and editorial expressing 'doubts' about Soviet policy, *ibid.*, 13 October.

The effect of these Soviet efforts was at first to sharpen India's insistence that no progress could be made without the prior release of Sheikh Mujib. Eventually, however, they succeeded in extracting a declaration from India that—despite earlier endorsement of the goal of complete independence for Bangla Desh—she did not regard herself as being committed to any particular formula for a political settlement between the Pakistanis and the Bengalis—provided that the Sheikh was a party to the talks.

The first public Indian reaction to Soviet pressure had come on 4 October, when the Indian ambassador to the United Nations, Mr Samar Sen, repeated in the General Assembly the suggestion that Islamabad should negotiate a settlement with Sheikh Mujib. The Pakistani ambassador, Mr Agha Shahi, replied that this was in effect a demand that Pakistan 'should enter into negotiations with the same group that wanted to break the national unity of Pakistan'. Meanwhile, on 1 October an injunction had been issued to the Pakistani Press denouncing 'speculations and rumours' concerning 'the trial and release of Sheikh Mujibur Rahman . . . negotiations with secessionist elements in East Pakistan, and other matters'.[159] Perhaps encouraged by these indications that Pakistan would not accommodate herself to the course being pressed on her by the Russians and the Americans, the Indian government then decided to fall in with the Soviet view. On 8 October Mr Swaran Singh publicly stated that India did not hold that sovereign independence was necessarily the only solution for the Bangla Desh problem and that she was not committed to any one of the three possible solutions—independence for Bangla Desh, to provincial autonomy for East Pakistan within Pakistan, or the reintegration of East Pakistan. 'The Indian stand,' he declared, 'had always been based on the need for a political solution acceptable to the already elected representatives of Bangla Desh.'[160]

---

[159] *Dawn*, 2 October.
[160] *The Times of India*, 9 and 10 October and editorial on 11 October, condemning these developments in Soviet policy. Although the Russians may have been telling the Indian Government in private that it was necessary for the Soviet Union to make at least a show of action in the sub-continent in order to impress the Americans, the Soviet diplomatic campaign was interpreted by many Indians as an indication that the strategy underlying the Indo–Soviet treaty had not paid off. On a number of occasions during the first week of October the exiled Bangladesh political leaders reaffirmed their commitment to complete independence; and in a reference to the lack of support from some other powers Mr Tajuddin Ahmed spoke of their pursuit of their 'narrow self-interest and world strategy'. *The Statesman*, 9 October; *Hindustan Standard*, 3 October.

SEPTEMBER–NOVEMBER: THE APPROACH OF WAR

The Indian government evidently adopted this position unwillingly, in the face of heavy pressure from their Russian ally; and Mr Swaran Singh perhaps deliberately chose to make his declaration before the All-India Congress Committee, where the opposition of Indian public opinion to any compromise over East Bengal would be most forcefully displayed. Nevertheless, Russia's efforts had brought Delhi to accept publicly that the outcome of negotiations within the framework of Pakistan between Yahya and the 'already elected representatives' of the East Bengalis might fall short of complete independence for Bangla Desh. This development was perhaps rightly regarded in Moscow as sufficient evidence of the Soviet commitment to 'restraint'. Now it was a matter for Pakistan and her friends to address themselves seriously to the question of whether to treat with Sheikh Mujib. As an aid to this reconsideration, on 10 October *Pravda* published an editorial condemning the trial of Mujib as a 'judicial reprisal', and declaring that 'the experience of Pakistan's own history demonstrates that persecution for political motives never led to constructive solutions of that country's problems'.

Two days later, on 12 October, President Yahya indirectly answered the Russians, in a televised address to the people of Pakistan.[161] Although he did not refer to Sheikh Mujib, he reiterated his plans for the holding of by-elections in East Pakistan and for the summoning of the National Assembly in December. In these circumstances, it was clear that he did not envisage any negotiations with Sheikh Mujib or with any of the Awami League exiles. Thus, although he 'welcomed' Mr Kosygin's speech on 28 September, he regretted that 'Premier Kosygin made no mention of the various positive steps taken by me to transfer power to the elected representatives of the people'. Moving the issue on to a new level, the President declared that India had been making 'feverish military preparations' which opened up a 'serious possibility of aggression by India against Pakistan'. But Pakistan was preparing to defend herself. The crisis might, he suggested, be resolved by mutual troop withdrawals from the borders; and in this connection he went on to revive the proposal which had first been made in July for the 'posting of United Nations observers to facilitate the return of displaced persons and defuse the explosive situation on the borders'. Finally, President Yahya insisted that 'the international community should impress upon India the need to desist from interfering in our internal affairs and withdraw her forces from our borders. . . . Unilateral efforts by

[161] See Appendix 11, p. 199. *Dawn*, 13 October.

SOUTH ASIAN CRISIS

us alone in such a situation are not enough and there has to be a response and reciprocity from India.'

President Yahya's decision not to be deflected from his plan for a 'transfer of power' to the National Assembly without the participation of Sheikh Mujib or the Awami League was an unequivocal rebuff for the Soviet efforts to bring about a settlement. Even more serious, in order to give substance to his demand for international action to avert an impending war it was necessary for Yahya to dramatize the threat of conflict. His statement was therefore accompanied by the movement of Pakistani forces towards the borders both in East Bengal and in West Pakistan. The Indians immediately seized the chance which Yahya's decision gave them to escape from the position which they had just taken up under Soviet pressure. On 14 October Mrs Gandhi stated that Mr Swaran Singh's declaration that India would be ready to accept a political settlement 'even within the framework of Pakistan' had been 'misquoted'. India, she declared, would not start a war with Pakistan. 'But it is up to Pakistan to see that war is not thrust upon us.' Meanwhile, although the Soviet Press commented favourably on President Yahya's remark that there was still time to prevent an outbreak of war, it blamed Islamabad's unwillingness to respond to Russia's diplomatic efforts on 'the presence in Pakistan of advocates of a hard line towards India'. On 16 October *Pravda* claimed that 'certain representatives of the Pakistani military administration continue to make statements fomenting tension and preventing a normalization of the situation'. The hard-liners in Pakistan, it continued, presented 'the main obstacle in the way of settling the conflict by solving its cardinal problem—that of East Pakistan'.[162]

On 15 October President Yahya confronted President Podgorny in Persepolis, amid the splendid celebrations of the 2,500th anniversary of the Persian Empire. It was reported by the Pakistani Press that Yahya had repeated his offer to withdraw his forces from their positions on the borders. In return, India should withdraw her forces from the East Pakistan border and stop 'sending infiltrators

---

[162] *The Statesman*, 17 October. For Mrs Gandhi's statements, see *The Times of India*, 15 October. President Yahya acknowledged these difficulties by implication in an interview published in *Le Monde* on 17 October. By mid-October the trial of the Sheikh seems to have been concluded. Commenting on the question whether Mujib would be executed if the military tribunal passed sentence of death, Yahya declared: 'Before taking any decision I would have to know the feeling of the country. If the people want clemency, I would grant it.' *The Statesman*, 19 October.

SEPTEMBER–NOVEMBER: THE APPROACH OF WAR

and committing other hostile acts'. Five days later the government of the Soviet Union publicly repeated what Yahya had been told. On the 20th Mr Kosygin stated that at the meeting in Persepolis President Podgorny had urged that steps should be taken to restore democracy in East Pakistan. Those steps should include the release of Sheikh Mujib.[163]

During the early weeks of October, while these events were being played out at the level of high diplomacy, the tension in East Pakistan was deepening. The response of the Bangla Desh government-in-exile to the pressures being brought to bear on India by the Russians was to insist that even though outside powers might hold back—because of their 'narrow self-interest and world strategy'—the Bangla Desh movement remained irrevocably committed to the goal of complete independence.[164] On 1 October the leader of the Bangla Desh delegation to the United Nations repeated that the three conditions of any political settlement must be the recognition of his country as an independent state, the release of Sheikh Mujib, and the withdrawal of Pakistani occupation forces from the East. This position was also affirmed by the Bangla Desh National Liberation Struggle Co-ordination Committee on 2 October, and it was repeated by the acting President and the Prime Minister on the 9th. 'We are progressively realizing,' Mr Tajuddin Ahmed told the Press, 'that the war has to be fought by us, our freedom earned by ourselves and that the answer to the Bangla Desh question lies on the battlefield.'

These brave words were followed by an announcement that the *Mukti Bahini* would now direct themselves to sabotaging the by-elections which were to be held in East Pakistan early in December.[165] On the 13th a series of political assassinations began with the murder of Abdul Monem Khan, a former Governor of East Pakistan and a leader of the Muslim League.[166] The success of these efforts was

---

[163] *The Statesman*, 16 and 17 October; *Hindustan Standard*, 23 October. It should be noted that the announcement of a final decision confirming President Nixon's visit to the Soviet Union was also made on 12 October: it was perhaps now easier for the Russians to relax their efforts.

[164] Mr Tajuddin Ahmed, quoted in *The Statesman*, 9 October. See note 160 above.

[165] *The Statesman*, 17 October. On the 13th an interestingly hesitant endorsement of this strategy was given by the moderate Mr A. H. M. Kamaruzzaman, the Bangla Desh Home Minister – 'I hope Yahya Khan will not dare to hold the farce of by-elections. If, however, he really does go ahead with his design, the Bangla Desh guerrillas will no doubt foil this conspiracy.'

[166] *Hindustan Standard*, 15 October. Mr Monem Khan was reported to

attested on the 23rd, when it was officially announced that 18 of the 78 vacant East Pakistan seats in the National Assembly would not be contested and that the candidates had consequently been returned unopposed.[167]

Meanwhile, the Indian and Pakistani armies were moving up to forward positions along the borders of both parts of Pakistan. In the West, these movements probably began on the Pakistani side before the end of September; and after Yahya Khan's broadcast on 12 October they were rapidly completed.[168] The Indians, who were already establishing themselves in forward positions along the eastern borders during September, now also moved forward in the West. On 17 October President Yahya repeated his suggestion that the forces on both sides should be withdrawn and a system of international supervision introduced. This renewed proposal was fiercely attacked by Mr Jagjivan Ram, the Indian Defence Minister. He declared that 'if war is thrust upon us by the Pakistani military junta, we will not withdraw from occupied Pakistani territory, come what may'.[169] Two days later Mrs Gandhi herself rejected the suggestion of a mutual withdrawal of forces.[170] On the 17th it was stated in Islama-

---

[167] *Dawn*, 23 October. The Election Commission announced that five seats had been taken by the People's Democratic Party, led in East Pakistan by Mr Nural Amin, another five by the Jamaat-i-Islami, while the Pakistan Convention Muslim League had two. The Pakistan Muslim League (Qayyum group) and the Council Muslim League got one each, and three seats were taken by the Nizami-i-Islami Party. On 22 October Mian Mahmoud Ali Kasuri, the leader of a visiting Pakistan People's Party delegation in Dacca, attacked the six-party electoral alliance which had emerged in East Pakistan. He confirmed that the PPP would contest eight or ten seats in the by-elections; but he added: 'the PPP may be compelled at some stage to review the entire situation.' *Dawn*, 23 October.

[168] *Hindustan Standard*, 13, 16 October, which cites a despatch from the Associated Press correspondent in Pakistan. See also Sydney Schanburg in the *International Herald Tribune*, 14 October.

[169] *The Statesman*, 17, 18 October.

[170] Indira Gandhi, *India and Bangla Desh*, pp. 44–7 – interview in New Delhi, 19 October 1971.

> It seems very simple and plausible to say that Pakistan troops will withdraw. But the situation had not begun a week ago; it has been

---

be working for a merger of the three factions of the Muslim League to take a share of power in East Pakistan. After his assassination, there were reports of a crisis in Dr Malik's civilian Bengali cabinet in Dacca. *Hindustan Standard*, 16 October.

SEPTEMBER–NOVEMBER: THE APPROACH OF WAR

bad that Indian artillery had started shelling the border villages in East Pakistan with medium guns in addition to the field guns and mortars to which they had limited themselves in earlier shelling incidents. During the rest of October and November there was an increasing number of complaints by both sides, alleging shellings across the border, violations of air space and the construction of fortifications along the cease-fire line in Kashmir.

A final round of diplomatic activity began on 20 October against the background of this accelerating deterioration in India–Pakistan relations. U Thant took up President Yahya's suggestion of 12 October that there should be a mutual withdrawal of forces from both borders, and in identical memoranda addressed to President Yahya and Mrs Gandhi and to the Indian and Pakistani ambassadors at the United Nations, he 'placed the United Nations and its facilities at their disposal in view of the threat of war in the sub-continent'. He also remarked that along the international frontiers in East and West Pakistan there was no equivalent to the safeguard mechanism provided by the United Nations military observers in Kashmir. This initiative was immediately welcomed by the Pakistanis, and President Yahya replied on the 21st, repeating his proposal of mutual troop withdrawals to a 'mutually safe distance on either side of the border' and suggesting that United Nations observers should be placed on both sides of the borders in East and West 'to over-see the withdrawals and supervise the maintenance of peace'. He also expressed the hope that U Thant would immediately pay a visit to the sub-continent.[171]

The Secretary-General's initiative coincided with Mrs Gandhi's departure from India for a three weeks' tour of Western capitals. On 22 October, two days before she left, a Soviet Deputy Foreign Minister, Mr Nikolai Firyubin, arrived in Delhi at the head of a delegation which was said to be for the purpose of initiating a routine annual series of bilateral discussions. No response to U Thant's initiative emerged from these consultations, either from the Soviet or from the Indian government. Instead, there was a joint statement on the 27th, declaring that the consultations between the two governments had

---

[171] *Pakistan Horizon*, XXIV, No. 4, p. 151.

an escalating situation, and the Pakistani 'hate India' Campaign, their call for a *jehad* on the basis of religion—all these things have to be considered ... Furthermore, Pakistan's line of withdrawal to their bases is very close to the borders, whereas our bases are very far.

been held under Article IX of the Indo–Soviet treaty—which provides for consultations in the event of either party being subject to an attack or threat of attack. The two countries declared that they were in agreement in their assessment of the tensions in the sub-continent. Fortified by this statement, Mrs Gandhi made her first public comment on the Secretary-General's suggestion in Vienna on 28 October. She indicated that India would not agree to the stationing of United Nations observers on Indian soil to supervise the withdrawal of troops from the borders. On the same day U Thant stated that he was offering 'good offices' and not mediation—which would require the consent of the Security Council. Mrs Gandhi, however, argued in London on 31 October that the effect of the Secretary-General's proposals was once again 'to equate India with Pakistan, although the situation was entirely a Pakistani creation, and although Pakistan's actions had threatened our security'. She added that there were already in India a number of representatives of the United Nations High Commission for Refugees, free to go where they wished. Their presence had not brought about any disposition among the refugees to return to East Bengal.[172]

The main purposes of Mrs Gandhi's tour were to explain the development of Indian policy to the Western governments, to win acceptance, if not approval, and to demonstrate that the Indo–Soviet treaty need not necessarily impair relations between India and the West.[173] She sought to bring home to Western public opinion the size of the refugee burden, and the justice of India's determination that it should be lifted from her shoulders. Mrs Gandhi also insisted on the growing urgency of the situation. The strain upon the resources of the neighbouring Indian states was rapidly becoming socially and politically insupportable—although many of the costs had been met by Western relief aid. She argued that President Yahya's plans for the transfer of power were not adequate; and evidence for this view was conveniently provided by the announcement in Islamabad on 30 October that a total of 35 candidates had been elected unopposed to vacant seats in the East Pakistan Provincial Assembly.

[172] On American television on 7 November, Mrs Gandhi remarked: 'So far as U Thant is concerned, he is always welcome, but we should be clear as to what can be achieved, what the United Nations wants to achieve. It was we who drew his attention to this question first, and we were not able to move anybody here. Now they want to come on what seems to us President Yahya Khan's terms.' Indira Gandhi, *India and Bangla Desh*, p. 92.

[173] *Ibid.*, pp. 49–99, gives extracts from speeches in Britain, the United States and West Germany.

SEPTEMBER–NOVEMBER: THE APPROACH OF WAR

In London her arguments made a considerable impression on the British government, which was reluctant to see India fall under the exclusive influence of the Soviet Union. And on her departure from Washington on 8 November, after she had spent three days in the United States, it was mistakenly felt that Mrs Gandhi and Mr Nixon had reached a better understanding of each other's position. On 8 November it was announced in Washington that, with the agreement of the Pakistan government, the remaining licences for the export of American arms to Pakistan were being suspended.[174] The Americans later argued that it was their understanding of these talks with Mrs Gandhi that the Indians had accepted the importance of 'restraint', and that they had agreed that the United States government should pursue yet another attempt to bring about a settlement by negotiation between Yahya Khan and the East Bengalis.[175] However, in Paris on the 8th, Mrs Gandhi reiterated that 'it was perhaps inevitable today that Bangla Desh should become independent'; and despite American blandishments the substance of her position remained as stated in the Lok Sabha on her return to India on the 13th—that there was a growing urgency in the situation, and that the release of Sheikh Mujib was essential if any political solution of the Bangla Desh problem was to be achieved.[176] On 16 November, in her belated formal reply to U Thant's communication of 20 October, she remarked that the root of the problem:

> is the fate of 75 million people in Bengal . . . this is what must be kept in mind, instead of the present attempt to save the military regime . . . The problem of East Bengal can be solved only by peaceful negotiations between the military rulers of West Pakistan and the elected and accepted leaders of East Bengal. The first step towards the opening of such negotiations is the release of Sheikh Mujibur Rahman.

India's negative response to U Thant's formulation of Yahya's proposal of mutual troop withdrawals left four courses open to Pakistan. The first was to build up a diplomatic and military deterrent to an outright Indian invasion of East Pakistan. If this could be achieved the Bangla Desh movement could probably be held back indefinitely by the army. The second possibility was to be guided by the United States down the long and dusty road towards an agreement with the

---

[174] Text in *Pakistan Horizon*, XXIV, No. 4, p. 172.
[175] See Dr Kissinger's Press briefing of 7 December, printed in the *New York Herald Tribune*, 6 January 1972. See Appendix 13, p. 207.
[176] Indira Gandhi, *India and Bangla Desh*, pp. 103–6.

East Bengali leaders, which would almost certainly lead eventually to the secession of East Pakistan. The third course was to continue the strategy of escalation which Yahya had embarked upon early in October, seeking to bring about a situation in which the great powers and the United Nations would somehow be obliged to take action to prevent or to stop a war—perhaps by voting to instal United Nations forces in East Pakistan. During the course of November and early December each of these courses in turn was tried by Islamabad. The Pakistanis did not, however, try the fourth possible line of action (or, rather, of inaction): the willingness to accept delays and humiliation and to avoid provocative gestures until the refugees began to drift back.

Pakistan's attempts to deter India from open attack developed on two levels. On the military level a threatening posture was adopted in the West, while defensive operations were undertaken in the East. The post-monsoon advance of the Pakistani army to the East Bengal border during September and October was followed during late October and November by the withdrawal and concentration of the bulk of the troops behind prepared defensive positions. At the same time as Indian tactics in support of the Bangla Desh forces became increasingly aggressive, Pakistani tactics against incursions were toughened, and the weight of the forces deployed against the raiders was increased. As the month of November wore on these confrontations at the border therefore gave rise to a growing number of sharp engagements, involving Indian and Pakistani tanks and aircraft in open conflict.

On the diplomatic level, Pakistan's attempts to deter India could now only be carried out in co-operation with China. Ever since the Chinese had defined their position on 13 April Islamabad's object had been to win a credible public commitment from the Chinese that they would act against India if she openly attacked East Pakistan. If such a commitment could not be obtained, the next best thing would be to secure China's support in fostering doubt and uncertainty about her intentions. During October this became especially important in view of the improvement which took place in relations between China and India. Peking's willingness to receive an Indian ping-pong team, and the favourable publicity given in China to Mrs Gandhi's messages on the National Day of the People's Republic, and on the entry of the People's Republic into the United Nations on 25 October, had been interpreted in India as a series of deliberate gestures indicating Peking's desire to improve relations with Delhi. Throughout the later phases of the crisis every Chinese reference to the situation in the sub-continent was exhaustively analysed in the Indian Press and com-

SEPTEMBER–NOVEMBER: THE APPROACH OF WAR

pared with the very much more biting Chinese comments during the 1965 crisis.[177]

As the urgency of engaging the Chinese more deeply became more and more acute Mr Bhutto's star again began to rise in Islamabad. After the scene had been set by a sharp note to the Soviet government over the joint Soviet–Indian statement after Mr Firyubin's visit to Delhi, on 5 November the leader of the Pakistan People's Party was sent at the head of an official Pakistani delegation to Peking. Although he held no public position, his delegation included the Foreign Secretary, the Commander-in-Chief of the Air Force, the Chief of the Army General Staff and the Naval Chief of Staff. To reinforce Mr Bhutto's efforts, five days before he left President Yahya told *Newsweek* that war between India and Pakistan was imminent, and that China would supply Pakistan 'with all the weapons and ammunition we need'. On 5 November he told an American television interviewer that China would help Pakistan in any way she could in the event of an Indian attack on Pakistan.

It was Mr Bhutto's task to give some substance to the President's statements—or, in any event, to ensure that the impression they were intended to create was not dispelled by the Chinese. But although the discussions were conducted at a high level, and the delegation was greeted at Peking airport by Mr Chou En-lai himself, the result was disappointing. The Chinese did not depart from the position which they had consistently maintained since 13 April; and in the major public statement on the Chinese side, made on 7 November by the acting Foreign Minister, Mr Chi Peng-fei, there was no sign of the desired commitment to the 'unity' or 'integrity' of Pakistan. The only reference to these concepts was the somewhat equivocal remark that 'we *believe* that the broad masses of the Pakistani people are patriotic, want to safeguard national unity and the unification of the country, and oppose internal splits and outside interference'. China's precise commitment remained as before: 'our Pakistani friends may rest assured that should Pakistan be subjected to foreign aggression the Chinese government and people will, as always, resolutely support the Pakistan government and people in their struggle to defend their state sovereignty and national independence'.[178] No joint statement was issued at the conclusion of the talks on 7 November and

---

[177] See Subrahmanyam, pp. 113–16, 117–27, 128–33, 167–70. Chinese policy is assessed from a Pakistani point of view in Nehrunnisa Ali, 'China's Diplomacy during the Indo–Pakistan War'. *Pakistan Horizon*, XXV, No. 1, pp. 53–62.

[178] Text in Naik, pp. 155–6. See Appendix 12, p. 205.

it was left to the Pakistanis to put the most favourable construction they could upon the Chinese position. The two sides, said Mr Bhutto, had not found the need for a joint communiqué. Complete understanding had been achieved on all matters. The visit of the delegation would be a deterrent to the further escalation of the difficulties between India and Pakistan. 'The visit was a complete success—complete in the complete sense of the word.'[179]

In essence the Chinese view seems to have been that they could take their stand with reasonable safety and some likelihood of effectiveness in defence of the independence and sovereignty of Pakistan in the West; but that over East Pakistan they could only restate their position and allow the Pakistanis to make the best of it. The Indians took this point immediately, and at Chandigarh on 10 November Mr Swaran Singh declared that there was no indication that China would intervene on Pakistan's side in a conflict with India. Later in the month the Pakistani authorities sealed off the Karakoram highway into China, ostensibly to allow for military traffic. By 24 November they prepared an elaborate welcome for the visit of the Chinese Minister for Machine-building, who was coming to attend the inauguration of the Taxila heavy mechanical engineering complex, which had been built with Chinese help. But in the event these efforts did not create the desired effect. When open war broke out in December several of India's divisions from the Himalayan front were in position for the invasion of East Pakistan.

The failure of Mr Bhutto's attempt to win reassurance from China coincided with Mrs Gandhi's visit to Washington and paved the way for a renewed effort by the United States and other Western powers to persuade President Yahya to attempt a political settlement in East Pakistan by winning over the moderate elements in the Awami League which still looked to Sheikh Mujib. During the open war which broke out on 3 December American spokesmen were to claim that these attempts were in some sense approaching success when they were frustrated by the intensification of India's pressure upon Pakistan in East Bengal during the last week of November.[180]

Throughout the period since 25 March it had been an essential part of the Indian view that no progress towards a political solution to the crisis in Pakistan could be brought about until Sheikh Mujib had been released. The Indians insisted—after 10 October with

[179] *Pakistan Horizon*, XXIV, No. 4, p. 118.
[180] See below, Chapter 5, pp. 106–45.

SEPTEMBER–NOVEMBER: THE APPROACH OF WAR

public Russian support—that President Yahya must negotiate with him and with the other 'already elected representatives of the people', most of whom were now established in India, where they had firmly committed themselves to the goal of complete independence for Bangla Desh. For their part, since 9 August the Pakistani authorities had repeatedly made it clear that negotiations with Sheikh Mujib were out of the question. The problem for the United States and her friends was to bridge the gap between these two positions.[181]

Informal contacts between American officials in Calcutta and Delhi and some of the Awami League exiles had been established in May and June, during the earlier phase of American efforts to press President Yahya towards 'a political solution'. But after Yahya's statement of 28 June these contacts had lapsed. At the end of October it was reported by Associated Press that 'the United States authorities have pressed their peace-making exercise to the point of establishing informal contacts with the leaders of the Bangla Desh regime'. The Bangla Desh Home Minister, Mr A. H. M. Kamuruzzaman—regarded as a moderate—immediately denied that the American authorities had contacted the Bangla Desh government either informally or formally. 'Our people have but one objective,' he said, 'and that is to liquidate the occupation army and liberate the motherland. They are committed to complete independence.'[182]

However, in November the Americans sought—apparently with Mrs Gandhi's knowledge—to bring about talks between the Pakistani authorities and members of the Awami League 'specifically approved by Sheikh Mujib'.[183] It is possible to gather something about the nature of these efforts from the American official papers published in January 1972 by the newspaper correspondent Mr Jack Anderson. Thus, on 7 December Dr Kissinger told the Press that the United States had been privately expressing its agreement with the Indians at least since the end of August that 'political autonomy for East Bengal was the inevitable outcome of political evolution and that we favoured it'. In mid-November, he declared, the Indian ambassador in Washington was told that 'we were prepared even to discuss

---

[181] In the House of Commons on 4 November, Sir Alec Douglas-Home defined the task: 'to explore the possibilities of dialogue between those in West Pakistan who hold the power now and those who can command confidence in East Pakistan, and also dialogue between India and Pakistan.'

[182] *The Statesman*, 24 October.

[183] Dr Kissinger's briefing of 7 December, see Appendix 13, p. 207; see also p. 125.

with them a political timetable, a precise timetable for the establishment of political autonomy in East Bengal'.

But according to Mr Anderson's revelations Dr Kissinger's account of this aspect of American policy was immediately challenged in a telegram from the American ambassador in Delhi. Ambassador Keating declared that 'he was aware of our repeated statements that we had no formula for a solution, and our belief that the outcome of negotiations would probably be autonomy if not independence. But he regretted that he was uninformed of any specific statement favouring autonomy.' He added that the official State Department account of the conversation in mid-November with the Indian ambassador had not made it clear that 'Washington and Islamabad were prepared to discuss a precise timetable for establishing political autonomy for East Pakistan'. He went on to say that he had not been informed of any evidence for believing that significant progress had been made in agreeing a basis of principle for the discussions between the Pakistani authorities and the representatives of the Awami League; and he challenged Dr Kissinger's account of the nature of the personal contacts around which it was intended that talks should be conducted.[184]

The American plan seems to have been to obtain President Yahya's permission to approach Mr A. K. Brohi, Sheikh Mujib's defence counsel, and to persuade him to act as a channel through which Sheikh Mujib could convey his 'specific approval' of those 'members of the Awami League' who should negotiate with President Yahya. If this plan was to succeed it was necessary to secure Yahya's approval for the opening of a link, through Mr Brohi and the Americans, between Sheikh Mujib and the Awami League exiles; to persuade Mr Brohi and the Sheikh to agree to establish a contact of this sort; to induce members of the Awami League in India to accept Mr Brohi as an interlocutor; to get them to enter into discussions with the Pakistanis on the basis of his report of Sheikh Mujib's 'specific approval'; and to persuade the authorities in Islamabad to negotiate with the Awami League members so approved. In respect of most of these conditions the extent of American progress in November remains obscure. But, according to Mr Keating's account of the reports sent to him of the crucial discussions concerning Mr Brohi, on 29 November, President Yahya was prepared to countenance a meeting between Mr Brohi and the American ambassador to Pakistan, Mr Joseph Farland—but only for the purpose of obtaining from Mr Brohi 'at least his general impressions as to the state of the trial and its conduct'. Four days later,

[184] See Appendix 13, p. 209.

SEPTEMBER–NOVEMBER: THE APPROACH OF WAR

on 2 December, President Yahya apparently told Mr Farland 'that Brohi allegedly was not interested in seeing him'.[185]

Islamabad does not seem to have actively discouraged the United States and other Western powers from continuing to think in terms of establishing a basis for talks between Pakistan and certain members of the Awami League—and even perhaps with Sheikh Mujib. But the government of Pakistan itself preferred to continue to look for a solution in the direction which it had been exploring since the middle of July—the establishment of an international presence on the India–Pakistan borders which would shield Pakistan's sovereignty in the East. In pursuit of this purpose, early in November Islamabad again put this proposal directly to the Soviet Union. Early in the month what was said to be a conciliatory Soviet response had been received after Pakistan had sought 'clarification' from the Russians of the joint statement issued after Mr Firyubin's visit to Delhi in late October. Commenting on this reply an official spokesman in Islamabad publicly declared on 5 November that 'the big powers should play a constructive role in strengthening the initiative of the United Nations Secretary-General in order to defuse the explosive situation in the sub-continent, by making an objective assessment of the point of view of the two countries immediately involved'.[186]

But there was no response in Moscow to this public challenge to them to support U Thant's proposal of 20 October that he should immediately visit the sub-continent. In his speech on 7 November the Chinese acting Foreign Minister also attempted to revive the project for mutual troop withdrawals which had been launched by

---

[185] In her letter of 15 December to President Nixon, Mrs Gandhi referred to these discussions:

> Lip service was paid to the need for a political solution, but not a single worthwhile step was taken to bring this about ... There was not even a whisper that anyone from the outside world had tried to have contact with Mujibur Rahman. Our earnest pleas that Sheikh Mujibur Rahman should be released or that, even if he were kept under detention, contact with him might be established were not considered practical, on the ground that the USA could not urge policies which might lead to the overthrow of President Yahya Khan. While the US recognised that Mujib was a core factor in the situation and that unquestionably in the long run Pakistan must acquiesce in the direction of greater autonomy for East Pakistan, arguments were advanced to demonstrate the fragility of the situation and Yahya Khan's difficulty.

Indira Gandhi, *India and Bangla Desh*, pp. 146–9.

[186] *Pakistan Horizon*, XXIV, No. 4, p. 116.

President Yahya in his broadcast of 12 October. Once again the Indians refused to respond. A week later, on 15 November, the Pakistani Foreign Secretary—who was visiting the United States—warned that his country faced a state of war on the India–Pakistan borders. Two days later, on the 17th, Pakistan and the United Nations announced that they had reached an agreement allowing relief workers freedom of access and movement throughout East Pakistan. This was followed on the 18th by the announcement that the Pakistan government had asked the Secretary-General to direct United Nations personnel in East Pakistan to investigate the 'false allegations' concerning the 'continued movement of displaced persons into India'. Underlying these efforts was the hope in Islamabad that, as the situation along the borders moved from a 'state of confrontation to a state of conflict', the unwillingness of the great powers to act to restrain India would be correspondingly reduced and eventually overcome.[187]

In East Pakistan the situation was indeed becoming increasingly tense. As we have seen, in September and early October, after the monsoons, the Pakistani army and para-military forces had moved up to the borders, where the *Mukti Bahini* were starting to operate in larger and better equipped groups. These developments were accompanied in late September and October by the concentration of Indian regular forces in strength in the frontier zones. It was at this stage in early October that the exchanges of fire across the border between the two armies began, first with small guns and mortars, then with larger guns. During late October and early November the Pakistani forces were regrouped in fortified centres to the rear to meet the anticipated large-scale Indian and *Mukti Bahini* attacks. At the same time they continued to resist the incursions which the *Mukti Bahini* were making in increasing strength from across the Indian border. Shellings and other border incidents intensified and increased as the Indians sought to give covering fire to these incursions and retirements across the border and the Pakistanis sought to prevent them. Locked in this situation, both sides moved with increasing speed towards full-scale hostilities.

The Indians were, of course, since April, very content with the drift of events. Since April India had been giving indirect assistance to the activities of the *Mukti Bahini*, and during the monsoon period

---

[187] The phrase comes from a speech by the Pakistani Foreign Secretary in Paris on 18 November. For these various Pakistani initiatives, see *Pakistan Horizon*, XXIV, No. 4, pp. 120–23.

SEPTEMBER–NOVEMBER: THE APPROACH OF WAR

it is possible, as alleged by Pakistan, that individual members of the Indian border security forces and even the Indian army and navy had 'unofficially' participated in the incursions into East Pakistan. After the end of the monsoon in September, and the replacement of the border security force by the Indian army along the borders, Indian participation became increasingly direct. At some time in the period immediately after Yahya Khan's broadcast of 12 October and the consequent breakdown of Russian attempts to bring about a compromise, the decision seems to have been made in Delhi deliberately to step up the military pressure on Pakistan in the East. On 22 October Indian army reservists were called up; and in the course of the next week, before Mrs Gandhi's departure for her tour of the Western capitals, the decision in principle seems to have been taken that Indian forces should be permitted to cross over into East Pakistan to counter Pakistani offensive-defensive operations.

The first of these military engagements took place on 30–31 October, near Kamalpur, where Indian troops acted to silence Pakistani guns which had been shelling across the border. Although it was not yet admitted that Indian forces had crossed over the frontier, the official Indian spokesman described the action as 'the first of its kind', and stated that casualties had been suffered on both sides. Pakistani sources claimed that similar actions, resulting in heavy Indian casualties, took place in the Mymensingh area on 4 November, and near Belonia on the 11th. Spokesmen for both sides also made conflicting claims about border crossings by regular forces in the area of Shikarpur in West Bengal.

This growing military confrontation in the East set the scene for the diplomatic developments which we have already discussed— Mrs Gandhi's tour of Western capitals and the Pakistani project for mutual troop withdrawals accompanied by international supervision of the East Pakistan border. In India it was widely expected that Mrs Gandhi's return on 13 November would be the signal for all-out war. But the account she gave of her tour before the Indian Houses of Parliament on 15 November was pacific in tone.[188] The Indian government had evidently decided that India should not put herself in the position of being clearly seen to be the aggressor in a full-scale international war between two members of the United Nations. Its strategy was that Delhi and Moscow should continue to act together to deny President Yahya the international protection he sought. Meanwhile, under the cover of the *Mukti Bahini* the military pressure upon Yahya's position in East Pakistan would continue to

[188] Indira Gandhi, *India and Bangla Desh*, pp. 103–6.

be built up until the expected crisis in Pakistan's internal or external policy provided an opportunity for India to take decisive action.

After 20 November the speed of the drift to war suddenly accelerated. The confrontation reached a new level of intensity, notably on 21 November in the Boyra sector opposite Jessore, and later, on the 27th, in the sector opposite Hilli. At Boyra Indian tanks crossed the border, allegedly after a Pakistani attack directed against the *Mukti Bahini* positions on the Indian side. In the engagement which followed the Pakistanis lost some thirteen *Chafee* tanks; and, in a brief air battle on the same afternoon, either two or three Pakistani *Sabre* jets were shot down. On 24 November Mrs Gandhi gave an account of the affair to the Indian parliament, and that evening an Indian spokesman stated that in future the army was under instructions to repulse Pakistani 'offensive' operations, if necessary by crossing the border. In this operation Indian forces had entered Pakistan to a depth of some eight miles. On 23 November the *Mukti Bahini* attacked Chaugacha, a road junction north-west of Jessore, and on the 29th it was captured. It was reported that Colonel Osmani had set up his headquarters near Jessore, and that the Bangla Desh provisional government was making arrangements to move there. On the same day there were reports of Indian troops fighting on East Pakistan soil near Hilli.[189]

Nevertheless, the Indian military commitment remained as carefully limited as their political commitment to the Bangla Desh government—which they had not yet recognized. On 29 November an Indian Defence Ministry spokesman defined the official position on the fighting: 'Whenever our people are shelled, or whenever the integrity of our territory is threatened, we shall cross the border to take defensive action. If there is a direct threat to our positions and our citizens, then we shall cross the border, and if necessary we shall stay put.' On the 30th the Indian Defence Minister, Mr Jagjivan Ram, made it clear that Indian troops were not being permitted to penetrate more than eight to ten miles—the distance represented by the range of the Pakistani guns which they had been ordered to silence.

In a series of protests and memoranda Pakistan claimed that these developments represented a massive Indian attack on East Bengal. On the other hand, the Indians put the blame on Pakistan's allegedly aggressive tactics against the *Mukti Bahini*—shellings, the violation of Indian air space, and the sending of saboteurs across the border.

---

[189] The text of a Pakistani statement on the fighting, issued on 23 November, is in *Pakistan Horizon*, XXIV, No. 4, pp. 158-9.

SEPTEMBER–NOVEMBER: THE APPROACH OF WAR

Nevertheless, the Indians could not deny that the *Mukti Bahini* had launched an offensive, nor that it was being supported by Indian forces to the extent that Pakistani guns and defensive actions on the soil of Pakistan were being attacked by the Indian army and air force. As events after 3 December were to show, on both the military and diplomatic levels the Indians had made very thorough plans for an all-out assault on East Pakistan.

On the diplomatic level the pivot of the Indian position was the Soviet Union. After mid-October the Russians felt that they had gone as far as they could—or as far as they needed to go—to enjoin 're-straint', when the Indians temporarily retreated under Soviet pressure from their commitment to the complete independence of Bangla Desh to the less exacting demand for the unconditional release of Sheikh Mujib. As we have seen, when President Yahya had implicitly rejected this approach in his broadcast of 12 October the Russian pressure on the Indians had stopped; and the Indian and Russian plans for a concerted strategy for the next phase were probably confirmed during Mr Firyubin's visit to Delhi in late October. The formal position of both parties was that they would accept a political settlement negotiated between President Yahya and Sheikh Mujib and the Awami League. The Indians had also repeatedly affirmed that the only outcome of this could be independence for Bangla Desh. For her part, the Soviet Union undertook to keep the issue out of the United Nations by frustrating Pakistan's proposals for internationally supervised troop withdrawals and her appeals for a visit by the Secretary-General to the sub-continent and for the stationing of United Nations observers at her borders. During November the Russians played no part in the efforts to prevent the growth of tension in the sub-continent, and Soviet influence helped decisively to exclude the United Nations from the role cast for it in Islamabad and Washington. Throughout the penultimate phase of the crisis the Soviets supported the Indian position that the situation in East Pakistan did not have the character of an international conflict, and that it was therefore not properly a matter for the United Nations. And when the open international war began, after 3 December, they continued to shield India with their veto in the Security Council. Nevertheless, the possibility that Russia would return to a more balanced position after the end of the war was foreshadowed at the same time in several Soviet attempts at the United Nations during the Fourteen Days' War to give Islamabad an opportunity to accept a solution short of the unconditional surrender of the Pakistani army in the East.

Meanwhile, throughout the first weeks of November the Western powers, and particularly the United States, were deeply engaged in the attempts we have already outlined to persuade President Yahya to talk with the Awami League. During the last days of the month these efforts were overtaken by the rapid deterioration of the military situation along the East Pakistan borders and by Pakistan's response to this development. On 23 November, two days after the Boyra incident and the opening of the *Mukti Bahini* movement towards Jessore, a state of emergency was proclaimed in Pakistan. Yahya addressed a stream of letters to various Heads of State and Government, to U Thant, and to the President of the Security Council, informing them of the new situation along the borders.[190] Whatever interest President Yahya may earlier have had in the American proposals for talks with the Awami League now evaporated (though it is possible this was not reflected in Ambassador Farland's reports to the White House). Yahya continued to press ahead on the road towards the 'internationalization of the conflict' along which he had been travelling with growing determination since July. On 29 November he again wrote to U Thant proposing that United Nations observers should be sent to report on border violations. Now he suggested that they should be stationed on the Pakistan side of the East Pakistan border only. However, the Indians were confident of Soviet support for the rejection of this proposal—which would require the consent of the Security Council if it were to be put into effect. The Indian government and the provisional government of Bangla Desh therefore immediately condemned this latest version of President Yahya's long-standing project. It was, said Mr Tajuddin Ahmed, 'a planned conspiracy and a foul attempt to protect the military regime by the back door'.

The last week of November confirmed the pattern of international alignments which was to surround the third full-scale war between India and Pakistan since 1947. Although the Chinese position had been perhaps the most clearly stated, it was generally regarded as the most obscure among those of the major powers, mainly because of Pakistan's attempts to give an account of it which might serve to deter the Indians. At the end of November Peking publicly endorsed the view that the military developments in East Pakistan were the result of 'foreign aggression'. But, although on 29 November China once again gave her support to the Pakistani proposal for troop withdrawals, Peking made no attempt to alter the precise terms of her general commitment to Pakistan. Nevertheless, the following day President Yahya ordered that the Karakoram highway should be closed to

[190] The text of the last of these letters is reproduced in *Pakistan Horizon*, XXIV, No. 4, pp. 152–3.

SEPTEMBER–NOVEMBER: THE APPROACH OF WAR

foreigners—a gesture which was intended to draw a conspicuous cloud of concealment across the overland route between China and Pakistan. In the tense and conspiratorial atmosphere which prevailed in Pakistan this gesture immediately acquired more substance than it warranted—even, perhaps, in the minds of those who had made it. The same kind of misconstruction may have been attached by the Pakistanis to the development of the American position in the last week of November. For, as the crisis lurched into its final stages before the all-out war, a growing divergence began to emerge between the policies of the Western powers. Over the previous month, they had given their support to the American efforts to arrange talks between Islamabad and the Awami League. Now the French and the British began to talk in terms of a scheme for the imposition of United Nations control in East Pakistan, to be followed by fresh elections. On the other hand, the Americans joined the Chinese on 24 November in giving public support to the Pakistani proposal for mutual troop withdrawals; and a week later, on 1 December, Washington implicitly endorsed the Pakistani view that India was responsible for the tension along the East Pakistan border by announcing that licences for arms exports to India were to be suspended, and that existing licences were being cancelled. By the first day of December all the pieces had been assembled on the board. The endgame was due to begin.

Chapter 5

December: 'The Fourteen Days' War'

WHEN the open war between India and Pakistan at last began on the night of 3 December 1971 the two were unequally matched. Since the 1962 border war with China India's forces had greatly improved in size, training and equipment, and an indigenous armaments industry had been developed with help both from the Soviet Union and from the Western powers. Consequently India was less affected than her rival when Western arms aid to both India and Pakistan was terminated after the 1965 war. She also received large-scale military supplies from the Soviet Union, which continued after 1965. On the other hand, despite very considerable Chinese help, Pakistan had not been able to escape from the effects of her previous reliance on Western supplies, especially from the United States. Although she had benefited from a limited resumption of military aid by both the United States and the Soviet Union in the late 1960s and from the continuing grant of licences for arms purchase in the West, the military balance in the sub-continent between 1965 and 1971 had been shifting steadily against Pakistan and in favour of India.[191]

In 1971 the Indian army was composed of thirteen infantry divisions, a further ten divisions especially trained and equipped for mountain fighting, six independent infantry brigades, and two parachute brigades, as against Pakistan's twelve infantry divisions, with two more being raised. Pakistan's two armoured divisions and one independent armoured brigade were equipped with American *Patton* and *Sherman* tanks, and Russian and Chinese-built T-55s and T-59s. The Indian armoured division and two armoured brigades deployed *Centurion* tanks, *Shermans,* T-54s and T-55s, and Indian-built *Vijayanta* medium tanks. In the air, India disposed of three *Canberra* light bomber squadrons, eight *Gnat* interceptor squadrons, and fifteen fighter-bomber squadrons mainly equipped with Su-7s and *Hunter* F-56s. A substantial aid-transport capability was provided by a fleet of transports and helicopters. Against the Indian air force, the Pakistanis deployed three light bomber squadrons (Il-28 and B-57B), two

---

[191] *The Military Balance, 1971–1972* (London: International Institute for Strategic Studies, 1971), gives an authoritative survey of the sub-continental military balance in 1971.

DECEMBER: 'THE FOURTEEN DAYS' WAR'

Mirage IIIE fighter-bomber squadrons, and thirteen fighter-bomber/interceptor squadrons using F-86s and Chinese-built MiG-19s. India's naval forces were also larger than the Pakistan navy. In addition to their surface vessels, each side had four submarines, while the Indians also operated an aircraft carrier—the *Vikrant*—and a number of Russian missile boats.

During 1971 both the two countries had sharply increased their military efforts, but there do not seem to have been any last-minute acquisitions of equipment by either side capable of affecting the balance of forces. With Chinese help the Pakistanis strove to bring their two new divisions—the 17th and the 33rd—into service before the end of the year. But neither of them was at full readiness when the war began. The Indians had also acquired a great deal of equipment during the year, mostly from the Russians. But although the Indian SAM missile systems were improved, no major technological innovations occurred; and neither were there any major transfers of arms to either side during the war itself.[192]

During the development of the crisis over the previous months the morale of the Pakistani forces had been seriously impaired. In the East the conditions of counter-terrorist civil war had brutalized many army units, and in the West the defection of Bengalis in the armed services, and the wariness with which those who remained were treated, had damaging consequences for the fighting capability of many Pakistani units. This was especially true of the Pakistan air force, which had many Bengalis among its ground staff. In both parts of the country one of the most serious effects of the decade since 1958, in which the armed services provided the source and sanction of political power, had been the diversion of their officers from military to civilian concerns. Apart from the south Indian contingents of the Indian army the character and background of the two armed forces was very similar. But in the circumstances of 1971 the Indian officer class was often both more rigorously professional and rather more closely identified with the rank-and-file of the army than its Pakistani counterpart.

Military rule in Pakistan had also affected the character and capacities of the central management of the military machine. As seen in Chapter 1, the conflation of military and civil power—which had been resisted by Ayub Khan—was carried very much further under Yahya's martial law administration after March 1969. Considerations of efficiency had been increasingly subordinated to the requirements

---

[192] The Indians may have acquired a superior make of rocket for their Russian *Osa* missile boats during the last months of 1971.

of the political balance which maintained the power of the leadership. In 1965 Ayub Khan had co-ordinated Pakistan's war effort through a joint chiefs-of-staff system derived from the old British model, and similar to that which was also employed in India. But in 1971 political circumstances compelled Yahya Khan to retain the rank of Army Commander-in-Chief—by virtue of which he had become Chief Martial Law Administrator and President—alongside the rank of Supreme Commander—which had come to him by virtue of his position as President. The structure of command which resulted was excessively centralized; and at the same time it was dominated by the army. Thus the functions of the supreme direction of the war and detailed operational control over all units in the west were alike carried out from the army's general headquarters in Rawalpindi. At G.H.Q. President Yahya was in overall command, supported by his Principal Staff Officer, General Pirzada, by the Army Chief of Staff, General Hamid Khan, and by the Chief of the General Staff—also an army officer—General Gul Hassan. While the army thus dominated the overall headquarters in Rawalpindi, Air Marshal Rahim Khan's airforce headquarters were located 300 kilometres away in Peshawar; and the naval headquarters under Vice-Admiral Muzaffar Hasan were even further removed at Karachi. In East Pakistan, General Niazi's Eastern command was theoretically independent, and, indeed, it does not seem to have been informed by Islamabad of the decision to open up the front in the West on 3 December. But in practice, as events showed, the nature and extent of General Niazi's powers were unclear to him in relation both to the Centre, and to the Governor of East Pakistan and his military affairs adviser, Major-General Rao Farman Ali Khan. Relations between each of these different elements in both West and East and between them and the units in the field were difficult and uneasy—fraught with personal and inter-service rivalries, with misunderstandings, and with simple incomprehension.

On the Indian side the relations between the different elements in the command system were much more clearly defined and better understood. The three services were of equal status. Each of them was equally subject to political direction by the civilian ministers in a cabinet collectively responsible to the Indian Parliament; and the services headquarters were located alongside the Ministry of Defence in Delhi. The Chiefs of Staff Committee brought the heads of the different services together regularly on a basis of equality. The heads were, Air Marshal P. C. Lal, Admiral Nanda, and General Manekshaw, who acted as chairman of the Committee by virtue of seniority of membership. Below the Chiefs of Staff Committee a Joint Planning Staff in the Ministry of Defence provided co-ordination at the centre;

DECEMBER: 'THE FOURTEEN DAYS' WAR'

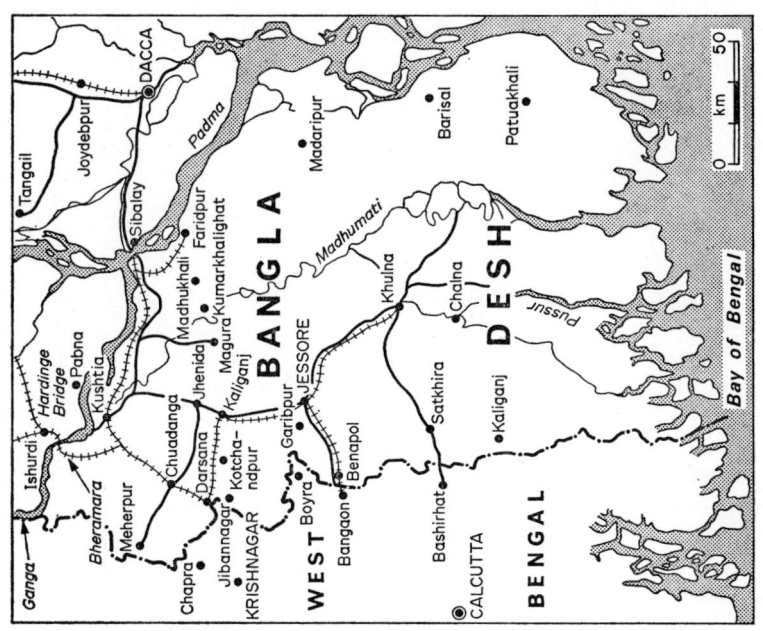

B. South-West Sector

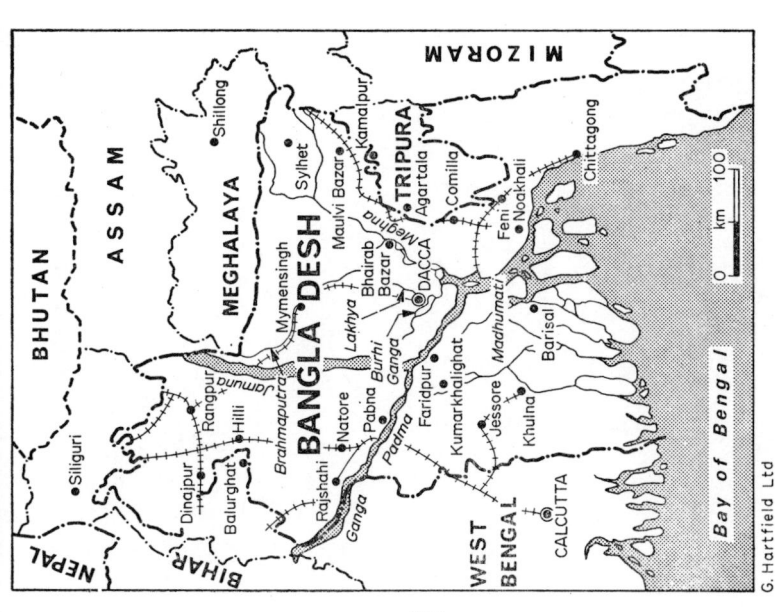

A. Bangla Desh

The Eastern Front I

SOUTH ASIAN CRISIS

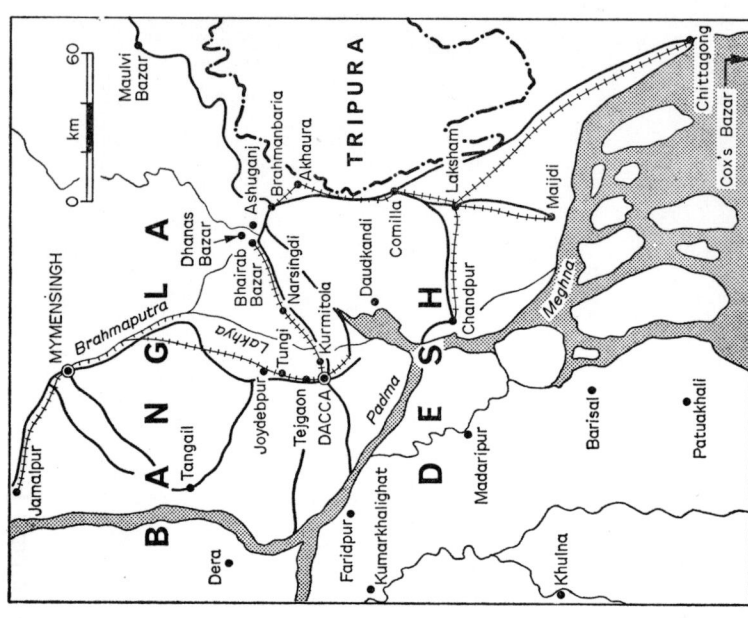

B. South-East Sector

The Eastern Front II

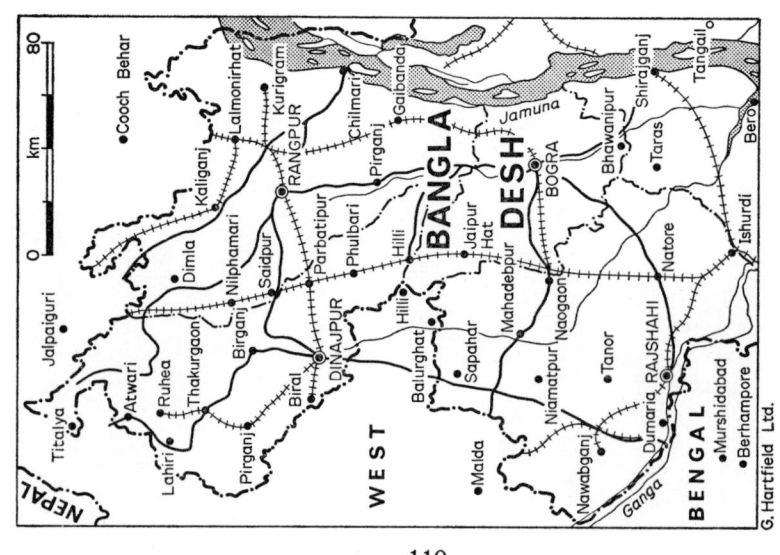

A. North-West Sector

DECEMBER: 'THE FOURTEEN DAYS' WAR'

and within the area commands in different parts of the country there was further machinery for co-ordination—notably, in respect of air–ground liaison, through the Tactical Air Commands attached to army HQs. This firmly established system—combined with good personal relations at the highest level and with the well-managed overall political direction of the war—provided a clarity of purpose and a quality of operational management far superior to that available to the Pakistan military machine in the circumstances of 1971.

Pakistan's disadvantage at the end of 1971 did not consist only of her relative weakness in numbers, equipment, organization and morale. Of possible strategic conditions those under which the war took place were the worst for her and the best for India. Since the 1950s the Indian forces had been organized on the assumption that they must be deployed on at least two fronts, against China in the Himalayas and against Pakistan in the West. On the other hand, Pakistan's military forces had been organized on the assumption that they would only need to be deployed on a single front, against India along the western border. Thus while a large part of the Indian army was normally on duty in the mountains, Pakistan had built up forces suitable for action on the plains, and during the 1960s she had acquired two armoured divisions as against India's one.

But none of these strategic asumptions held true during the third India–Pakistan war. Pakistan was compelled to divide her forces between East and West; and the prospect of a third front—between India and China in the Himalayas—was averted by Indo–Soviet diplomacy, by Chinese restraint, by the climatic conditions in the Himalayan passes, and by India's caution in the West. It is doubtful that much military significance can be attributed to the fourth front which it seemed might open up in the second week of the war, when the United States *Enterprise* task-force was detached from the Seventh Fleet and sent into the Bay of Bengal.

As we saw in the previous chapter, the full-scale Indo–Pakistani war which broke out on 3 December arose out of the pressure on Pakistan's military and political position in East Bengal, which became increasingly intense when the Indians began to reinforce the efforts of the *Mukti Bahini* after late October. Despite the defensive positions General Niazi had built up against the *Mukti Bahini* in the East, and despite Pakistan's military and diplomatic weakness and the dangers of the overall strategic outlook, it was the Pakistani authorities in Islamabad who took the fateful decision to launch the attack in the West which unleashed the full weight of Indian military resources against East Pakistan.

The motives behind this decision and the weight to be given to the various possible explanations are likely to remain uncertain. President Yahya had frequently threatened that the mounting Indian engagement in the East would be met by 'final war'. After the incident at Boyra at the end of November it seemed that his bluff was being called. In the heated atmosphere of Islamabad, failure to accept the Indian challenge could easily have been represented as cowardice—and it also risked a further intensification of India's efforts. Yahya's freedom inside Pakistan to pursue a policy of conciliation or disengagement had of course always been limited by the influence of the 'hardliners'. In an interview published in the *Washington Post* at the end of November General Farman Ali referred to these divergent views in Islamabad, predicting that in spite of them there would be no general war. 'If the President will not go to war, then these lieutenant-colonels and majors can't go to war.' But when the President's attempts to pursue an alternative policy with American support failed —as they seemed to have done by late November—the party of 'the lieutenant-colonels and majors' grew stronger, and it became more and more difficult for Pakistan to accept the implications of General Farman Ali's wise opinion : 'A nation can take a hell of a lot. You say "I can't tolerate that", and then it happens, and you do.'

The decision may also have been influenced by the logic of Pakistan's established defensive strategy, which had been based on the proposition that the East Wing could only be defended in the West. This doctrine had been successfully applied in the 1965 war. If the policy of deterrence failed and war occurred, it was assumed that captured Indian territory along the western front could be exchanged against any Indian advances in East Pakistan. Thus, in line with this strategy Yahya decided in September and October that India was to be deterred by the threat of a Pakistani offensive in the West, linked with diplomatic action to limit the scope of the war in the East by invoking the possibility of Chinese support in the Himalayas.

Moreover, after the events of 1971 the traditional strategy may have suggested another possibility to some: that of accepting the loss of East Pakistan and making up for it by securing an extension of Pakistani territory in the West—especially in the disputed territory of Kashmir. It also indicated a diplomatic strategy—a continuation of President Yahya's policy since October: that of playing up the dangers of war in the West until the deadlock in the United Nations had been broken and the great powers and the United Nations had been forced to act to put an end to the threat of full-scale international war in the sub-continent. This policy seems to be that advo-

DECEMBER: 'THE FOURTEEN DAYS' WAR'

cated by General Farman Ali. As he told the *Washington Post*: 'when the whole world knows that the entire game is political, I think they will not allow a war.' Accordingly, during November the key to the diplomatic defence of East Pakistan came to be seen more and more to lie with military action in the West.

After the failure of the United Nations to respond to the incidents along the East Bengal border in late November these different currents of opinion in Pakistan joined together in the accelerating movement towards war. The common element in each analysis was the idea that Pakistan should be willing to take the initiative in opening up the western front. But, apart from this, each argument had its own logic which contradicted that of the others. The logic of a war to capture territory for exchange in subsequent negotiations pointed to the occupation by Pakistan of the greatest possible extent of territory, in whatever sector of the front was most convenient. A war for the permanent acquisition of new ground indicated a concentration of Pakistan's efforts on Muslim territory in Kashmir. But, on the other hand, a war to 'internationalize' the conflict implied that an impression of restraint and reluctance on Pakistan's part should be given.

As we have seen, Pakistan's military and political organization was not well adapted to harmonizing such varied points of view. When war came, each of the three courses were pursued at the same time—which made it impossible to realize any one of them. At the same time the capacity of the forces in East Pakistan to hold out was overestimated. And—a more fundamental misjudgement—the ability of the great powers to stop the war was overrated, and the extent of the Soviet commitment to give India the cover she required in the Security Council was underestimated.

For, protected by the Soviet veto in the United Nations, the Indian strategy was to act as swiftly and decisively as possible to render Pakistan's position in the East untenable; and at the same time to defend India in the West, as far as possible on Pakistani soil. Although there must have been Indian contingency plans for an extended assault on West Pakistan, and some detailed consideration may have been given to them as the war progressed, there does not seem to be any genuine evidence that it was ever the serious intention of the Indian leadership to put them into effect—a policy which would have involved a serious risk of Chinese intervention, and which would have strained Russian support beyond its limits. Thus from the beginning of the war the strategies of the two sides on the two fronts were the mirror-image of one another. In the West, India was on the

SOUTH ASIAN CRISIS

defensive and Pakistan took the offensive; and in the East, the Pakistani strategy was defensive, and the Indian offensive had been long and carefully prepared.

Any description of the events of the Fourteen Days' War must both take account of the interrelation of diplomacy and military action, and at the same time follow the pattern of events as they occurred. The order of our narrative is indicated by this pattern.[193] First, on the military level the initial stages of the war were dominated by Pakistan's efforts on the western front, while the diplomatic conflict was concentrated at the United Nations. On both levels it became apparent more or less simultaneously at the end of the first week that the war in the West was deadlocked, and that the United Nations was not going to be able to achieve a settlement. Then the focus of the war shifted to East Pakistan, where the Indians were racing to Dacca against mounting American pressure for a cease-fire. Finally, after the fall of Dacca on 16 December there was a brief period of suspense while it remained uncertain whether the Indians would take the offensive in the West, or whether President Yahya would accept a cease-fire. The war on the western front finally came to an end at 8.00 p.m. on 17 December.

On the western front the 1,500-mile border between India and Pakistan falls naturally into four sectors. In the north, the cease-fire line through the disputed territory of Jammu and Kashmir runs in a broad arc through the mountainous country from the Karakoram Pass to the Ravi river. On the Indian side this front was held by XV Corps, commanded by Lt.-Gen. Sartaj Singh. Facing him were the 112th (Pakistani) Azad Kashmir Division in the heights around Kargil and Tithwal in the far north; the 23rd Azad Kashmir Division under Maj.-Gen. Iftikhar Khan Janjua on the Kotlien Poonch front in eastern Kashmir; and I Corps commanded by Lt.-Gen. Tikka Khan with his headquarters at Sialkot. The Pakistan I Corps front included the Chhamb area in southern Kashmir, and the Shakargarh salient which lay in recognized Pakistani territory stretching

---

[193] My account of the military history of the war is drawn partly from the interviews which I conducted in Pakistan, India and Bangla Desh, and partly from three Indian books. The official Indian account is contained in *The Annual Report 1971-2* of the Ministry of Defence, Government of India, 1972. There is an excellent brief narrative in Dilip Mukerjee, *Yahya Khan's 'Final War'*. Major-General D. K. Palit's *The Lightning Campaign, Indo-Pakistan War 1971*, was even more rapidly written and published, and it is important to consult the later impressions, in which some of the errors of the first impression are corrected.

DECEMBER: 'THE FOURTEEN DAYS' WAR'

out towards Pathankot and Dera Baba Nanak in the northern Punjab. The units under General Tikka Khan's command included the 8th, 15th and 17th Infantry Divisions and the 6th Armoured Division. In the Shakargarh salient opposite Pathankot he was opposed by the Indian I Corps, under Lt.-Gen. K. K. Singh.

Immediately south of Kashmir, the Punjab front stretched from Dera Baba Nanak in the south of the Shakargarh salient, to Fazilka on the Indian side of the Sulemanke bridge across the Sutlej river. Over most of this front two rivers constitute a natural barrier—the Ravi between Gurdaspur and Amritsar, and the Sutlej between Ferozepore and Fazilka. But, as the 1965 war had demonstrated, the country is highly suitable for tank warfare; and in December 1971 the struggle centred on the three enclaves with bridges traversing the rivers—at Dera Baba Nanak, where Pakistan controlled the bridge across the Ravi; at Hussainiwala, where the Indians possessed an enclave across the Sutlej around the Bhagat Singh Memorial, next to a Pakistani enclave at Sehjra; and at Sulemanke, where the Pakistanis controlled the bridge across the Sutlej to Fazilka. The Indian front was manned by the XI Corps under Lt.-Gen. Rawlley, which, together with XI Corps and XV Corps in Kashmir, made up the Indian army's Western Command under Lt.-Gen. K. P. Candeth. Facing General Rawlley's XI Corps was the Pakistani IV Corps under Lt.- Gen. Bahadur Sher, based on Lahore, comprising the 10th and 11th Infantry Divisions and the 8th Armoured Brigade.

Further south, where northern Rajasthan abuts on the Punjab, the front opposite Multan stretched across the desert between Fazilka and Anupgarh. Although in many places the sand is too soft, this country is also suitable for tank warfare. On the Pakistani side II Corps under Lt.-Gen. Irshad Ahmad Khan had its headquarters at Multan. It comprised the 7th and 33rd Infantry Divisions, the 25th Armoured Brigade, and—a threatening feature—the 1st Armoured Division. General Rawlley's Indian XI Corps—including the 1st Armoured Division—covered the northern part of this front. The southern part fell within the Indian Southern Command in Rajasthan, under Lt.-Gen. G. G. Bewoor.

Still further south, the Rajasthan front ran on through the desert areas around Anupgarh in the north to the marshes of the Rann of Kutch stretching down towards the ocean. The 18th Infantry Division and two armoured regiments manned the Pakistani side, with headquarters at Hyderabad in Sind. On the Indian side this front also fell within General Bewoor's Southern Command, which consisted of two divisions.

The Pakistani offensive in the West began abruptly at 5.47 on the afternoon of 3 December, when the Pakistan air force struck simultaneously at the Indian airfields at Amritsar, Srinagar, Avantipur and Pathankot, and at the landing ground at Faridkot and the radar station at Amritsar. According to the Indians only six *Starfighters* and ten *Sabres* took part in this attack—apparently designed to damage runways and impede the Indian response to Pakistan's subsequent ground attack. Exploiting the evening light, the PAF was able to escape interception by Indian planes, which were held up on the ground where it was already dark. But although the Pakistanis succeeded in evading the Indian early-warning system by flying low over Rajasthan, the forces employed were not sufficient to do much damage. Only at Agra—which was bombed by three Pakistani B-57s later in the evening—was much damage done to the runways. Eight hours after the Pakistani air attack the India air force counter-attack was under way, and the Pakistani airfields at Murid, Mianwali, Sargodha, Chander, Risalwala, Shorkot and Masrur were raided by the Indian *Canberra* force. At first light the following morning the Indians anticipated further Pakistani attacks by mounting a series of raids, especially on Peshawar—the PAF headquarters—and, in co-operation with the Indian navy, on the oil-storage depots at Karachi. Thereafter, the Pakistanis never recovered the initiative in the air war, which was dominated by the Indian offensive effort.

On the evening of the 3rd, the Pakistan army also began ground operations in Kashmir and the Punjab, and set on foot a long-range armoured operation in Rajasthan. In Kashmir, the Pakistani attack was concentrated at Poonch and Chhamb. At Poonch, the 26th infantry brigade thrust southwards through the hilly country from Kahuta, while commandos of the Pakistan Special Services Group infiltrated behind the Indian lines towards the bridge to Mendhar over the Kalni river. But the IAF's counter-attack helped the Indian ground forces to prevent a juncture between these two forces, and the first Pakistani assault on Poonch ceased on the 5th. On the night of the 9-10th a second Pakistani attack was frustrated by Indian bombing, in which An-12 transports and *Vampire* trainers were used to break up the opposing forward concentrations. Thereafter, the Indians mounted a local offensive which secured several tactical posts west and north of Poonch. Casualties on both sides were heavy.[194]

[194] See also the report by the Secretary-General submitted to the Security Council of the United Nations, on the situation along the cease-fire line in Kashmir: United Nations Security Council Documents S/10412 (4 December), and S/10412 *addendum* 1 (5December), *add*. 2 (6 December).

DECEMBER: 'THE FOURTEEN DAYS' WAR'

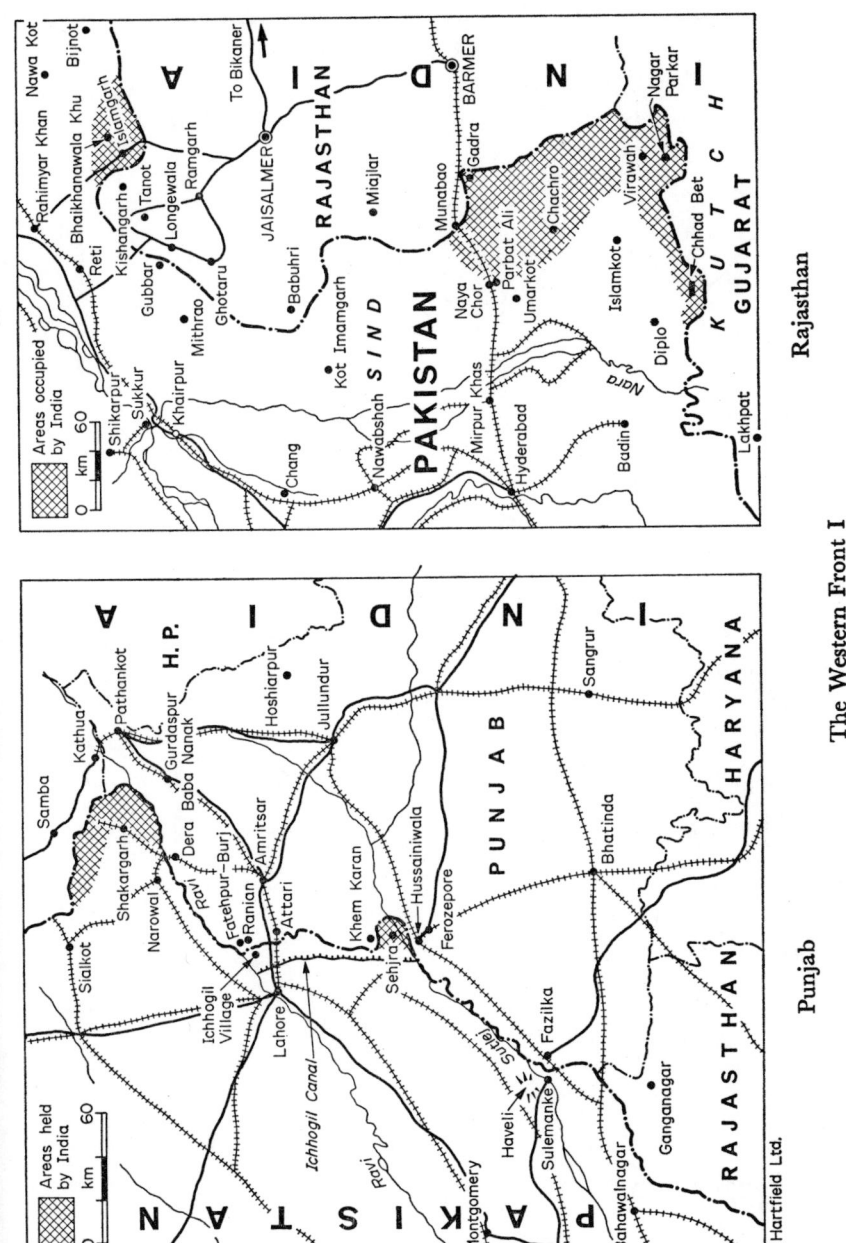

The Western Front I

SOUTH ASIAN CRISIS

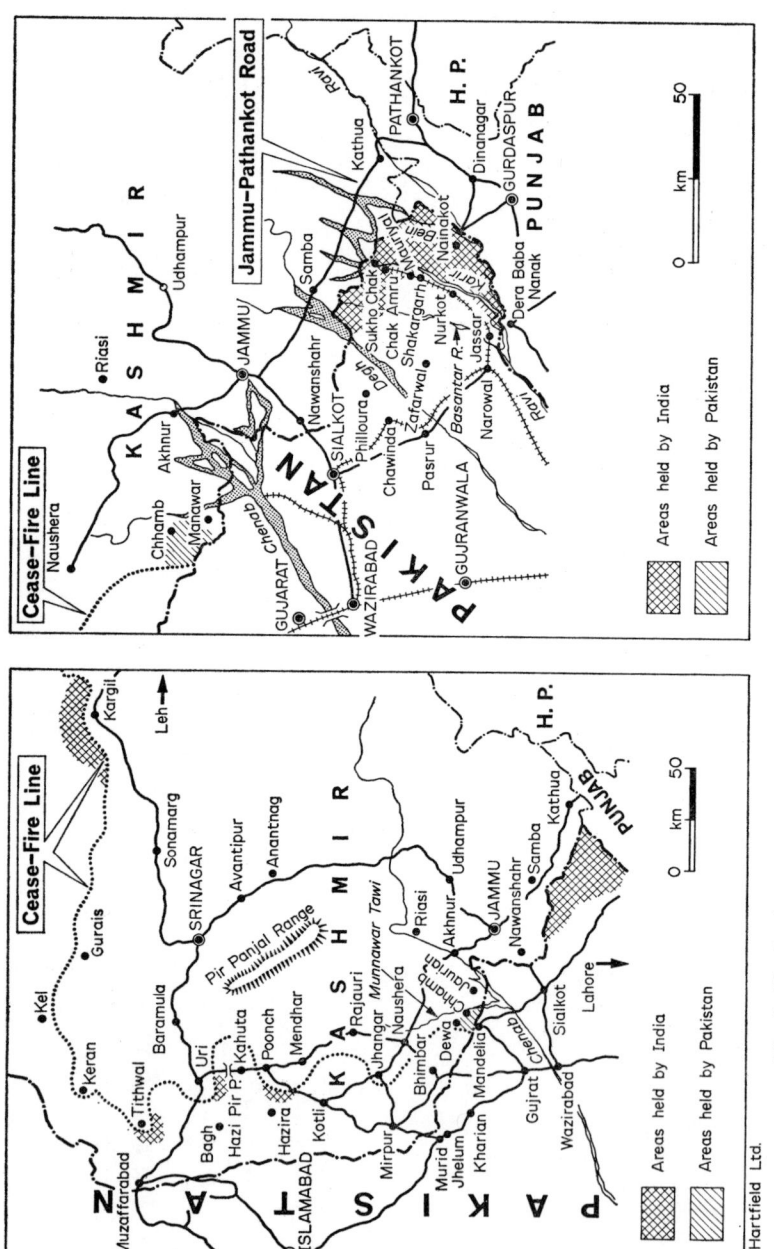

The Western Front II

DECEMBER: 'THE FOURTEEN DAYS' WAR'

Immediately to the south, a major Pakistani attack opened up on the 3rd in the Chhamb sector with extensive air support being provided for four infantry brigades, an armoured brigade and eight artillery regiments. In the 1965 war this sector had been of key importance because of the vulnerability of the bridge across the Chenab river near Akhnur—where the road to Naushera and Poonch in the Indian portion of upper Kashmir runs close to territory held by Pakistan. But since 1965 the strategic importance of this sector had been reduced by the construction of alternative rearward Indian routes into upper Kashmir. Nevertheless, the Pakistani forces under General Tikka Khan did not exploit the alternative position which they held in the salient towards Akhnur, where heavy fighting had also taken place in 1965. They concentrated their attack almost exclusively on the Indian positions at Chhamb, on the Pakistani side of the Munnawar Tawi river. After seventy-two hours they had made the Indians withdraw from their positions in the open country west of the Munnawar Tawi. But the Pakistanis had lost more than twenty of their T-59 tanks. On the 8–9th they took Chhamb and established a lodgment on the eastern side of the river—but by the evening of the 10th they had been driven back to the western bank after three days of fierce fighting. By this time the Indians estimate that the Pakistanis were deploying a whole division of infantry along the 10,000-metre battlefront. Several more assaults were launched before the front stabilized on the 12th. The Indian estimate of casualties in this sector is that they lost 17 tanks and about 440 men killed, as against Pakistani casualties estimated to be 36 tanks and 1,350 men killed.

Elsewhere in Kashmir the Indian forces exploited the opportunity to make tactical improvements to their positions along the cease-fire line. In the south, the Pakistani salient towards Akhnur was captured on 5–6 December. Further north fifteen Pakistani posts above Kargil at a height of over 16,000 feet were captured after night attacks in winter conditions; in Itthwal and Uri a further twenty-one posts were taken.

But on a larger scale there was also a carefully prepared Indian counter-offensive further south in the Sialkot-Shakargarh sector south and west of Chhamb. Within the Shakargarh bulge the Pakistanis had constructed elaborate fortifications manned by units of Tikka Khan's I Corps—including the 8th and 17th Infantry Divisions, the 6th Armoured Division and the 8th Armoured Brigade. On the night of 5–6 December the Indian I Corps moved forward to relieve the pressure on Chhamb and to counter the Pakistani threat to the Pathankot–Jammu road, which ran close to the cease-fire line. The Indians mounted two thrusts, one from the north designed to cut the road between Shakargarh and Zafarwal—which was not reached until the 15th. The other, from the east, struck out towards Shakargarh. The assault was held up by mine-fields; and a stout Pakistani resistance culminated in the largest tank battle of the war on the night of the 15th and on the following day. Two Pakistani tank regiments of *Pattons* were thrown against an Indian tank force of *Centurions*. When the cease-fire came, the Indian I Corps had captured 750 sq. km of territory in the Shakargarh bulge, with a loss of 301 men against an estimated Pakistani loss of 285.

Meanwhile along the Indian XI Corps front in the northern Punjab between Dera Baba Nanak and Anupgarh both sides fought fiercely to improve their positions in anticipation of the major Pakistani strategic offensive which was expected in that area. Neither the Pakistani 1st Armoured Division—part of II Corps based on Multan —nor its Indian equivalent within General Rawlley's XI Corps were however brought into action at any stage of the war. Nevertheless, at Ranian and Fatehpur, and at the enclaves traversing the Ravi and Sutlej rivers—at Dera Baba Nanak, at Hussainiwala, and at Fazilka —the Pakistanis mounted a series of determined attacks with heavy casualties. At Dera Baba Nanak a surprise Indian attack on the Pakistani enclave on the eastern bank of the Ravi was launched on the night of 6–7 December, and the bridge was secured against an anticipated Pakistani assault. Further south, in the area of Fatehpur, an initial Pakistani attack on the night of the 3rd captured four Indian posts, which were retaken one by one over the following two weeks. The repeated Pakistani attacks on the Indian defensive canal at Ranian were beaten back without loss of territory. At Hussainiwala on the Sutlej, however, the Indians abandoned their enclave on the western bank after a brief tank battle on 4 December. On the other hand, the near-by Pakistani enclave at Sehjra near Khem Karan was taken by the Indians on the night of 5–6 December: during the 1965 war it had housed a Pakistani armoured brigade. At Fazilka—the enclave nearest Multan and Montgomery, where the Pakistan 1st Armoured Division was reported to have taken up its position—a strong Pakistani attack was launched on the first night of the war, across the bridge over the Sutlej at Sulemanke. After an initial success in gaining a lodgment on the Fazilka side of the Indian defensive moat, the Indian defending force counter-attacked and retrieved the position. Casualties on both sides were heavy. The air superiority the Indians established apparently enabled them to make use of the lumbering An-12 transport aircraft for bombing operations in the wooded area round Changa Manga near Haveli opposite

DECEMBER: 'THE FOURTEEN DAYS' WAR'

Fazilka, where it was believed that the Pakistan Armoured Division was located.

Further south, the battles along the Rajasthan front of the Indian Southern Command were subordinate to these more important confrontations along the Punjab front. Both sides sought to draw out the enemy's reserves from further north. On the night of the 3–4th a powerful Pakistani force made up of one infantry brigade, an armoured regiment of T-59 tanks and a squadron of *Shermans* made its way undetected across the desert to the Indian border opposite Ramgarh, north-west of Jaisalmer. It crossed the border on the night of the 4–5th, but it was observed near Longewala post early on the morning of the 5th. The Pakistani thrust was not provided with air support, and the IAF *Hunters* spear-headed an Indian counter-attack which destroyed some 37 tanks in the course of the day. Between the 5th and the 10th the Indian counter-offensive at Gubbar and in the bulge of Pakistani territory around Islamgarh captured some 640 sq. km of Pakistan soil.

The Pakistani attack on Longewala was paralleled by similar but more successful Indian thrusts south of the Punjab into Sind and the Rann of Kutch. In military terms the advance in this sector opened up the prospect of cutting the main Pakistani lines of north–south communications through Hyderabad to Karachi. It also held out the political opportunity of possibly being able to exploit Sindhi separatist sentiment. On the night of the 4–5th the Indian 11th Infantry division moved into Pakistan along the axis of the old Barmer–Hyderabad railway line towards Nyachor, which was reached on the 8th. Heavy fighting went on outside the town until the cease-fire. Moving southwards, long-range raiding parties overwhelmed the Pakistani posts towards Chachro. In Kutch, an Indian commando raided Virawah, and three Indian Border Security Force battalions and a regular infantry battalion took Nagar Parkar on 5 December and Chhad Bet on the 12th. At the cease-fire the Indian forces in Kutch and Sind had occupied 4,765 square miles of Pakistani territory. Perhaps more important, the Pakistani 33rd Infantry division, which had been kept as part of the strategic reserve in II Corps, had been drawn south to the defence of the Rahimyar Khan–Hyderabad sector along Pakistan's Rajasthan front.

Although the number of troops employed was comparatively small, these operations in Sind represented the most successful Indian ground offensive effort against Pakistan in the West. But in the air and at sea the Indians remained on the offensive throughout the war. On the first night after the Pakistani raid on the airfields in the

SOUTH ASIAN CRISIS

West, the IAF mounted 500 sorties along the front and at strategic targets further into Pakistan; and over the fourteen days of open war the Western Air Command of the IAF carried out more than 4,000 sorties. The PAF was driven back into a defensive role; and the air support given to the Pakistani efforts on the ground was very patchy. It seems probable that, although the PAF ground staff had been weakened by the exclusion of Bengalis—who constituted nearly a fifth of its technicians—the main reason for the deficiency of the Pakistani effort in the air was that a deliberate decision had been made at PAF headquarters that its strength should be conserved after the heavy losses in the first few days of the war. Like the tanks of the 1st Armoured Division, which remained in reserve, the PAF's *Mirages* were very little used, except at Chhamb. There was no prospect of Pakistan being able to replace them, and precious little of securing replacements for any American *Sabres* and *F–104*s that might be lost. On the other hand, the Indians knew that they were able to throw everything into the battle, secure in their access to Soviet equipment and in their own supply of domestically built *Gnats* and MiG-21s. In addition to harrying the PAF bases and the Pakistani ground forces, the IAF mounted a sustained offensive against Pakistani communications and petroleum supplies. On the nights of the 4–5th and 8–9th combined Indian air–naval operations were also carried out against the oil-storage facilities at Karachi, and the Indian navy deployed its eight recently delivered Russian *Osa*-class 200-ton boats armed with *Styx I* missiles.

Thus in 1971 India fought her first full-scale naval war. She maintained an effective blockade against both East and West Pakistan, and she carried out a full naval control operation over all Indian shipping. A number of offensive raids were also mounted against the Pakistan navy and Pakistani shipping in harbours in both parts of the country. On the late afternoon of the 3rd the Pakistani submarine *Ghazi* was detected off Vizakhapatnam harbour and sunk by depth-charge: the Indian navy had already put to sea in anticipation of a surprise attack. From the forward naval base at Okha in Gujarat the first Indian raid on Karachi harbour was mounted on 4 December, sinking one Pakistan navy destroyer, a minesweeper, and a neutral merchant ship. The second raid, under the command of Rear-Admiral E. C. Kuruvilla in the cruiser *Mysore*, took place on the 8th. The oil installations were again hit, and among the ships sunk in Karachi harbour was the British merchant ship *Hamrattan*. As the Indian navy squadron withdrew the anti-submarine frigate *Khukri* was sunk by a Pakistani submarine.

But the decisive battles were, of course, fought on land, and the

DECEMBER: 'THE FOURTEEN DAYS' WAR'

turning-point of the land war in the West came towards the end of the first week, on about 10 December, when it became apparent that the Indian defensive–offensive strategy was being successfully implemented and that the Pakistani offensive had come to a halt. In Chhamb the front was being stabilized. In the Shakargarh bulge the Indian advance was drawing Pakistani forces away from the Chhamb sector. In the Punjab, Pakistani pressure across the bridgeheads was being successfully resisted, and the threat to Fazilka had been warded off. Along the Rajasthan front and in Sind a powerful Indian attack with small forces was penetrating deep into sensitive territory. The IAF had established its dominance in the air war, and at sea the Indian blockade had been enforced. Pakistan's hope of relieving the East Wing by action in the West had been frustrated.

In the Eastern war also, as we shall see, the decisive moment had been reached at the same time as the Indian army drew breath along the Meghna river. But meanwhile a decisive engagement had also taken place in New York during the first week of the conflict. By 10 December it was apparent that the hope that the great powers would be able to intervene to stop the war was illusory. The Soviet Union had twice exercised its veto in the Security Council. And the overwhelming approval given in the General Assembly to a resolution unfavourable to India had no effect on Pakistan's deteriorating military situation in East Bengal. Before 10 December the international reaction to the war was focused on the American attempts to secure a cease-fire through the United Nations; but after the 10th the great powers became more directly involved. For Pakistan's friends it was no longer a question of securing international action to cover Pakistan in East Bengal. The issue seemed increasingly to be, how to safeguard West Pakistan itself from disaster.

Between 4 and 10 December, the East Pakistan question dominated the first phase of the diplomatic confrontation in the United Nations. The Pakistani representatives argued that their country was being forcibly dismembered by the intervention of a fellow-member of the United Nations, and that the political solution being demanded by India and her supporters amounted to an instruction to Pakistan to 'dismember herself'. Pakistan, they declared, was willing to explore political solutions in the East—but the basic principle must be autonomy within Pakistan, not sovereign self-determination for East Bengal under a system imposed by external intervention. India, for her part, maintained that the military repression carried on since the end of March inside East Pakistan had destroyed the possibility of that country remaining voluntarily within Pakistan. Bangla Desh, the Indians declared, was now a 'nation' with its own government, duly constituted by representatives freely chosen in the elections held in Pakistan in December 1970. President Yahya's refusal to release Sheikh Mujib was conclusive evidence of the unreality of his proposed political solution. Pakistan had irrevocably lost the allegiance of a large section of its people and could not bring them under its sway. As for the objective of Indian policy—on 12 December Mr Swaran Singh declared in the Security Council that India had 'no territorial ambitions in Bangla Desh or in West Pakistan'. She was willing to 'discuss any cease-fire or withdrawal which would ensure the freedom and aspirations of the people of Bangla Desh, and which would ensure the vacation of Pakistani troops from Indian territory'.[195]

The Russians supported the Indian case, on the argument that Pakistan had failed to take the only satisfactory course, which they defined as the 'renunciation of the policy of repression, the release of Sheikh Mujib-ur Rahmann and the immediate resumption of talks with the aim of finding such a resolution as would accord with the will expressed by the population of East Pakistan at the elections'. On this basis the Soviet Union proceeded to veto all resolutions which did not link the establishment of a cease-fire with the 'unconditional' recognition of the will of the East Pakistan population. This was the principle embodied in the Soviet resolutions of 5 and 7 December, which, had they been adopted—as the Russians were later able to argue—might have saved the Pakistani army in the East.

For China, this was her first crisis in the United Nations, and the inexperience of her representatives was revealed in a certain lack of skill in operating the Security Council procedures.[196] China opposed all resolutions which did not 'strongly condemn the aggressive acts of the Indian government and demand that the Indian government immediately and unconditionally withdraw all the Indian armed forces from Pakistan'. She was also anxious that the 'Soviet social imperialists' should be pilloried.

Apart from nuances of vocabulary the Chinese position was identical with that taken up by the United States, who took the lead in urging support for Pakistan within the United Nations. The American government strongly supported the Pakistani position on two stated

---

[195] There was of course a scarcely veiled menace in the Indian refusal to give any assurances over the *status quo* in Kashmir. But it was hardly to be expected that India would abandon her 25-year-old position on Kashmir at the height of her victory in 1971.

[196] At one point they cast a veto against a motion which had already failed to win sufficient support.

DECEMBER: 'THE FOURTEEN DAYS' WAR'

grounds. First the Americans argued that their mediation in November had brought Pakistan to the point where she had been prepared to discuss 'a precise timetable for the establishment of political autonomy in East Bengal', that Mrs Gandhi had known this, and that she had given assurances that she would do all she could to avert war. These contentions were advanced at Dr Kissinger's Press briefing on 7 December; but they were immediately sharply disputed within the Administration—notably by Mr Kenneth Keating, the American Ambassador in India.[197] Dr Kissinger's second argument was less controversial. It was based upon the principle that the 'attempt to dismember a sovereign state, a member of the United Nations' would lead to 'international anarchy' which would jeopardize world peace.

Although American public opinion was very largely favourable to India, the White House policy prevailed.[198] On the 4th a State Department spokesman declared that 'Indian policy, in a systematic way, has led to the perpetuation of the crisis, a deepening of the crisis, and India bears a major responsibility for the broader hostilities which have ensued'. On the 6th, the American Ambassador to the United Nations, Mr George Bush, stated on television that India was guilty of 'clear-cut aggression'. On 3 December all outstanding licences for military sales to India were revoked. On the 6th all United States economic aid to India was suspended, while at the same time it was made clear that the remaining aid facilities for Pakistan had not been discontinued. As 'the next turn of the screw', on the 8th it was ordered that no provision should be made for India in the following year's AID budget. While a State Department spokesman declared on the 8th that 'the effort we have been making may have got a bit out of focus', throughout the crisis the administration sought to make it plain that 'India has jeopardized relations with the United States; and on 6 December President Nixon himself publicly indicated sympathy for President Yahya's 'efforts . . . to move to reduce tensions on the sub-Continent'.

As a consequence of Pakistan's attack on 3 December, India was able to make the first move in the United Nations—in the form of a complaint lodged with the Secretary-General on the evening of the

---

[197] Dr Kissinger's briefing was printed in the *New York Herald Tribune*'s Paris edition on 6 January 1972, along with Mr Keating's cable to the American Secretary of State. See Appendix 13, p. 207.

[198] There is a fascinating record of the development of American policy in the so-called 'Anderson Papers' – the minutes of Dr Kissinger's Washington Special Action Group, published by the newspaper columnist Mr Jack Anderson in the *New York Times* on 5 and 14 January 1972. See Appendix 14, p. 212.

3rd.[199] At the same time it was stated in Delhi that India did not propose to take the matter to the Security Council, because of her past unhappy experiences with United Nations intervention in the case of 'previous Pakistani aggressions'. On the 4th the Security Council was called into emergency session on a request from Argentina—who was to play an important diplomatic role throughout the crisis in the United Nations—supported by Burundi, Italy, Japan, Nicaragua, Somalia, the United Kingdom and the United States. The debate that day opened with a proposal from the Soviet Union and Poland that representatives of 'the Government of Bangla Desh' should be invited to address the Council. Mr Huang Hua (China) denounced 'this rebellious organization', and for the moment Mr Jacob Malik (USSR) allowed the proposal to rest. The United States Ambassador, Mr George Bush, then took the initiative by submitting a resolution after the opening speeches had been made by Mr Agha Shahi (Pakistan) and Mr Samar Sen (India).[200] Mr Bush's proposal called for an immediate cease-fire and the withdrawal of all armed personnel to their own side of the border. His resolution also attempted to bring to life again the long-standing project for the placing of United Nations observers along one or both sides of the frontier. Early the following morning the Soviet Union and Poland voted against the resolution. This was the first of the Soviet vetoes. Britain and France abstained, and eleven nations voted in favour of the resolution (Argentina, Belgium, Burundi, China, Italy, Japan, Nicaragua, Sierra Leone, Somalia, Syria and the United States).

Later the same day, the debate was resumed, with three draft resolutions before the Council. A Chinese proposal called for a cease-fire and the withdrawal of troops, and for the condemnation of 'Indian aggression'.[201] A Soviet resolution required 'a political settlement in East Pakistan which would inevitably result in a cessation of hostilities'.[202] And an Argentinian resolution along the same lines as the American proposal of the previous day was supported by seven nations.[203] The Soviet motion was vetoed by China after Poland and the Soviet Union had voted in its favour and twelve nations had ab-

---

[199] On 3 December the Secretary-General issued a report to the Security Council (S/10410) summarizing the development of events since 20 July, and quoting from the official United Nations correspondence with India and Pakistan.

[200] For the text of the American Resolution see S/10416 *ibid.*

[201] S/10421, *ibid.*

[202] S/10418, *ibid.* See also the Tass statement circulated as a Security Council document on 5 December, S/10422.

[203] S/10419, *ibid.*, and S/10423.

DECEMBER: 'THE FOURTEEN DAYS' WAR'

stained. The Chinese resolution was withdrawn. On the 6th there was a further deadlock, accompanied by furious mutual recriminations between the Russians and Chinese—whose representative was described by Mr Malik as 'the imperialists' court jester'. A French resolution was withdrawn after the Soviet Union, China, and the United States had each objected. Another Soviet resolution was submitted, calling for a cease-fire and effective action by the Pakistan government towards a political settlement 'giving immediate recognition to the will of the East Pakistan population as expressed in the elections of December 1970'.[204] It was not voted upon—although as we shall see, the Pakistani authorities in Dacca realized that it represented a way of extricating the Pakistani army in the East. The Council could agree only to refer the issue to the General Assembly under the 'uniting for peace' procedure which had only been used four times since it was instituted in 1950. Eleven nations voted in favour of this resolution; none voted against, and France, Poland, the Soviet Union, and Pakistan abstained.[205]

On 6 December the Indian government at last recognized the Provisional Government of Bangla Desh, thereby finally committing itself irrevocably to the complete expulsion of Pakistan from East Bengal. After the 6th India could no longer accept any 'political settlement' which retained East Bengal within the framework of Pakistan. Accordingly, Pakistan immediately broke off diplomatic relations with India. Yahya's attempt to secure United Nations intervention through the Security Council had failed; and on the 7th the General Assembly met in New York. Almost exactly the same resolution as that submitted by Argentina to the Security Council on the 5th was put before it, supported by fourteen nations headed by Argentina. Its main features were a demand for a cease-fire and the withdrawal of armed forces to their own sides of the border. It also insisted that 'efforts be intensified in order to bring about, speedily and in accordance with the purpose and principles of the Charter of the United Nations, conditions necessary for the voluntary return of the East Pakistan refugees to their homes'.

In the debate which followed some 47 nations took part. The British and the French restated their positions, Sir Colin Crowe declared that the United Kingdom would abstain once again, because the resolution would not contribute to the task of 'halting the fighting,

[204] S/10428, *ibid.* This resolution originated as an amendment to S/10425, a resolution submitted the previous day by Belgium and five other states.

[205] S/10429, *ibid.* Resolution moved by Argentina, Burundi, Japan, Sierra Leone, and Somalia.

and finding peaceful solutions to the desperately complicated issues which gave rise to the outbreak of war'. The French representative, M. Kosciusko-Morizet, similarly argued that 'the only realistic measure would be to obtain before anything else a cessation of hostilities, of all the hostilities, without prejudice to what may be decided subsequently'. On 8 December the Argentinian resolution was adopted by the General Assembly, by a vote of 104 to 11, with 10 abstentions—Afghanistan, Chile, Denmark, France, Malawi, Nepal, Oman (the only Arab power not to support Pakistan), Senegal, Singapore and the United Kingdom. Along with China, Rumania and Yugoslavia were the only Communist powers who voted in support of the resolution. A Soviet motion repeating the proposal she had made in the Security Council on the 6th was not put to a vote.

Thus in the United Nations, as well as on the ground in West and East Pakistan, the end of the first week of the war marked a turning point. On 9 December Mr Agha Shahi informed the Secretary-General that Pakistan was willing to fall in with the terms of the resolution adopted by the General Assembly. But it was already plain that India would not accept it, and some days later, on the 12th, Mrs Gandhi affirmed that Indian troops would not be withdrawn from Bangla Desh until a Pakistani military withdrawal had been accomplished. In the week after the General Assembly had passed its resolutions the zones of high diplomatic pressure consequently shifted away from New York—to Washington and the Bay of Bengal, to Peking and the mountains of Ladakh, to Moscow and Delhi and Islamabad. For the remaining week of the war the United Nations became merely a mirror of events in the sub-continent; although during this second phase the drama of the debates in the Security Council was heightened by the arrival of two new principal actors, namely the Indian Foreign Minister, Mr Swaran Singh, and Mr Bhutto, the newly appointed Deputy Premier and Foreign Minister of Pakistan.

In this second phase the problem for Pakistan's friends now seemed to be, how to protect *West* Pakistan from Indian attack. On 12 December, the United States returned the issue to the Security Council, and there was a statement from the White House to the effect that 'with East Pakistan virtually occupied by Indian troops, a continuation of the war would take on increasingly the character of armed attack on the very existence of a member-State of the United Nations'.[206] Presenting a resolution based on that passed on the 8th

---

[206] S/10444: letter of the American permanent representative to the President of the Security Council, 12 December.

DECEMBER: 'THE FOURTEEN DAYS' WAR'

in the General Assembly, Mr Bush called for 'a clear and unequivocal assurance that India does not intend to annex Pakistan territory and change the status quo in Kashmir'. Mr Swaran Singh replied with an assurance—which ignored the point about Kashmir—that 'India has no territorial ambitions in Bangla Desh or in West Pakistan'. Mr Bhutto declared that 'we will fight for a thousand years'.

On 13 December the United States resolution was put to a vote.[207] The Soviet Union and Poland opposed, and Britain and France again abstained. The Russians again proposed that the Bangla Desh representative should be invited to appear before the Council. The Chinese ambassador again objected, and the Russian proposal was again withdrawn. On the 14th brief consideration was given to a draft resolution submitted by Italy and Japan.[208] The debate was adjourned without a vote. The next day at another meeting of the Council Mr Bhutto tore up his notes and walked out of the chamber. An Anglo–French resolution was then submitted, calling for an immediate cease-fire and the negotiation of a comprehensive political settlement.[209]

But diplomatic intervention, which had been powerless to prevent the war, did not prove effective either in bringing it to an end. On the 16th Mr Swaran Singh informed the Council that a cease-fire had been negotiated between the Indian and Pakistani forces in Bangla Desh. He added that a unilateral cease-fire would be undertaken by the Indian armed forces in the West, starting the following morning. On 22 December, Argentina had the last word. Another of her resolutions was adopted by 13 votes without opposition—the USSR and Poland still abstaining.[210] The most important feature of this final resolution was a call for the cease-fire line in Kashmir to be fully respected.

Meanwhile, although these diplomatic efforts affected the course of the war at several points, the decisive factor in determining the timetable of the war was the rapid advance of the Indian army in the East to total victory. While India's success was inevitable from the moment the general war broke out—unless diplomatic intervention could frustrate it—the Indian campaign in East Bengal was nevertheless a striking feat of arms. Those features of East Bengal which had most favoured the guerrilla tactics of the *Mukti Bahini* impeded more orthodox military operations, both offensive and defensive.

[207] Text of the resolution in S/10446.
[208] S/10451.
[209] S/10445.
[210] S/10465.

Surrounded on three sides by Indian territory, the borders of the province were immensely exposed and difficult to defend. But for the same reason the Indian lines of communication were also strung out around the three sides of the deep salient of Pakistan territory. From Calcutta to Agartala, the main Indian overland communications through the narrow Siliguri corridor south of Sikkim and China ran by railway to Dharamnagar, and thence to Agartala and Belonia over a largely single-track road. Similar roads provided the only access to the Meghalaya border across the Garo hills. Agartala, with its primitive air-strip was the only important centre of air communications on the whole of the eastern side of Bengal.

Inside East Pakistan the marshy terrain with its many streams and rivers—which had benefited the *Mukti Bahini*—imposed severe handicaps on the mobility of the Indian and Pakistani armies alike. On the other hand, it favoured the defensive strategy adopted by the Pakistanis. Three major rivers between one and five miles wide divide East Bengal into four parts, with the central point lying at Dacca. Running north to south, cutting the country in half, is the Jamuna, which is joined below Dacca by the Surma–Meghna waters flowing south-west from the area of Sylhet. There are, however, no major river obstacles north of Dacca in the triangle formed by the Jamuna and the Meghna, with its apex at Dacca and its base along the Indian border in Meghalaya. East of the Meghna lie Sylhet, Ashuganj, Comilla, Noakhali and Chittagong, all connected by a railway line which rarely lies any further than twenty miles from the Indian border. West of the Jamuna the country is divided by the Padma or Ganges, which flows south-eastwards into the Jamuna above Dacca. North of the Padma lie the major towns of the north-west region of East Bengal—Rangpur, Dinajpur, Bogra and Rajshahi. To the south lie Kushtia, Jessore, Khulna and Chalna. As on the eastern side, the main towns are connected by a north–south railway which runs very close to the Indian border at many points, with the main crossing-point on the Padma located at the Hardinge bridge immediately north of Kushtia.

These internal rail and road communications were of key importance for regular formations operating normally. But, traversing so many rivers, they were also very vulnerable to disruption—whether for offensive or defensive purposes—at a few key points and many minor ones. The indispensable requirement therefore of any Indian offensive strategy designed to do more than merely to provide support for the *Mukti Bahini* was the development of a capacity for rapid movement capable of by-passing the natural obstacles—marshes, wide rivers with blown bridges, river-systems already fortified by the

DECEMBER: 'THE FOURTEEN DAYS' WAR'

Pakistani army. The attacking troops had to travel on foot, provided with only light vehicles and light artillery supplemented by air support. They had to be supplied with bridging equipment and helicopters for air-transportation. The only advantage of war of this kind was that it enabled the Indians to some extent to discount the weakness of their infrastructure around the eastern front.

The consequence of these tactics was that once the full-scale war had begun the Indians would necessarily undertake a deep penetration into East Bengal. Politically, this opened up two alternative prospects: a cease-fire with Indian troops already deep inside Pakistani territory, or—if time was available—an advance to Dacca followed by the unconditional surrender of the Pakistani forces. During the planning of these operations in the months before 3 December it was decided that once they were fully involved the Indian forces should not confine themselves to capturing a few major centres in the border regions and leaving them in the hands of the Bangla Desh government. Hence the need for cover at the United Nations—reinforced by the fact that before the war began the Indians seem to have expected that it would take at least three weeks to get to Dacca. Once a satisfactory international atmosphere had been assured by the Russians, it was decided that the Indian forces should be disposed so as to penetrate as deeply and as fast as possible into East Bengal on all sides. Nevertheless, the weakest thrust and the slowest to advance was in the northern central area opposite the Meghalayan border—the area which offered the best prospect of a rapid advance to Dacca. It was not until 11 December that this prospect was realized, when the Indians brought in their reserve paratroop battalion at Tangail in order to cut off the Pakistani retreat from the north towards the capital.

The same geographical circumstances in East Bengal which determined the form of the Indian offensive also determined the nature of Pakistan's defensive posture. In October as the political conditions were ripening for Indian-supported *Mukti Bahini* attacks on major centres near the borders, the Pakistani forces had largely withdrawn from scattered border-protection duties into cleverly fortified defensive positions at the major centres inside the frontiers, where they held all the major 'place names' against *Mukti Bahini* attacks, and blocked the routes of entry from India. It was politically impossible for General Niazi simply to abandon the border areas in favour of a general concentration around Dacca. Nor would it have been appropriate to his strategy of defence against the *Mukti Bahini* in the border areas. But once the full-scale war had begun, because of the difficulties of communication there was very little prospect that his troops would be able to make a fighting withdrawal in the direction of the capital. When the war came, Dacca was defended only by scattered security forces because priority had been given to the defence of the border towns and strongholds. The Pakistani troops had little choice but to hold out at these strong points, hoping that international pressure would compel the Indians to confine their operations at most to supporting the *Mukti Bahini* in expanding their enclaves. The disappointment of this hope, and the speed with which most of the Pakistani lines of withdrawal were secured by the Indians, goes far to explain the rapid collapse of Pakistani morale, both in those outlying strongholds which were abandoned without a struggle, and in Dacca itself at the end of the war.

General Niazi's forces in the Pakistani Eastern Command comprised approximately 35 infantry battalions, one armoured regiment, two armoured squadrons equipped with Walker *Bulldogs* and American light *Chaffee* tanks, six artillery regiments, and a number of independent mortar and field batteries. There were also several Special Services Group commando units, equivalent to one battalion. The Pakistani air force was represented by some twenty *Sabre* jets, and a naval force of gun-boats for coastal and inland waterway patrol. In addition, since April 1971, some 4,000 members of the West Pakistan Frontier Corps organized in seven 'wings' had been brought into East Bengal, together with 4,000 West Pakistani police. Some 35,000 armed *razakars*—mostly drawn from the Bihari community—had been organized in *mujahid* battalions, and 25,000 East Pakistan Civil Armed Forces in seventeen 'wings' had also been raised in East Pakistan.

The Pakistani Eastern Command headquarters were located in Dacca, where there were no regular infantry formations directly available to General Niazi—although there were about 5,000 assorted troops. The 9th division's headquarters were located at Jessore, with one brigade at Jessore and another at Jhenida. After the Boyra incident in this sector on 22 November the Pakistanis had been left with only one squadron of tanks west of the Padma. In the north-west, the 16th division was based at Natore, with a brigade at Natore, another in the Hilli area, where it had been engaged with the Indians on 24 November, and a third at Rangpur, where the Pakistanis had also based their only armoured regiment in East Bengal. In the north there was one brigade at Mymensingh, with a formation at Jamalpur, coming under the command of Maj.-Gen. Jamshed's 36th division skeleton headquarters at Dacca, which also controlled the para-military formations. Near the Coronation bridge across the Meghna, the

DECEMBER: 'THE FOURTEEN DAYS' WAR'

14th division was centred on Ashuganj, with a brigade at Sylhet, another in the area of Maulvi Bazar, and a third at Brahmanbaria on the line of rail running along the Tripura border and south to Comilla and Chandpur. The 39th division was located at Chandpur, with brigades at Comilla, Feni, and Chittagong.

The situation along the borders was very fluid during October and November as the *Mukti Bahini* attacks mounted and the Pakistani forces were regrouped. By early December the Indian Eastern Command headquarters in Calcutta had at its disposal a total force consisting of two divisions which had been posted in Bengal since the beginning of the year (the 9th and the 4th divisions), two divisions drawn in October from the depth reserve formations (the 20th and 23rd divisions), and two divisions withdrawn from anti-insurgency operations (the 8th and 57th divisions). These forces were lightly equipped, but they had been carefully trained for their task and they were supported by bridge-building platoons and by overwhelming air superiority. In addition the Indian forces were supported by the *Mukti Bahini* organized in eight regular infantry battalion formations, and tens of thousands of *'Gono' Bahini* irregulars and freedom fighters.

The Indian II Corps, with its newly established headquarters at Krishnagar, under Lt.-Gen. Raina, consisted of the 9th and 4th divisions, two tank regiments equipped with *T-55s* and *PT-76s*, and one medium artillery regiment using 130mm. long-range Russians guns. Its task was to drive to Jhenida, Magura, Faridpur and the Hardinge Bridge, and to the Madhumati beyond Jessore and Khulna. In the north-east XXXIII Corps had its headquarters at Siliguri. It consisted of the 20th division and two extra brigades from Nagaland, together with one light armoured regiment. Its task was to take Bogra, cutting off the Pakistani communications into the Dinajpur/Rangpur sector.

In the northern sector in Meghalaya two infantry brigades were placed under '101 Communication Zone', a special field headquarters with a staff equivalent to a skeleton divisional headquarters, coming under Eastern Command in Calcutta. Although their route to Dacca, along the eastern bank of the Brahmaputra, was clear of river obstacles, difficulties of communication in Meghalaya—and perhaps some doubts about the wisdom of further troop deployments away from the Himalayan mountain front—caused this thrust to be the weakest of all. It was directed primarily towards Jamalpur, with a diversionary movement towards Mymensingh.

In the east, IV Corps with its headquarters at Agartala consisted of three divisions—the 8th, the 57th and the 23rd—with the 8th division operating towards Sylhet and Maulvi Bazar, and the other two being given the major task of taking the line of the Meghna bulge. The 57th division was to move through Akhaura in the direction of Bhairab Bazar and the Coronation bridge, and the 23rd division was to by-pass Comilla and move across country to Chandpur.

The Jessore Sector

In the Jessore sector the main concentration of Pakistani forces from Maj.-Gen. Ansari's 9th division was located at Jessore itself. It consisted of one infantry brigade group supported by tanks and artillery. There were subsidiary units at a number of centres from Chuadanga, Jhenida and Kushtia in the north of the sector, to Khulna and Chalna in the south. The Indian 9th division under Maj.-Gen. Dalbir Singh thrust south of Jessore towards Khulna, Chalna and Barisal. But its main forces had been drawn out at Boyra in the last week of November, and they were now directed north of Jessore through Garibpur. The 4th division, under Maj.-Gen. M. S. Brar, passed in a number of columns around Darsana on the border, towards Kaliganj, Jhenida, Magura and Kushtia. Moving mostly across dirt tracks, the Indians reached the railway at Kotchandpur on the 5th, after heavy fighting at Suadhi village. On the 7th this column took the road centre at Jhenida, after a cross-country advance supported by the air-dropping of supplies.

After the fall of both Kaliganj and Jhenida the Pakistani forces in Jessore began a piecemeal retreat north-eastwards to Magura and the road link to Dacca, and southwards towards Khulna and the anchorage at Chalna. But as soon as the war began the Indian navy had established control of the coasts. On 10 December Chalna fell to Indian troops landed from the sea. Further upstream Khulna held out until General Niazi signed the instrument of surrender on the 16th. Meanwhile, on 8 December, Magura fell to units of the 9th division after it had made a rapid advance across country from Kaliganj. On the 11th Kushtia fell to an Indian thrust from Magura after a sharp tank battle inside the town, which caused heavy Indian losses. Later that afternoon the Indians reached the Hardinge bridge from Kushtia. Three days later, units of the 9th division crossed the Madhumati; and on the morning of the 15th they entered Faridpur on the Padma.

The Indian xxxiii Corps Front

In the north-west, Lt.-Gen. M. L. Thapan's Indian XXXIII Corps with its headquarters at Siliguri faced the Pakistani 16th division with brigades at Natore, Hilli, and Rangpur. One Indian brigade

DECEMBER: 'THE FOURTEEN DAYS' WAR'

thrust south from Cooch Behar towards Rangpur; another crossed the border at Jalpaiguri, moving towards Dinajpur. The strongly held defences of both of these places were reached on 9 December. The Pakistanis had prepared for an Indian thrust to be directed against the two lines of rail running through the narrow waist between Gaibanda on the Jamuna and Hilli—where there had been a heavy engagement on 24 November. But while a section of the Indian 20th division invested Hilli, where there was heavy resistance, an Indian column passed eastwards across country north of Hilli towards Pirganj, which they reached on the 7th. It then advanced from Pirganj towards the communications centre at Bogra, which fell on the 13th.

THE EASTERN SECTOR

The most spectacular Indian advances occurred in the IV Corps sector east of the Meghna, possibly because the Pakistani forces did not expect an attack on such a scale to come in the most remote sector of the Indian front. Under Lt.-Gen. Sagat Singh the 8th, 57th and 23rd divisions faced the Pakistani 14th division with its headquarters at Ashunganj, and the 39th division with its headquarters at Chandpur. The 8th Indian division in the north crossed the border opposite Karimganj. One column moved south towards Maulvi Bazar, and another advanced on Sylhet. When the Indians reached Maulvi Bazar on 8 December the Pakistani commander withdrew northeastwards towards Sylhet. Further south, on the next day the Indian 57th division reached the Meghna at Ashunganj after advancing towards Brahmanbaria through a salient opposite Akhaura held by the *Mukti Bahini*. Another column passed north of Comilla towards Daudkandi on the Meghna, which was reached on the 9th. The Indian 23rd division by-passed Comilla and made for the important rail junction at Laksham, heading for Chandpur, which controlled access from Dacca to the sea. This column reached Chandpur on the 9th, the same day as units of the 57th division reached the Meghna at Ashuganj. Another column of the 23rd division headed south from the Belonia salient towards Chittagong.

The rapidity of this Indian advance towards the Meghna demonstrated that a conclusive result could be achieved more quickly than had been expected by either side; and it eliminated the possibility of evacuation of Pakistani forces without Indian co-operation. By the 10th the Indians had reached the banks of the Meghna at three points: at Ashuganj, at Daudkandi—less than 40 air kilometres from Dacca—and at Chandpur, which dominated the route from Dacca to the sea. At the same time, in the Jessore sector they had reached Magura and were thrusting towards Faridpur on the Padma. Within the first three days of the war the Indian air force had virtually eliminated the small force of Pakistani *Sabres* in East Pakistan, by air battle, destruction on the ground, and by putting Dacca airfield out of action. Pakistani troop movements along the river routes were rendered almost impossible by the Indian command of the air; and along the coasts the Indian navy—notably the aircraft-carrier *Vikrant*—had established a totally effective blockade. As the implications of this situation became apparent to them at the end of the first week of the fighting, the Pakistani authorities in Dacca decided to press seriously for a cease-fire; and the Indians grasped the possibility of rapid and complete military victory in the East.

As we have seen, on 6 December Mrs Gandhi had announced India's recognition of the provisional government of Bangla Desh. On the 10th an agreement was signed by Mrs Gandhi, Mr Tajuddin Ahmed, and Syed Nasrul Islam—respectively the Prime Minister and the Acting President of Bangla Desh—placing the *Mukti Bahini* under the command of Lt.-Gen. Aurora, Commander-in-Chief of the Indian Eastern Command. These political developments, and the consolidation of the Indian position on the Meghna on the 10th, coincided with the turning point of the war on the West Pakistan borders, and the breakdown of Pakistan's attempts to secure a cease-fire through the United Nations. There now seemed to be little prospect of relieving the situation in East Pakistan by action at the diplomatic level. The question now was how conclusive the Indian victory on both the eastern and the western fronts was to be. For Pakistan's friends in the United States and for China this question had two aspects: how to save something from the wreckage of Pakistan in the East; and even more important, how to safeguard Pakistan in the West from being overwhelmed.

From the published minutes of the meetings of the Washington Special Action Group (WSAG)[211] it is clear that in Washington there was some scepticism about the proposition that India had either the intention or the capacity to 'extinguish' West Pakistan once the operations in the East were completed. At the meeting on 4 December no dissent was registered from the view expressed by Mr Richard Helms (Central Intelligence Agency), that 'the Soviet assessment is that there is not much chance of a great power confrontation'. On the 6th, General William Westmoreland (Joint Chief of Staff) declared that it might take 'as much as a month' to move all or most of the Indian forces from the East to the West. His assessment of the

[211] See above, p. 125.

DECEMBER: 'THE FOURTEEN DAYS' WAR'

position on the western front was that the Indians were 'in relatively good shape'. While they would be striking towards Hyderabad so as to cut the main line of communication to Karachi,' they probably did not intend to go all the way to Karachi. The Indian move in that direction 'could very well be diversionary in order to force the Pakistanis to pull reserves back from the Kashmir area'. It was suggested that the Indian thrust into Sind was essentially for a political purpose —conceived to be the capture of some Pakistani territory to compensate Indian public opinion for losses in Kashmir.

However, by the 8th the American assessment of Indian intentions in the west was becoming sterner. Mr Helms stated: 'It is reported that prior to terminating present hostilities, Mrs Gandhi intends to attempt to eliminate Pakistan's armour and air force capabilities'; and General John Ryan of the Joint Chiefs of Staff declared that while it would take a 'reasonably long time' to shift Indian forces from east to west, the airborne brigade could be moved within a matter of five or six days.

In the course of the WSAG meeting on the 8th these comparatively moderate assessments were erected by Dr Kissinger into the proposition that 'if the Indians smash the Pak air force and the armoured forces we would have a deliberate Indian attempt to force the disintegration of Pakistan'. Mr Joseph Sisco (State Department), immediately expressed his doubt that this was the Indian purpose, and referred to the Indian statements disclaiming the intention to take any Pakistani territory. Kashmir, it was pointed out, was really disputed territory; and 'we must also consider the fact that the Paks may themselves be trying to take Kashmir'. Dr Kissinger's response was to ask for an assessment of the Pakistani capabilities and prospects in Kashmir.

This discussion on 8 December of Indian intentions in West Pakistan arose from an attempt to find an answer to the question posed earlier in the meeting by Dr Kissinger, 'what the next turn of the screw might be?' Most of the readily available steps to demonstrate that 'India has jeopardized relations with the United States' had already been taken. The White House was evidently searching for more: the possibilities of protesting against the Indian blockade of Pakistan, and of acceding to Jordan's request for permission to lend weapons and aircraft to Pakistan, were discussed in this connection, along with the suggestion that any occurrence of massacres of Biharis in East Pakistan should be the subject of an immediate protest to India.

The decision to send the *Enterprise* task-force from the Seventh Fleet into the Bay of Bengal was probably the result of this casting about for means of 'registering our position'.²¹² By the end of the first week of the war the diplomatic possibilities seemed to be exhausted. On the 4th, Dr Kissinger had enquired whether there were any treaty obligations which might arise between the United States and Pakistan 'outside the SEATO context'. The answer which he received at the time must have been the same as that publicly given by State Department officials on 14 December, when it was stated that there were no such commitments binding America to Pakistan. At the WSAG meeting on the 8th it was pointed out that the United States had no legal obligations to Pakistan arising out of the CENTO agreement. Dr Kissinger responded sharply that 'neither did we have legal obligations towards India in 1962 when we formulated the air defence agreement'. By the 9th the diplomatic exercise in the General Assembly had been completed, and at the meeting of the WSAG on the 8th, Dr Kissinger was told that the United States did not have 'a legal case to protest the Indian blockade'. In connection with the Jordanian request for permission to transfer *F-104s* to Pakistan, it was pointed out: 'We could not authorize the Jordanians to do anything that the United States government could not do. If the United States Government could not give the *104s* to Pakistan, we could not allow Jordan to do so'.²¹³

The project for naval intervention was probably contemplated at the time of the discussion of evacuation problems at the meeting of 6 December, when it was briefly reported that 'the Dacca evacuation

---

²¹² This was Dr Kissinger's phrase at the WSAG meeting of 4 December. A similar deployment of a United States naval force into the Bay of Bengal for an essentially political purpose was worked out by Professor Galbraith in 1962 when he was American ambassador to India: 'I revived an idea yesterday which had been in the back of my mind for some time— that of having a carrier make a courtesy visit to Madras. This would have a calming effect on India and a deterring effect on China.' Diary note of 27 November 1962: *Ambassador's Journal*, p. 443.

²¹³ Nevertheless, the American government deliberately sought to encourage Indian fears that the United States might supply weapons to Pakistan. Mr Jack Anderson has published an extract from a telegram addressed by the Under-Secretary of State, Mr John Irwin, to the American embassies in Saudi Arabia and New Delhi.

> In view of intelligence reports spelling out Indian military objectives in West Pakistan, we do not want in any way to ease Indian government concern re help Pakistan might receive from outside sources. Consequently the Embassy should give India no assurances re third country transfers – *Daily Telegraph*, 12 January 1972. See Appendix 15, p. 232.

DECEMBER: 'THE FOURTEEN DAYS' WAR'

had been aborted'. At that stage it was not yet clear how rapidly the Indians would complete their victory in East Bengal. Another possible rationale for American naval intervention was implicit in General Westmoreland's remark at the same meeting, that there was 'no means of evacuating West Pakistani forces from the East Wing, particularly in view of Indian naval superiority'. Further, on the 7th, according to Mr Anderson, it was reported in Washington that 'three Soviet naval ships, a seagoing mine-sweeper and a tanker have begun to move north-eastward into the Bay of Bengal' near Ceylon.

On 10 December a naval task-force consisting of the aircraft-carrier *Enterprise*, an amphibious assault ship, four guided-missile destroyers, a guided-missile frigate and a landing craft was detached from the Seventh Fleet off South Vietnam. During the night of the 13th–14th it passed through the Straits of Malacca. On the 15th its entry into the Bay of Bengal was reported. Meanwhile on the 13th its movements had become public. The following day the Defence Secretary, Mr Melvin Laird, announced that the government had contingency plans for the evacuation of American citizens in East Pakistan, where some 47 American citizens had chosen to remain after the evacuation of 114 United States nationals by the (British) Royal Air Force on 12 December. On the 15th it was officially stated in Washington that the task force might help to evacuate Pakistani forces from the East after a cease-fire.

This dramatic American intervention was the most spectacular of the reactions among the great powers to the deadlock in the United Nations. It was accompanied by Russian and Chinese moves, also outside the United Nations, to ensure that India would act with restraint after her victory in the East. On 12 December Mr Vasily Kusnetsov, the Soviet First Deputy Foreign Minister responsible for sub-continental affairs, arrived in Delhi for a visit planned to last for two days. He remained until the 16th.[214] At the same time, Mr D. P. Dhar, Chairman of the Indian Policy Planning Committee and the

---

[214] This must be the same Kusnetsov whose part in the visit by Nehru and his daughter to the USSR in 1955 is picturesquely described by K. P. S. Menon in his autobiography. In the Crimea:

> the 100-kilometre road from Simferopol to Yalta was lined by crowds holding flowers in their hands, and they would fling the flowers into the car in which the Prime Minister and Indira were travelling. Kusnetsov sat beside them in order to ward off these floral attacks and, in doing so, the thorns on the roses hurt his fingers, which started bleeding. 'Today,' he said, 'I have shed some blood in the cause of Indo–Soviet friendship.'

K. P. S. Menon, *Many Worlds*, p. 284.

official responsible for Indian policy towards Bangla Desh, visited Moscow between 11 and 15 December. The Russian efforts at this stage were praised by President Nixon in an interview published on 26 December. 'We had differences with the Soviets in South Asia at the beginning of the war, although not at the end, when both sides used restraint.' The President commented that Soviet restraint had helped to bring about 'the cease-fire that stopped what would inevitably have been the conquest of West Pakistan as well'.

The Chinese also took a hand. On the 9th it was reported that Mr Chou En-lai had toasted 'Pakistan's victory' with the Pakistani ambassador at a diplomatic reception in Peking. According to the 'Anderson Papers' the Central Intelligence Agency reported that after the 8th 'the Chinese [had] been passing weather data for locations in Tibet and along the Sino–Soviet border'. This was considered unusual, and it implied the threat of a possible Chinese intervention in Ladakh. But it was not until after the cease-fire in the East on 16 December that the Chinese government intervened directly, with a note to India alleging that Indian armed personnel had crossed the Sikkim border on 10 December.[215] This step was clearly designed to warn India against extending the war in the West. But the final cease-fire followed shortly afterwards, and the possibility of a Russian counter-demonstration in Sinkiang—foreshadowed by Mr Richard Helms at the WSAG meeting on 8 December—was never seriously put to the test.

By the same token it is impossible to establish whether or not 'the Indians' had ever intended to carry on the war in the West until the destruction of Pakistan had been accomplished. In his interview on the 26th President Nixon's remarks on this point were ambiguous:

> I would not like to contend that the Indians had a definite plan to do that [conquer West Pakistan]. But once these passions of war and success in war are let loose they tend to run their course. ... It is my conviction based on our intelligence reports as to the forces that were working on the Indian government, that they would have gone on to reduce once and for all the danger that they had consistently seen in Pakistan.

But other powers, also informed about 'the forces working on the Indian government', were doubtful of this assessment. While the Indians refused to give a commitment which would compromise their

---

[215] The note is printed in *Pakistan Horizon*, XXV No. 1, first quarter 1972, p. 156. A long statement was also issued by China on the 16th: *ibid.*, pp. 156–8, and also S/10461, United Nations Security Council Documents.

DECEMBER: 'THE FOURTEEN DAYS' WAR'

traditional position over Kashmir, there was no evidence from the disposition of Indian forces that Delhi was preparing to act decisively to alter the *status quo* across the cease-fire line. The other Western powers—notably Britain and France—did not see any reason to doubt that Indian policy would depart from the course publicly reaffirmed by Mr Swaran Singh at the United Nations on 12 December, when he confirmed that India had no territorial ambitions in West Pakistan, and by Mrs Gandhi, who repeated the assurance in her letter to President Nixon on 15 December.

The chief effect of the despatch of the *Enterprise* task-force occurred not in India but in Pakistan—where it encouraged the government to pursue the war in the East for several days longer than it might otherwise have done. On the afternoon of 10 December, Maj.-Gen. Rao Farman Ali Khan, Military Adviser to the Governor of East Pakistan, called at the office of the Secretary-General's representative, M. Paul-Marc Henri. He asked him to transmit through the United Nations communications network a request to President Yahya that he should approve steps which the Pakistani authorities in Dacca proposed to take which might 'be considered as a firm offer to comply with the terms of the Soviet resolution to the United Nations'. General Farman Ali proposed an immediate cease-fire, the arrangement of facilities for the repatriation of the Pakistani army in the East, withdrawal of Indian forces 'as well', and the summoning of the elected representatives of East Pakistan to accomplish the 'peaceful transfer of power'. He stated that General Niazi had been consulted, and that the Governor had transferred 'the responsibility for taking the final and fatal decision' to him.

This last point seems to have been misunderstood by the Secretary-General's representative in Dacca, and by the Secretariat officials in New York. Although the General was clearly asking for President Yahya's 'approval', the note was taken to be a firm offer of a cease-fire by the Pakistani authorities in Dacca, and the Security Council was immediately informed. But on the 11th word reached Dacca from Islamabad that there should be no cease-fire. A Pakistani official spokesman stated in Islamabad that Pakistan had invoked its 'understandings' with friendly powers to come to its assistance. Dacca was told that 'help' from 'friends' was expected, and this was understood by the authorities in East Pakistan to refer to Chinese support and to an American naval–air intervention.

The Pakistani Eastern Command's proposals for a cease-fire were thus abandoned. Meanwhile on 11 December the problem of evacuation of foreign nationals from Dacca came to a head. After two failures to accomplish the evacuation on 6 and 7 December, the

Indians agreed on the 10th to a 24-hour bombing pause at Dacca airfield, starting that evening. This period was to allow for the clearing of the runway, and it was to be followed by a further six-hour period in which the evacuation was to be carried out by three Royal Air Force *Hercules* transports and one United Nations chartered Canadian C-130, operating from Calcutta. Although on the 11th the runway was cleared, the evacuation was repeatedly delayed by the Pakistani authorities. At one point, the aircraft were airborne at Calcutta when they were ordered to turn back. That evening the United Nations Secretariat in New York ordered their transport to return to Bangkok on the ground that conditions in Dacca made it necessary to suspend the evacuation effort until a meeting of the 22 countries with nationals involved could be held. But despite the withdrawal of the United Nations element, the British persisted in their efforts. On the night of the 11th the Pakistani command in Dacca relented. The Indian government was persuaded to extend the truce until the afternoon of the 12th. By tea-time on the 12th the evacuation had been accomplished.

Although the Pakistanis of course had every reason for trying to spin out the truce at Dacca airport, it is possible that this delay in effecting the evacuation was intended to encourage American intervention and to provide a pretext for it. And it is certain that Islamabad's decision not to give approval to General Farman Ali's project for a cease-fire was connected with the hope of some material support from the United States and China. Nevertheless, over the following four days it became apparent to the Pakistani leadership in Dacca that the position was hopeless, and that a cease-fire in East Pakistan could not be further delayed.

By 10 December the Indians had two possible approaches to Dacca: from the east—across the Meghna—and from the north, where there were no major river obstacles between the Meghalaya border and Dacca. In the eastern sector the units from the 57th division which had reached Ashuganj were held up on the eastern side of the mile-wide river after the bridge across the Meghna at Bhairab Bazar had been blown up. On the 10th they began an unopposed crossing, using local river-craft and a force of Mi-4 helicopters. The following day Indian forces reached Narsingdi, 35 kilometres from Dacca on the line of rail from Bhairab Bazar. The river Lakhya lay between this small column and the East Pakistan capital. By 15 December the Indian units had crossed the Lakhya at four points and were 12 kilometres outside Dacca.

But the most dramatic developments in this final phase of the war

DECEMBER:' THE FOURTEEN DAYS' WAR'

occurred in the northern sector. In the first week of the war, 101 Communications HQ's attack with one brigade from Tura towards Jamalpur had been successfully held up by a Pakistani infantry brigade supported by a squadron of tanks. Jamalpur was not reached until 9 December, when a by-passing column crossed the Brahmaputra and cut off the Pakistani garrison. When the officer commanding at the 101 Communications HQ was wounded, Maj.-Gen. G. S. Nagra brought up another brigade which struck out for Mymensingh —which fell on 11 December. But the way still lay open for the retreat of the Pakistani brigade from Jamalpur and Mymensingh towards Dacca.

On the afternoon of 11 December a battalion of an Indian parachute brigade was dropped in the Tangail area, so as to cover the road between Jamalpur, Mymensingh and Dacca. Some elements of the Pakistan brigade had already passed through Tangail, but the Indian forces intercepted the rest and after a fierce night-battle extending into the morning of the 12th the Pakistani forces from the north disintegrated. Later that day the paratroop units were joined by the brigades coming down from Jamalpur. On 13 December they forced their way through Joydebpur into Tungi, and the following day General Nagra moved the regrouped paratroop battalion along the highway towards Dacca. Early on the morning of the 16th they entered the outskirts of the capital.

Two days before, in the early afternoon of the 14th, the Governor of East Pakistan had resigned along with the civilian ministers of his cabinet. They took refuge in the neutral zone supervised by the United Nations at the Intercontinental Hotel in Dacca. Later that same afternoon General Niazi and General Farman Ali called upon the American Consul, Mr Herbert Spivack. On his own authority, General Niazi asked Mr Spivack to transmit to the Indians a proposal for a conditional cease-fire. He requested facilities for the regrouping of his forces for repatriation to West Pakistan, and guarantees of the safety of the paramilitary forces and all those who had co-operated with the martial law administration. This proposal was not passed to General Manekshaw until a day later, on the afternoon of the 15th. He replied that the air attacks on Dacca would be suspended at five o'clock that afternoon; but that unless the Pakistani forces in the East surrendered unconditionally the Indian offensive would be resumed on the morning of the 16th. Later that afternoon General Niazi requested an extension of the truce, to take account of delays 'owing to communications difficulties and the isolation of my forces'. The next morning General J. F. R. Jacob flew into Dacca with the terms of the surrender. On the afternoon of 16 December the instrument of surrender was ceremoniously signed at Dacca racecourse by General Niazi and by Lt.-Gen. Jagjit Singh Aurora, 'G.O.C.-in-C. Indian and Bangla Desh forces in the Eastern Theatre'.[216]

While the second week of the war was dominated by the dramatic advance of the Indians in the East towards Dacca, in West Pakistan there was something of a lull. The Indian forces continued their slow advance in the Shakargarh bulge and expanded their holdings in Sind. The Pakistan Air Force increased its care to avoid risks. On the ground the main strategic reserves of both sides still held aloof.

In Islamabad, one of the earliest political effects of the war had been the creation of a coalition government on 7 December, which brought in Mr Bhutto as Deputy Prime Minister and Foreign Secretary, with the senior Bengali politician, Mr Nurul Amin, as Prime Minister. At the end of the first week of the war Mr Bhutto flew to New York to preside over Pakistan's presentation of her case at the United Nations. President Yahya continued to elaborate his proposals for a new constitution, which would confirm him in office as President and Commander-in-Chief of the army for a further five years, and leave in his hands the power to proclaim martial law and to override his ministers.

After the news of the cease-fire in the East came on the afternoon of the 16th, the President broadcast to the nation at 8.30 p.m., announcing his intention to continue the war and at the same time to proceed with his timetable for the promulgation of the constitution on 20 December and the formation of representative governments at the centre and in the provinces. 'In such a great war a setback on any one front does not at all mean that the war has come to an end... have confidence, the war continues.' Privately, the President told visitors that Pakistan had lost a battle, but not the war. He drew an analogy with the situation of France after 1940. 'We are not alone in this historical struggle. We gratefully acknowledge the support of the People's Republic of China and the United States...'[217]

But later that evening, in a broadcast statement, Mrs Gandhi announced that she had ordered a unilateral cease-fire on the western front, to begin at 8 p.m. on the evening of 17 December. That morning the inner circle of President Yahya's administration debated whether Pakistan should continue the fight. Until late in the morning the issue was uncertain. Finally, at 3.30 in the afternoon of 17 De-

---

[216] See Appendix 16, p. 233.
[217] The text of President Yahya's broadcast is printed in *Pakistan Horizon*. XXV, No. 1, pp. 143–4.

DECEMBER: 'THE FOURTEEN DAYS' WAR'

cember a statement was read out over Pakistan radio, in which the President declared that he had ordered that Pakistani forces should reciprocate the cease-fire from 7.30 p.m. that evening.[218] The last of Yahya's confusions was the preface to this final statement: 'I have always maintained that war solves no problems.' The victors in Dacca knew otherwise.

[218] *ibid.*, p. 144.

Chapter 6

Conclusion

THE coming into existence of a new state with 75 million citizens in circumstances of civil war and war between nations poses an historical problem of the first magnitude: beyond the conscious decisions and deliberate policy of the various parties to the conflict out of which Bangla Desh was born we can discern the complex interplay of historical and geographical circumstances shaping the crisis and lending it an aspect of pathos and tragedy. We might say that the significance for posterity of such an historical episode lies in its balance between the two elements of conscious choice and ineluctable necessity. In this perspective, the most important questions posed by the crisis of 1971 in the sub-continent are, therefore, whether the disintegration of Pakistan could have been avoided by wiser policy in Islamabad or by a different policy on the part of India; or whether Pakistan—and perhaps India also—are caught up in an inexorable logic of mutual antipathy and internal division and subdivision. And from the point of view of international politics the significance of the crisis may be summed up in the question of why and how it was that the great powers were caught up or chose to be involved in the internal crisis of Pakistan, and how the crisis was resolved without the threat of hostilities on a wider scale being realized.

As we saw in the first chapter of this account, the origins of Pakistan's disintegration lay deep in her history. Beneath their unity-in-Islam the Indian Muslims are divided into a number of different racial and cultural communities of which the furthest removed from the heartland of Islam in the Near East are the native Muslims of Bengal. Advancing in prosperity and education under British rule in India, the Bengali Muslim descendants of the original Bengali converts to Islam found that their identity as a community was defined by two inherently contradictory forces: on the one hand, their cultural and racial kinship with the Hindus of Bengal and, on the other hand, the Muslim faith which they share with other north Indian peoples of quite different stock and civilization. The conflict between these two different elements began to emerge in the 1930s when provincial self-government was introduced in Bengal. But during the Second World War and the approach to independence in the sub-continent, the

CONCLUSION

Islamic allegiance of the East Bengalis took first place and they rallied to the Muslim League and the concept of Pakistan.

While this development owed a great deal to the accidents of war and famine in Bengal and to the hectic manoeuvrings which went on during the independence negotiations, there is no suggestion that East Bengal was forced into Pakistan against her will. Islam was at that time—as it is today—one of the most powerful elements in the makeup of the people of East Bengal. But, for the reasons analysed in Chapter 1, over the twenty years after 1947 the establishment of a stable political order, capable of reconciling the conflicting principles of unity and consent, proved to be beyond Pakistan's reach. The internal divisions naturally engendered by the geographical separation of the two wings and by their differences of culture and language were deepened first by a feeling of political grievance on the part of the Bengalis, and then by the development among them of a sense of social and economic deprivation relative to the West Wing. They traced these deficiencies to the structure of the state itself, whose precarious unity was increasingly strained by the centralization of government under martial law and presidential rule after the abrogation of the 1956 constitution. When Ayub's regime dissolved in 1969 President Yahya attempted to restore the principle of consent, but by that time it was too late. The elections which he held in December 1970 brought the movement of opinion in East Bengal to a head. And although the Awami League's six points retained the idea of Pakistan as a loose framework of association, they amounted to a charter for virtual secession by the Bengali Muslims.

The development of East Bengali nationalism to the pitch which it reached in the December 1970 election—assisted by the accident of the cyclone disaster—might perhaps have been avoided if a constitutional structure had been evolved in Pakistan after 1947, capable of engaging the consent of the Bengalis and ensuring their access to power and to the fruits of economic expansion and communal self-expression. But, unlike India, Pakistan failed to tap the integrating powers of democracy. Yahya Khan's promise came too late. From the beginning of 1971 he was faced with a fatal choice: on the one hand he could act to maintain the concept of Pakistan, with which he and his subordinates in the martial-law administration identified the integrity and unity of the nation; on the other hand he could continue with his policy of affecting a transfer of power to popular forces that were committed to a fundamental transformation of the relationship between East Bengal and the rest of the country.

The discussions and negotiations that went on inside Pakistan between December 1970 and March 1971 revealed that there was no middle way out of this dilemma. At first the President seems to have hoped that when he was confronted by the prospect of a share of power over the whole of Pakistan Sheikh Mujib would retreat from the more extreme implications of the six points. But this solution was unacceptable to important elements in the army, to the forces in the West Wing represented by Mr Bhutto, and to the radical and nationalist elements in the Awami League. Nor were Mr Bhutto and Sheikh Mujib willing or able to find a common cause in the alliance for social reform pressed upon them by some elements of the left in both wings. This was a situation which could not have been made any more difficult by covert intervention from India; and our account suggests that significant Indian intervention in East Bengal did not begin until after President Yahya attempted to resolve his dilemma by the use of military force in order to suppress the Bangla Desh movement.

Thus during the period between December 1970 and 25 March 1971 there was very little room for manoeuvre available to the different sides to escape from the collision course set by the logic of their respective positions. In the weeks after the military 'crackdown' it was also inevitable that by virtue of its superior power the Pakistani army would succeed in its attempts to re-establish martial law in East Bengal. But the strength of the Bengali resistance over the four weeks after 25 March was not anticipated by the Pakistani authorities. This resistance was a development of the highest significance. It aroused an unappeasable public excitement in India; and in the shape of the millions of refugees displaced by the struggles inside East Pakistan it provided a justification for Indian intervention.

The Indian government might have chosen not to allow the events in East Bengal to damage relations between Delhi and Islamabad. Despite the probably unfounded charges of interference which Pakistan levelled against her immediately after the 25th, it would have been possible for India to remain aloof and to act to settle the refugee problem as soon as it began to arise at the end of April. Nevertheless, just as Pakistan's fate was written in her history, so India was also driven by the pressures of the past to seek to exploit her neighbour's crisis. The hostility of Pakistan and India originates in centuries of conflict; and since 1947 their antagonism has been expressed in the mutually incompatible principles upon which the two states are founded. The concepts of All-India secularism and modernization which underlie the Indian Union implicitly deny the claims of Islamic nationality upon which Pakistan was erected. Similarly, Pakistan's aspiration to speak for the 'nation' of Indian Muslims rebuked India's

CONCLUSION

hopes for a democratic society transcending religious and communal divisions. In the twenty years after the attainment of independence the main symbol of these fundamental antagonisms was the dispute over Kashmir, which caused the wars of 1947–9 and 1965. The same issues were also at stake in East Bengal in 1971, where Pakistan's founding principle of Islamic solidarity was meeting the severest test it had yet faced.

After 25 March, the instinctive Indian attitude to the situation in East Bengal was determined by this historically rooted hostility towards Pakistan. At the same time, Mrs Gandhi's government had just been strengthened by its success in the March 1971 general election —a victory which would have been largely nullified in the eyes of Indian public opinion if it had been seen to acquiesce in Pakistan's repression of the Bengalis. The circumstances of Indian domestic politics pressed upon Mrs Gandhi with the same weight as those internal forces in Pakistan which pressed upon President Yahya, Mr Bhutto and Sheikh Mujib. And while it could be maintained—as Nehru had argued—that in the interest of her own unity India had a stake in the survival of the sub-continental states-system as it had been defined in 1947, it could also be urged that, after the events of March 1971, the eventual separation of East Bengal from Pakistan had become inevitable and that it was consequently in India's interest to take command of the logic of events. This was the position that Mrs Gandhi adopted at the end of March.

After 25 March, the deliberate choices of the Indian government became the decisive factor in the situation, and it is very probable that, without its skilful and determined intervention to assist the nationalists, the struggle in East Bengal would still be going on, or that the opposition would for the time being have been successfully overcome by the Pakistani authorities. For, although the necessities of Pakistan's inner history brought the crisis into being, it was by a conscious and sustained exercise of will on the part of India that the conflict in East Bengal was decided against Pakistan during 1971. Consequently the pattern of events after the end of March was shaped in the main by the impulses of Indian policy : by the increasing definition of its objectives and instruments, by the complex interrelation of India's actions with Pakistan's responses, by the mounting pressure of terrorism and guerrilla war inside East Pakistan and across its borders, and by the increasing diplomatic involvement of the United Nations and the great powers under pressure from India.

As we saw in Chapter 2, immediately after the events of 25 March, Pakistan's diplomacy was directed to forestalling the possibility of

Indian intervention by seeking to win the support of the outside powers for the principle that the problems of East Bengal must be regarded as exclusively an internal affair of Pakistan. On the other hand, once the Indians had rejected the possibility of immediate military intervention across the border, they began to use diplomatic means to press for international action against Pakistan to induce her to respect the rights of the East Bengalis and their duly elected representatives.

Thus the international line-up which was formed during the early weeks of April took shape around Pakistan's contention that there was no basis for the concern of outside powers in her domestic affairs, and India's counter-argument to the effect that world opinion, and the great powers in particular, had a right and a duty to condemn Pakistan's behaviour and to intervene to alter it. The first Soviet reaction on 2 April was to criticize Pakistan in terms which implied support for the Indian position. Britain and the United States refrained from condemning Pakistan, and endorsed the view that the crisis was an internal matter; but, at the same time, they pressed Islamabad to accept outside relief aid for East Bengal. And the Chinese note of 13 April gave full support to Pakistan's position by condemning India for 'carrying out gross interference in the internal affairs of Pakistan by exploiting the internal affairs of [the] country . . . The Soviet Union and the United States,' Mr Chou En-lai continued, 'are doing the same one after the other.'

However, although the situation in the sub-continent determined the precise issue around which the reactions of the great powers formed, the character of their reactions was determined by the circumstances of their own mutual relations. The internal history of the sub-continent supplied the logic of the sequence of events leading up to the crisis in Pakistan; but India's determination to make an international issue of the situation which had arisen in East Pakistan automatically engaged the sub-continent in a wider pattern of conflicts originating in conditions remote in time and place from South Asia and its deep-rooted antagonisms. There is thus a wealth of meaning behind the curious Chinese comment that the Soviet Union and the United States—in that order—were undertaking the interference in Pakistan's internal affairs 'one after the other'.

This brings us to the second of our questions about the significance of the sub-continental crisis of 1971—the question as to why and how the great powers chose to be involved or were caught up in these developments in Indo–Pakistan relations.

In the perspective of international politics the peculiar interest

CONCLUSION

of events in South Asia during 1971 is to be found in their connection with the fundamental reconstruction of the system of world politics which took place during that year. The rapprochement between the United States and the People's Republic of China opened up the prospect of a new balance of power in Asia—indeed a new global balance. The course of events in the sub-continent during this year of international transformation was deeply influenced by these changes in international relationships; and in its turn left its mark on the new structure of world power.

The underlying fact of Asian political geography is that the Soviet Union and China have a common frontier—at present disputed for much of its length—which runs for thousands of miles from the Pacific to the Himalayas. Despite the evidence of history it might be argued that this fact alone need not induce a state of permanent tension between the two powers. Nevertheless, the Sino–Soviet rivalry has for the present become one of the most prominent features in the international landscape; and the fact that there is a common frontier, taken together with the now sufficiently advanced state of development of nuclear military technology on both sides, has had the paradoxical—but historically predictable—effect of transferring the locale of active tension between China and Russia away from their mutual border to regions where the risk of direct confrontation is less acute. The Indian sub-continent is obviously one of the most important of these regions.

Here again geography takes a hand. The Soviet Union is still pent up behind the geo-political barriers erected around the sub-continent against the Tsars by the British Empire. Russia and Pakistan are still separated by that carefully negotiated strip of Afghan territory that gives Afghanistan a common frontier with China. And beyond the Wakhan strip, Pakistan and Pakistan-occupied Kashmir interpose yet another barrier between Russia and India. On the other hand, while China has a long frontier with India, her only link by land with Pakistan traverses the disputed territory of Azad Kashmir across the high passes of the Karakoram in the extremest corner of her remote far west.

Neither the Soviet Union nor China is impelled by these circumstances to try to alter the territorial settlement in the sub-continent to improve its position—although it is important to remember that the territorial settlement is not firmly established and that China's communications into Pakistan lie across disputed territory in Kashmir. However, the political geography of the north-western region of the sub-continent very largely determines the pattern in which

SOUTH ASIAN CRISIS

Sino–Soviet rivalry in the region is cast. For Russia it is a great gain to her diplomacy in Asia to secure the reliable diplomatic support of India against China; but the value of this gain is much reduced by the facts that throughout their brief history as modern states Pakistan and India have been mortal enemies—so reducing India's capacity to stand up to China—and that both Afghanistan and Pakistan straddle Soviet land communications into India. While Pakistan hold aloof from various Soviet projects for transit arrangements linking Russia, Afghanistan and India, the Soviet Union is compelled to rely on the unfamiliar ocean routes to maintain her relations with the sub-continent; and with the Suez Canal closed, her sea communications with both India and Pakistan via the south Atlantic and south-east Asia are even longer than those between the sub-continent and Western Europe, Japan, or the United States. In these circumstances Russia may be able to derive advantages from a diplomatic alignment with India. But the value of that alignment is reduced by Pakistan's constant pressure on India; and, because of the geographical separation between the Soviet Union and India which Pakistan imposes, Russia cannot in any event cement her advantages by the development of close and permanent economic and strategic ties—assuming, of course, that the Indians would want to enter into them.

Pakistan's refusal to participate in Soviet schemes for regional cooperation in the sub-continent thus prevents Russia from deepening her influence in the sub-continent as a whole. If Pakistan were to settle down to the 'good neighbourly' relations with India which Russia has been urging upon her for more than a decade, India's regional preponderance would be decisively confirmed and she would be that much better able to compete for regional influence with China, especially in the Himalayan states. For although India may not have the capacity to join China in the ranks of the super-powers, either independently or with Russian support, she would be able to play a more commanding part on the Asian stage if her disputes with Pakistan could be resolved.

Thus the system of 'good neighbourly' relations pressed by Russia upon Pakistan could—if realized—greatly benefit the Soviet Union, both in her confrontation with China and in the extension and practical application of her influence in the sub-continent (with the further prospect of engaging Indian support in extending a formal or informal Soviet-led system of 'collective security' into south-east Asia and the Indian ocean area). But very few of these benefits can be fully reaped without Pakistan's co-operation.

Ever since the emergence of the Sino–Soviet dispute in the early 1960s and the abandonment of Mr Khrushchev's earlier attitude of

CONCLUSION

exclusive support for India, Russian policy towards the sub-continent has therefore been shaped by the need to reduce the mutual hostility of the two sub-continental powers and to win the support of both together at the same time. Thus Mr Kosygin's mediation at Tashkent in 1966 was based on the concept of Soviet friendship with both states, leading eventually to co-operation between them and to the opening up of overland trade. But between 1966 and 1971 very little progress was made in this direction; and the dilemmas created by this concept continued to mark Russian policy throughout the crisis of 1971. At first, as we saw in Chapter 2, the events of 25 March were regarded in Moscow as an opportunity to improve relations with India. The Russians may also have been seriously concerned at that stage to induce India not to intervene by force in East Pakistan. But President Podgorny's letter of 2 April was swiftly followed by Mr Kosygin's moves to redress the balance of Soviet policy in the direction of Pakistan. Throughout the months of April, May and June, Russia pursued this attempt at even-handedness, making gestures in the direction of both of these sub-continental powers; and during September and early October there were signs of a reversion to this attitude after the marked shift towards India represented by the Indo–Soviet treaty.

Russia's decision at the end of July to move closer to India was a direct consequence of Mr Nixon's dramatic announcement of 15 July that the Chinese government had invited him to visit Peking early the following year. The Chinese decision for a rapprochement with the United States resulted from the deepening Sino–Soviet antagonism which, for several years, had been reflected not only in the confrontations on their mutual borders but in the sub-continent and elsewhere in Asia. The crisis in Pakistan touched on vital Chinese interests in this rivalry. For if Pakistan is Russia's gateway to India, it is also a central point in China's security system—for the reverse of the same reasons. As we have seen, so long as Pakistan refuses to improve its relations with India the prospects of a stronger position for India in her rivalry with China is diminished and the land route to the sub-continent is denied to the Russians. Pakistan is the crucial gap in what would otherwise be a ring of hostile powers encircling China's most vulnerable salient; and Peking's relationship with Islamabad has also provided useful support for China in extending her connections in the Indian Ocean and the Near East, and especially into the non-Arab Muslim world within which Pakistan is one of the leading powers.

The Chinese government's reappraisal of its attitude to the United

SOUTH ASIAN CRISIS

States had of course been going on for several months before the March crisis in Pakistan began; and it was largely determined by global considerations which went much wider than the issues immediately posed by the situation in the sub-continent. Nevertheless there was a coincidence between the first stages of the crisis in Pakistan and what appears to have been the decisive period in Peking's internal debate about the establishment of a new relationship with the United States. On 6 April—ten days after the storm in East Pakistan broke—the American table-tennis team competing in the world championships in Japan suddenly received an invitation from the Chinese team to visit the mainland. When its members were received by Mr Chou En-lai on 14 April—the day after his letter to President Yahya—they were told: 'With your acceptance of our invitation, you have opened a new page in the relations of the Chinese and American people.'

Mr Chou En-lai's pledge of China's support for Pakistan's 'independence and state sovereignty' rather than her 'national unity and territorial integrity' was a very exact statement of the nature of the Chinese stake in Pakistan. Peking was deeply concerned for the maintenance of a strong and independent West Wing. But China was interested in the East Wing only as a means of strengthening Pakistan, and only to the extent that support for President Yahya's position in East Bengal was necessary if India was to be deterred from intervention, and if Russian influence in Islamabad was to be kept to a minimum. It was also, of course, essential that China should not give commitments which she would be unable to honour. As it turned out, the Chinese had made a very accurate reading of the situation. Pakistan was unable to retain East Bengal; and, although during the first months of the crisis the Russians were able to make some headway in their efforts to improve their position in Islamabad, as the pressure of events intensified Russia and Pakistan drew apart, and China was left sharing possession of the field with the Americans. In the end, despite every plea from the Pakistanis, Peking did not move an inch from the precise commitment into which it had entered in April. And, although in December East Pakistan was overwhelmed by the Indians, the key stronghold in the West remained intact, China had avoided a losing confrontation with India, and Soviet–Pakistani relations had been decisively set back.

The sources of President Nixon's new policy towards China were even further removed from the particular exigencies of the South Asian balance than were the motives lying behind the Chinese response to his advances. The foreign relations of both China and the

CONCLUSION

Soviet Union are deeply influenced by the permanent facts of their geographical situation on the Asian continent; the United States enjoys relatively greater freedom of action, afforded by its insular position. After 1950 American policy in Asia was largely determined by the effort to construct a system of 'containment' around what was regarded as a 'monolithic' Communist bloc composed of the Soviet Union and her Chinese ally and their satellites. America's alliances with Pakistan came into being during this period. After 1962 the Sino–Soviet split and the growing American understanding with Russia led to a shift in United States policy towards an even greater concentration on the 'containment' of China—especially in south-east Asia. During the India–Pakistan war of 1965, the United States adopted a neutral attitude; after the war she cut off military assistance to Pakistan—who by then had established a growing intimacy with China—and tacitly encouraged the Soviet Union to extend her influence by mediation in the disputes of the sub-continent.

The main achievements of Mr Nixon's foreign policy during his first term of office were the reinstatement of the Soviet Union as necessarily the main rival of the United States, and the reduction of America's engagement against China around the periphery of the People's Republic. During 1969 and 1970 this reduction of the American presence in Asia began under the so-called 'Guam' or 'Nixon' doctrine; and by the beginning of 1971 the United States and China were both ready to undertake its complement—the improvement of Sino–American relations as a means of improving the positions of both states against their common rival.

In President Nixon's Foreign Policy Report of February 1972 we find a twofold definition of the wider United States interests in Asia and of the consequences for policy towards the sub-continent.[219] The most prominent of these formulations is that concerned with 'world order'. It asserts America's overriding concern for the settlement of international disputes according to the principles of the United Nations Charter. The concept of a stable, rational, legal world order articulated through the United Nations and its allied international agencies is still the central concept in the American philosophy of foreign policy—and it is one which, in the American view, imposes upon the most powerful nations a responsibility for defending those principles. In Asia, the application of this conception of a legitimate international order is conceived to be especially important at the present juncture, because there are so many areas of tension and

---

[219] For a discussion of these themes, see 'Mr Nixon's Philosophy of Foreign Policy', *The Round Table*, October 1972.

actual or potential conflict still to be settled. This was behind the President's argument that India's behaviour towards Pakistan was likely to make it more difficult to use the United Nations system to maintain whatever agreements might be arrived at in the Middle East and in Indo-China.[220] In his mind, these diverse problems were linked by the concept of the universal reception of the principles of the United Nations as the appropriate means of maintaining international order in Asia.

Thus the President attempted to rationalize his new China policy —and its relation to the crisis in the sub-continent—by setting it in the context of this higher American interest in the articulation of a comprehensive legal order in Asia. While the United States retains its commitment to world order, its previous 'containment' policy has been replaced with the new objective of integrating Communist China into the international system which has been built up around these principles since 1945. Moreover, beyond this interest in the consolidation of an international legal order there is also a less explicit American concern for the achievement of a balanced relationship with China, such that the United States can improve its own balance-of-power position in relation to the Soviet Union. At this point, considerations of world order merge into considerations of strategic balance : and in neither respect would it be appropriate for the United States to be much influenced by particular concerns and preoccupations of the sub-continental powers or by the rights and wrongs of their local disputes.

Hence, although India was able very appositely to quote the American Declaration of Independence at President Nixon in 1971, his policy in the event set a higher value upon the maintenance of Pakistan's sovereignty and the principle of the peaceful settlement of international disputes than upon the realization of self-determination in East Bengal by India's intervention in Pakistan's domestic affairs. And although India was also able to argue convincingly that it was in its national interest to liquidate the East Pakistan problem, President Nixon's response was merely to persist in his view that the American national interest involved a diplomatic rapprochement with China, with certain necessary consequences for American policy towards the less important region of the Indian sub-continent.

By coincidence the crisis in Pakistan began at the same time as the new relationship between China and the United States was about to be consummated. Having decided to effect a rapprochement with China, Mr Nixon was obliged for some time ahead to pursue policies

[220] See Dr Kissinger's comments: Appendix 13, p. 207.

CONCLUSION

which as far as possible would not bring him into conflict with vital Chinese interests. Hence the personal interest the President showed in the South-Asian problem from August onwards. Because of Chinese concern for Pakistan the possibility of supporting India's claims on behalf of the Bangla Desh liberation movement was necessarily ruled out. Consequently, the extension of Soviet influence in India could not be forestalled—indeed it might be said that the price of better relations between Washington and Peking was an improvement in relations between Moscow and Delhi.

From this position it is easy to see how the American movement to a strong 'tilt' towards Pakistan came about. In the crisis which developed between March and December 1971 the United States had nothing to gain by neutrality along the lines it had followed in 1965. Refusal to express a firm view would not only have incurred hostility in each of the affected capitals without any compensating gain: it would also have seemed like an abdication of American power—and as the crisis developed it also appeared more and more that the effectiveness of the United Nations was at issue. On the other hand, support for Pakistan's position conferred influence in Islamabad that it was hoped could be used to encourage progress towards a peaceful resolution of the crisis in East Bengal and to restrain Pakistan from provocative actions against India. In the end, of course, American influence was not sufficiently powerful to achieve either of these purposes. But perhaps their attainment would always have been less important than the fact that support for Pakistan showed China that on at least one Sino–Soviet issue of central importance to China the United States was willing to throw its weight on the Chinese side. For obvious reasons it was impossible for the moment to do this in the areas of long-standing Sino–American confrontation—in Formosa, Indo-china, Korea, or in relation to Japan. Only in the Indian subcontinent was America sufficiently uncommitted to be able to establish substantial common ground with the Chinese.

Thus American policy during the crisis started off by bringing heavy pressure to bear on Pakistan, first to permit a United Nations role in East Bengal, then to reach some kind of political settlement with an acceptable selection of Bengalis. But as the international tension mounted (Chapters 3 and 4), and as the long interval between President Nixon's China announcement and the actual date of his visit drew on, the United States moved with increasing determination to support Pakistan and Chinese influence in Pakistan. When full-scale war actually came in December (Chapter 5) the Americans took the lead in organizing world-wide diplomatic pressure against the Indians. And when that failed to have any effect, the United

SOUTH ASIAN CRISIS

States mounted its unilateral display of naval power in the Bay of Bengal.

Nevertheless, despite the drama of these great-power interventions and their connection with the evolution of world politics, the policies of the outside powers towards the sub-continent were essentially reactive—attempts to influence a situation which was developing with its own momentum according to conditions which were peculiar to the region. On this level the dialectic of relations between India and Pakistan was the decisive factor. Its unfolding may be briefly summarized.

As we have seen, the first Indian response to the events in East Pakistan after 25 March was to use diplomatic means to put pressure on Islamabad. Pakistan attempted to protect herself by insisting on her sovereignty in East Pakistan and by refusing to admit representatives of international relief agencies. During the course of April she secured general international assent to her position; and at the beginning of May her unilateral declaration of a six-month moratorium on debt repayments to the World Bank's Aid-Pakistan consortium demonstrated that the force of international opinion was not sufficient to impose an effective check on her policy. By the middle of May Islamabad was ready to respond to American pressure for the opening of East Pakistan to United Nations-sponsored relief and rehabilitation efforts.

By this time, however, Pakistan's position was already beginning to be undermined by the exodus of refugees into India. Their presence created a new opportunity for India, whose initial attempts to secure international intervention had now been frustrated by the readiness of the great powers and the United Nations to co-operate with the Pakistani authorities in East Bengal. The refugees provided recruits for the groups of 'freedom fighters' being formed with Indian encouragement and assistance. And they afforded India a basis— skilfully exploited by Indian propaganda—for insisting that she had become a party to the situation in East Pakistan and that the difficulties there should be resolved on terms that would satisfy the refugees and their representatives in Calcutta.

By the end of May it was clear that India was not interested in the unconditional return of the refugees and that she would not co-operate with the efforts of the United Nations to bring it about by providing international assistance at the borders. The Indians ceased to press for international intervention—save in the provision of relief for the refugees in India. The exiled leaders of the Bangla Desh movement began to condemn the international relief and rehabilitation

CONCLUSION

efforts inside East Pakistan. During June the so-called 'monsoon offensive' against communications and the movement of goods inside East Bengal began to get under way. Indian policy and official opinion in the United Nations started to diverge; and in the course of June there was a sharp deterioration in relations between India and the United States. The official source of these differences was the continuing flow of American arms exports to Pakistan. But behind the arms issue there was a growing conflict between India's determination to resolve the East Bengal situation in her favour—although the precise Indian objective was still unclear—and the mounting determination of the United States to help Pakistan to use the United Nations as a mean of maintaining her position and of relieving the pressures created by the outflow of refugees.

It is probable that the Soviet Union—and China—supported the United States in her efforts to encourage Yahya Khan to rebuild a basis of consent for his rule in East Bengal. During late May and June Yahya attempted to attract the support of moderate Bengali opinion by the promise of a restoration of political life; and he began to press for the establishment of United Nations representatives on both sides of the East Pakistan border to facilitate the return of the refugees. When U Thant officially placed this suggestion before the Security Council on 20 July it had already received wide international support at the meeting of the Economic and Social Council earlier that month. India was being placed in the position either of defying the Security Council, or of accepting the establishment of a United Nations 'shield' in East Pakistan.

At this point, however, the chain of events in the sub-continent was abruptly broken by the transformation in great-power relations which followed upon President Nixon's China statement of 15 July. For the reasons discussed in Chapter 3 the Soviet Union finally decided to abandon her policy of cautious support for Pakistan in order to establish her relationship with India upon a new foundation. After the signing of the Indo–Soviet Treaty of 9 August the Russians made it clear that they would oppose any attempt to invoke the United Nations on the East Pakistan borders. The way was opened for an intensification of the military activities of the *Mukti Bahini* and the Indian army across the borders into East Bengal. However, during the last week of September and the first two weeks of October the Soviet government made a final attempt to achieve a peaceful settlement by bringing heavy diplomatic pressure to bear on India to limit her commitment to Bangla Desh. This attempt ended abruptly after President Yahya's broadcast of 12 October, which indicated that the Pakistani leaders were still not willing to take the path which had been opened up for them—the release of Sheikh Mujib and the settlement of the crisis by negotiation with him on the basis of a loose association between the two wings. Instead, as we saw in Chapter 4, Islamabad continued to place her hopes in the United Nations, whose involvement she sought to bring about by countering the growing Indian military pressure at the East Pakistan borders with the build-up of forces in West Pakistan and by conjuring up the spectre of war in the sub-continent. This policy culminated in the Pakistani attack in the West on the evening of 3 December, and the subsequent unleashing of Indian power in the East.

The great powers were inexorably drawn into the mounting crisis by the logic of their mutual relations and by the unyielding strategy pursued by Pakistan in response to India's unyielding pressure. Despite Pakistan's hopes of intervention by the United Nations, throughout the Fourteen Days' War the Indo–Soviet diplomatic relationship stood up to all attempts to force a cease-fire. The failure of the United Nations opened up the prospect that the great powers would become directly involved in the crisis. The United States dispatched the *Enterprise* task force into the Bay of Bengal. China complained of Indian border violations on the north-east frontier. The Soviet Union kept Mr Kusnetsov's mission in Delhi throughout the second week of the war. Each of these efforts was directed to ensuring that India did not press her advantage against Pakistan in the West after the cease-fire in the East. If she had done so it is probable that she would have been compelled to operate in defiance of the United Nations, with the Soviet diplomatic umbrella withdrawn. She might then have faced the possibility of Chinese nuclear threats in defence of West Pakistan; and the Russians and the Americans 'one after the other' might have been compelled to consider making nuclear counter-threats. These dizzy eventualities may have opened themselves up before the minds of the policy-makers in Delhi and Islamabad during the second week of December. But they drew back from the brink; and when the war came to an end on the 16th–17th it was by means of a bilateral arrangement between India and Pakistan. In the East, India accepted the surrender of the local Pakistani forces. And in the West she offered a cease-fire and—apparently after some hesitation—it was accepted by the Pakistani government.

From the point of view of the student of international relations the historic significance of the crisis of 1971 in the sub-continent may perhaps be said to lie in the interrelation between the working out of deeply rooted historic processes on the regional level and the accomplishment of strategic shifts in the structure of world politics. Our nar-

CONCLUSION

rative has shown how the great powers were drawn into the conflict between India and Pakistan, and how their various policies affected the evolution of that conflict. The relationship between India and the Soviet Union, and the consequent paralysis of the United Nations, added a new chapter to the history of post-war relations between super-power and client powers; and it opens up a gloomy perspective on the future. For as the system of world politics becomes more complex with the emergence of 'multi-polar' balances there seems likely to be a relaxation of the international pressures favouring the maintenance of the existing states-system. The sub-continent is not unique in its internal strains. From Ulster and Yugoslavia in the Old World to Canada[221] and Brazil in the New World, and almost everywhere in the 'Third World', there are tensions in the relation of state to community that are analagous to those that brought about the disintegration of Pakistan. On the other hand, the location of many of these conflicts is further removed from the main areas of great-power rivalry than is the sub-continent; and while the Balkans, the Middle East, and south-east Asia are each areas in which local tensions may lead to the involvement of the great powers, it is unlikely that there will be an early recurrence of the uncertainty and instability in relations between the powers which arose in 1971 from the circumstances of the American rapprochement with China.

Nevertheless, the main lesson of the South Asian crisis of 1971 was that the working out of historic local antagonisms may prove too strong a force for the diplomacy of the great powers to arrest. The appropriate conclusion may be that it is unwise for any of the powers to invest too heavily in the preservation of states-systems whose future is cast in doubt by the operation of local forces.

[221] Both Canada and Yugoslavia voted with the majority in the General Assembly on 7 December; and throughout the development of the crisis both Yugoslavia and Canada had actively sought to influence India against intervention to support secessionism. See Canadian Department of External Affairs, 'The Indo–Pakistan Conflict', *International Perspectives*, March/April 1972.

Bibliography of Works Consulted

DOCUMENTS

Keesing's Contemporary Archives.

Monthly News Review on Pakistan/South Asia (New Delhi: Institute for Defence Studies and Analyses, 1971).

Pakistan Horizon – documentary and chronological appendices, Pakistan Institute of International Affairs, Karachi,
XXIV, No. 2, second quarter 1971,
No. 3, third quarter 1971,
No. 4, fourth quarter 1971,
XXV, No. 1, first quarter 1972.

JOURNAL ARTICLES

I have not listed newspapers consulted, to which full references are made in the footnotes to the text.

Ahmad, Aziz. 'Pakistan faces Democracy: A Provisional Nationality.' *The Round Table* (London), April 1971.

Berindranath, Dewan. 'Power Politics in Pakistan, One Year of the Yahya Regime.' *Journal of the United Services Institution of India* (New Delhi), Vol. C, No. 418 (January–March 1970).

Canadian Department of External Affairs. 'The Indo–Pakistan Conflict.' *International Perspectives* (Ottawa), March/April 1972.

Canadian Institute of International Affairs. 'India, Pakistan, Bangladesh.' *International Journal* (Toronto), XXVII, No. 3 (Summer 1972).

Chandrasekhara Rao, R. V. R. 'India and Non-aligned Summitry.' *The World Today* (London), September 1970.

Chopra, Pran. 'East Bengal: a Crisis for India.' *The World Today* (London), September 1971.

—— 'Indian Politics on a New Foundation.' *The World Today* (London), May 1971.

China Report (Washington). 'Special Number on Sino–American Thaw', July–August 1971.

Faruki, Kemal A. 'India's Role in the East Pakistan Crisis: Legal Aspects.' *Pakistan Horizon* (Karachi), XXIV, No. 2 (2nd quarter 1971).

Gupta, Bhabani Sen. 'Moscow, Peking, and the Indian Political Scene after Nehru.' *Orbis* (Philadelphia), XII, No. 2 (Summer 1968).

Gupta, Sisir. 'The Power Structure in South Asia.' *The Round Table* (London), April 1970.

—— 'Sino–U.S. Détente and India.' *India Quarterly* (New Delhi), XXIV, No. 3 (July/August 1971).

Hansen, G. Eric. 'Indian Perceptions of the Chinese Communist Regime and Revolution.' *Orbis* (Philadelphia), XII, No. 1 (Spring 1968).

BIBLIOGRAPHY

Hassan, Zubeida. 'Pakistan's Relations with the USSR in the 1960s.' *The World Today* (London), January 1969.

Hyder, Khurshid. 'Recent Trends in the Foreign Policy of Pakistan.' *The World Today* (London), November 1966.

Khan, Khan Wali, 'Pakistan from Within – a Threeway Split?' *The Round Table* (London), January 1972.

Kim, Jung-Gun. 'Defiance of UN Membership Obligations.' *India Quarterly* (New Delhi), April–June 1970.

Maniruzzaman, T. C. 'Political Activism of University Students in Pakistan.' *Journal of Commonwealth Political Studies* (Leicester), IX, No. 3 (November 1971).

Palmer, Norman D. 'Alternative Futures for South Asia and United States Policy.' *Orbis* (Philadelphia), XV, No. 1 (Spring 1971).

Rao, R. Rama. 'Pakistan re-arms.' *India Quarterly* (New Delhi), XXVII (April–June 1971).

Rashiduzzuman, M. 'The National Awami Party of Pakistan; Leftist Politics in Crisis.' *Pacific Affairs* (Vancouver), XLVIII, No. 3 (Fall 1970).

—— 'The Awami League in the Political Development of Pakistan.' *Asian Survey* (Berkeley, Calif.) July 1970.

—— 'The National Assembly of Pakistan under the 1962 Constitution.' *Pacific Affairs* (Vancouver), XLII, No. 4 (Winter 1969–70).

The Round Table (London). Editorial: 'Mr Nixon's Philosophy of Foreign Policy', October 1972.

Seth, S. P. 'China as a Factor in Indo–Pakistani politics.' *The World Today* (London), January 1969.

Sharma, B. L. 'U.S. Arms for Pakistan.' *Journal of the United Services Institution of India*, January–March 1971.

Sobham, Rahman. 'East Pakistan's revolt against Ayub.' *The Round Table* (London), July 1969.

—— 'Pakistan's Political Crisis.' *The Round Table* (London), May 1969.

Subrahmanyam, K. 'The Challenge of the Seventies to India's Security.' *India Quarterly* (New Delhi), XXIV, No. 2 (April/June 1970).

Syed, Anwar. 'The Politics of Sino–Pakistan Agreements.' *Orbis* (Philadelphia), XI, No. 3 (Fall 1967).

Wariavwalla, B. K. 'The Indo–Soviet Treaty.' *The Round Table* (London), April 1972.

Zinkin, Maurice. 'The Political Aftermath of the Indo–Pakistan War.' *Survival* (London), XIV, No. 2 (March/April 1972).

Pakistan Horizon. Various articles in XXIV, Nos 2, 3, 4, and XXV, No. 1. (1971–2).

SOUTH ASIAN CRISIS

BOOKS

Ahmad, Kamruddin. *A Social History of Bengal* (Dacca: Progoti Publishers, 1970).
Ahmad, Mushtaq. *Politics without Social Change* (Karachi: Space Publishers, 1972).
Ayoob, Mohammed, and K. Subrahmanyam. *The Liberation War* (New Delhi: S. Chand, 1972).
Bangla Desh Documents (New Delhi: Government of India, 1971).
Bhutto, Zulfikar Ali. *The Great Tragedy* (Karachi: Pakistan People's Party, September 1971).
Feldman, Herbert. *Revolution in Pakistan: A Study of the Martial Law Administration* (London: Oxford U.P., 1967).
—— *From Crisis to Crisis, Pakistan 1962–1969* (London: Oxford U.P., 1972).
Galbraith, J. K. *Ambassador's Journal* (New York: Signet Paperback edition, 1969).
Gandhi, Indira. *India and Bangla Desh: Selected Speeches and Statements March to December 1971* (New Delhi: Orient Longman, February 1972).
Government of Pakistan. *White Paper on the Crisis in East Pakistan* (Islamabad, 5 August 1971).
Government of Pakistan Planning Commission. *Reports of the Advisory Panels of the Fourth Five Year Plan 1970–75* (Islamabad, July 1971).
Habibullah, M. *The Tea Industry of Pakistan* (Dacca: 1964).
Hodson, H. V. *The Great Divide: Britain, India, Pakistan* (London: Hutchinson, 1969).
Indian Ministry of Defence. *Annual Report, 1971–72* (New Delhi: Government of India, 1972).
International Institute for Strategic Studies. *The Military Balance 1971–1972* (London: IISS, 1971).
International Journal. *India, Pakistan, Bangla Desh*, (Toronto: Canadian Institute of International Affairs, Summer 1972).
Kamal, Kazi Ahmed. *Politicians and Inside Stories: an Intimate Study mainly of Fazlul Haq, Suhrawardy and Maulana Bashani* (Dacca: Kazi Giasuddin Ahmed, 1970).
—— *Sheikh Mujibur Rahman and Birth of Bangladesh* (Dacca: Kazi Giasuddin Ahmed, 1972).
Kadar, A. H. *People's Commitment* (Lahore: A. H. Kardar, 1971).
Loshak, David. *Pakistan Crisis* (London: Heinemann, 1971).
Luard, Evan (ed). *The International Regulation of Civil Wars* (London: Thames and Hudson, 1972).
Mankekar, D. R. *Pakistan Cut to Size* (New Delhi: Indian Book Company, 1972).
The Marketing of Jute in East Pakistan (Dacca: Dacca University Press, 1961).

BIBLIOGRAPHY

Mascarenas, Anthony. *The Rape of Bangla Desh* (New Delhi: Vikas Publications, 1971).

Menon, K. P. S. *Many Worlds* (Bombay: Oxford University Press, 1971).

Mukerjee, Dilip. *Yahya Khan's 'Final War'* (New Delhi: Times of India, 1972).

Naik, J. A. *India, Russia, China and Bangla Desh* (New Delhi: S. Chand, 1972).

Nixon, Richard M. *US Foreign Policy for the 1970s: The Emerging Structure of Peace.* A Report to the Congress ... (Washington, 9 February 1972).

Palit, Maj.-Gen. D. K. *The Lightning Campaign, Indo-Pakistan War 1971* (New Delhi: Thomson Press (India) Ltd, January 1972).

Pirzada, Syed Sharifuddin (ed). *The Foundations of Pakistan* (2 vols. Karachi: National Publishing House, 1969).

Rushbrook-Williams, L. *The East Pakistan Tragedy* (London: Tom Stacey, 1972).

Siddiqui, Kalim. *Conflict, Crisis and War and Pakistan* (London: Macmillan, 1972).

Subrahmanyam, K. *Bangla Desh and India's Security* (Dehra Dun: Palit and Dutt, 1972).

Wheeler, Richard S. *The Politics of Pakistan* (Ithaca, N.Y.: Cornell University Press, 1970).

Appendixes

1. *The Awami League's Six Points*
EXTRACT FROM AWAMI LEAGUE MANIFESTO

Pakistan shall be a Federation granting full autonomy on the basis of the six-point formula to each of the federating units:

Point No. 1

The character of the government shall be federal and parliamentary, in which the election to the federal legislature and to the legislatures of the federating units shall be direct and on the basis of universal adult franchise. The representation in the federal legislature shall be on the basis of population.

Point No. 2:

The federal government shall be responsible only for defence and foreign affairs and subject to the conditions provided in (3) below, currency.

Point No. 3:

There shall be two separate currencies mutually or freely convertible in each wing for each region, or in the alternative a single currency, subject to the establishment of a federal reserve system in which there will be regional federal reserve banks which shall devise measures to prevent the transfer of resources and flight of capital from one region to another.

Point No. 4:

Fiscal policy shall be the responsibility of the federating units. The federal government shall be provided with requisite revenue resources for meeting the requirements of defence and foreign affairs, which revenue resources would be automatically appropriable by the federal government in the manner provided and on the basis of the ratio to be determined by the procedure laid down in the constitution. Such constitutional provisions would ensure that federal government's revenue requirements are met consistently with the objective of ensuring control over the fiscal policy by the governments of the federating units.

Point No. 5:

Constitutional provisions shall be made to enable separate accounts to be maintained of the foreign exchange earnings of each of the federating units, under the control of the respective governments of the federating units. The foreign exchange requirement of the federal government shall be met by the governments of the federating units on the basis of a ratio to be determined in accordance with the procedure laid down in the constitution. The regional governments shall have power under the constitution to negotiate foreign trade and aid within the framework of the foreign policy of the country, which shall be the responsibility of the federal government.

BIBLIOGRAPHY

Point No. 6:
The government of the federating units shall be empowerd to maintain a militia or para-military force in order to contribute effectively towards national security.

Source: the *Government of Pakistan White Paper*. The full text of the Awami League's 1970 Election Manifesto can be found in the collections of *Bangla Desh Documents*, pp. 66–82. On pp. 23–33 can be found a detailed exposition of the Six Points, made by Sheikh Mujib in March 1966.

SOUTH ASIAN CRISIS

2. President Yahya Khan's Broadcast of 26 March 1971

My dear countrymen,
Assalam-o-Alaikum,
On the 6 of this month I announced 25 March as the new date for the inaugural session of the National Assembly hoping that conditions would permit the holding of the session on the appointed date. Events have, however, not justified that hope. The nation continued to face a grave crisis.

In East Pakistan a non-co-operation and disobedience movement was launched by the Awami League and matters took a very serious turn. Events were moving very fast and it became absolutely imperative that the situation was brought under control as soon as possible. With this aim in view, I had a series of discussions with political leaders in West Pakistan and subsequently on 15 March I went to Dacca.

As you are aware I had a number of meetings with Sheikh Mujibur Rehman in order to resolve the political impasse. Having consulted West Pakistan leaders it was necessary for me to do the same over there so that areas of agreement could be identified and an amicable settlement arrived at.

As has been reported in the Press and other news media from time to time, my talks with Sheikh Mujibur Rehman showed some progress. Having reached a certain stage in my negotiations with Sheikh Mujibur Rehman I considered it necessary to have another round of talks with West Pakistani leaders in Dacca.

Mr Z. A. Bhutto reached there on 21 March and I had a number of meetings with him.

As you are aware, the leader of the Awami League had asked for the withdrawal of Martial Law and transfer of power prior to the meeting of the National Assembly. In our discussions he proposed that this interim period could be covered by a proclamation by me whereby Martial Law would be withdrawn, provincial Governments set up and the National Assembly would, *ab initio,* sit in two committees – one composed of members from East Pakistan and the other composed of members from West Pakistan.

Despite some serious flaws in the scheme, in its legal as well as other aspects, I was prepared to agree in principle to this plan in the interest of peaceful transfer of power but on one condition. The condition which I clearly explained to Sheikh Mujibur Rehman was that I must first have unequivocal agreement of all political leaders to the scheme.

I thereupon discussed the proposal with other political leaders. I found them unanimously of the view that the proposed proclamation by me would have no legal sanction. It will neither have the cover of Martial Law nor could it claim to be based on the will of the people. Thus a

APPENDIXES

vacuum would be created and chaotic conditions will ensue. They also considered that splitting of the National Assembly into two parts through a proclamation would encourage divisive tendencies that may exist. They, therefore, expressed the opinion that if it is intended to lift Martial Law and transfer power in the interim period, the National Assembly should meet, pass an appropriate interim Constitution Bill and present it for my assent. I entirely agreed with their view and requested them to tell Sheikh Mujibur Rehman to take a reasonable attitude on this issue.

I told the leaders to explain their views to him that a scheme whereby, on the one hand, you extinguish all source of power, namely, Martial Law and, on the other, fail to replace it by the will of the people through a proper session of the National Assembly, will merely result in chaos. They agreed to meet Sheikh Mujibur Rehman, explain the position and try to obtain his agreement to the interim arrangement for transfer of power to emanate from the National Assembly.

The political leaders were also very much perturbed over Sheikh Mujib's idea of dividing the National Assembly into two parts right from start. Such a move, they felt, would be totally against the interest of Pakistan's integrity.

The Chairman of the Pakistan People's Party, during the meeting between myself, Sheikh Mujibur Rehman and him had also expressed similar views to Mujib.

On the evening of 23 March the political leaders, who had gone to talk to Mujib on this issue, called on me and informed me that he was not agreeable to any changes in his scheme. All he really wanted was for me to make a proclamation, whereby I should withdraw Martial Law and transfer power.

Sheikh Mujibur Rehman's action of starting his non-co-operation movement is an act of treason. He and his Party have defied the lawful authority for over three weeks. They have insulted Pakistan's flag and defiled the photograph of the Father of the Nation. They have tried to run a parallel government. They have created turmoil, terror and insecurity.

A number of murders have been committed in the name of the movement. Millions of our Bengali brethren and those who have settled in East Pakistan are living in a state of panic, and a very large number had to leave that Wing out of fear for their lives.

The Armed Forces, located in East Pakistan, have been subjected to taunts and insults of all kinds. I wish to compliment them on the tremendous restraint that they have shown in the face of grave provocation. Their sense of discipline is indeed praiseworthy. I am proud of them.

I should have taken action against Sheikh Mujibur Rehman and his collaborators weeks ago but I had to try my utmost to handle the situation in such a manner as not to jeopardize my plan of peaceful transfer of power. In my keenness to achieve this aim I kept on tolerating one illegal act after another, and at the same time I explored every possible avenue for arriving at some reasonable solution. I have already mentioned the efforts made by me and by various political leaders in getting Sheikh

SOUTH ASIAN CRISIS

Mujibur Rehman to see reason. We have left no stone unturned. But he has failed to respond in any constructive manner; on the other hand, he and his followers kept on flouting the authority of the Government even during my presence in Dacca. The proclamation that he proposed was nothing but a trap. He knew that it would not have been worth the paper it was written on and in the vacuum created by the lifting of Martial Law he could have done anything with impunity. His obstinacy, obduracy and absolute refusal to talk sense can lead to but one conclusion – the man and his Party are enemies of Pakistan and they want East Pakistan to break away completely from the country. He has attacked the solidarity and integrity of this country – this crime will not go unpunished.

We will not allow some power-hungry and unpatriotic people to destroy this country and play with the destiny of 120 million people.

In my address to the Nation of 6 March I told you that it is the duty of the Pakistan Armed Forces to ensure the integrity, solidarity and security of Pakistan. I have ordered them to do their duty and fully restore the authority of the Government.

In view of the grave situation that exists in the country today I have decided to ban all political activities throughout the country. As for the Awami League, it is completely banned as a political party. I have also decided to impose complete press censorship. Martial Law Regulations will very shortly be issued in pursuance of these decisions.

In the end let me assure you that my main aim remains the same, namely, transfer of power to the elected representatives of the people. As soon as situation permits I will take fresh steps towards the achievement of this objective.

It is my hope that the law and order situation will soon return to normal in East Pakistan and we can again move forward towards our cherished goal.

I appeal to my countrymen to appreciate the gravity of the situation, for which blame rests entirely on the anti-Pakistan and secessionist elements, and to act as reasonable citizens of the country because therein lies the security and salvation of Pakistan.

God be with you. God bless you.

PAKISTAN PAINDABAD

Source: *Pakistan Horizon*, XXIV, No. 2, pp. 107–10.

APPENDIXES

3. Resolution of the Indian Parliament 31 March 1971 Moved by Mrs Indira Gandhi

This House expresses its deep anguish and grave concern at the recent developments in East Bengal. A massive attack by armed forces, despatched from West Pakistan, has been unleashed against the entire people of East Bengal with a view to suppressing their urges and aspirations.

Instead of respecting the will of the people so unmistakably expressed through the election in Pakistan in December 1970, the Government of Pakistan has chosen to flout the mandate of the people.

The Government of Pakistan has not only refused to transfer power to legally elected representatives but has arbitrarily prevented the National Assembly from assuming its rightful and sovereign role. The people of East Bengal are being sought to be suppressed by the naked use of force, by bayonets, machine guns, tanks, artillery and aircraft.

The Government and people of India have always desired and worked for peaceful, normal and fraternal relations with Pakistan. However, situated as India is and bound as the people of the sub-continent are by centuries-old ties of history, culture and tradition, this House cannot remain indifferent to the macabre tragedy being enacted so close to our border. Throughout the length and breadth of our land, our people have condemned, in unmistakable terms, the atrocities now being perpetrated on an unprecedented scale upon an unarmed and innocent people.

This House expresses its profound sympathy for and solidarity with the people of East Bengal in their struggle for a democratic way of life.

Bearing in mind the permanent interests which India has in peace, and committed as we are to uphold and defend human rights, this House demands immediate cessation of the use of force and the massacre of defenceless people. This House calls upon all peoples and Governments of the world to take urgent and constructive steps to prevail upon the Government of Pakistan to put an end immediately to the systematic decimation of people which amounts to genocide.

This House records its profound conviction that the historic upsurge of the 75 million people of East Bengal will triumph. The House wishes to assure them that their struggle and sacrifices will receive the wholehearted sympathy and support of the people of India.

Source: *Bangla Desh Documents*, p. 672.

4. President Nikolai Podgorny's Letter to President Yahya Khan of 2 April 1971

Esteemed Mr President,
  The report that the talks in Dacca had been broken off and that the Military Administration had found it possible to resort to extreme measures and used armed force against the population of East Pakistan was met with great alarm in the Soviet Union.
  Soviet people cannot but be concerned by the numerous casualties, by the sufferings and privations that such a development of events brings to the people of Pakistan. Concern is also caused in the Soviet Union by the arrest and persecution of M. Rehman and other politicians who had received such convincing support by the overwhelming majority of the people of East Pakistan at the recent general elections. Soviet people have always sincerely wished the people of Pakistan all the best and prosperity and rejoiced at their success in solving in a democratic manner the complex problems that face the country.
  In these days of trial for the Pakistani people we cannot but say a few words coming from true friends. We have been and remain convinced that the complex problems that have arisen in Pakistan of late can and must be solved politically without use of force. Continuation of repressive measures and blood-shed in East Pakistan will undoubtedly only make the solution of the problems more difficult and may do great harm to the vital interest of the entire people of Pakistan.
  We consider it our duty to address you, Mr President, on behalf of the Presidium of the Supreme Soviet of the USSR, with an insistent appeal for the adoption of the most urgent measures to stop the blood-shed and repression against the population in East Pakistan and for turning to methods of a peaceful political settlement. We are convinced that this would meet the interest of the entire people of Pakistan and the interest of preserving peace in the area. A peaceful solution of the problems that have arisen would be received with satisfaction by the entire Soviet people.
  In appealing to you we were guided by the generally recognized humanitarian principles recorded in the universal Declaration of Human Rights and by [concern for] the welfare of the friendly people of Pakistan.
  We hope, Mr President, that you will correctly interpret the motives by which we are guided in making this appeal. It is our sincere wish that tranquillity and justice be established in East Pakistan in the shortest possible time.

Source: *Bangla Desh Documents*, pp. 510–11.

APPENDIXES

5. Mr Chou En-lai's Letter to President Yahya Khan of 13 April 1971

I have read Your Excellency's letter and Ambassador Chang Tung's report on Your Excellency's conversation with him. I am grateful to Your Excellency for your trust in the Chinese Government. China and Pakistan are friendly neighbours. The Chinese Government and people are following with close concern the development of the present situation in Pakistan. Your Excellency and leaders of various quarters in Pakistan have done a lot of useful work to uphold the unification of Pakistan and to prevent it from moving towards a split. We believe that through the wise consultations and efforts of Your Excellency and leaders of various quarters in Pakistan, the situation in Pakistan will certainly be restored to normal. In our opinion, the unification of Pakistan and the unity of the people of East and West Pakistan are the basic guarantees for Pakistan to attain prosperity and strength. Here, it is most important to differentiate the broad masses of the people from a handful of persons who want to sabotage the unification of Pakistan. As a genuine friend of Pakistan, we would like to present these views for Your Excellency's reference.

At the same time, we have noted that of late the Indian Government has been carrying out gross interference in the internal affairs of Pakistan by exploiting the internal problems of your country. And the Soviet Union and the United States are doing the same one after the other. The Chinese Press is carrying reports to expose such unreasonable interference and has published Your Excellency's letter of reply to Podgorny. The Chinese Government holds that what is happening in Pakistan at present is purely the internal affair of Pakistan, which can only be settled by the Pakistan people themselves and which brooks no foreign interference whatsoever. Your Excellency may rest assured that should the Indian expansionists dare to launch aggression against Pakistan, the Chinese Government and people will, as always, firmly support the Pakistan Government and people in their just struggle to safeguard State sovereignty and national independence.

Source: *Pakistan Horizon*, XXIV No. 2, pp. 153–4.

SOUTH ASIAN CRISIS

6. President Yahya Khan's Broadcast of 28 June 1971

My dear countrymen,
Assalam-o-Alaikum,
The recent happenings in East Pakistan have caused anguish to all of us. For me personally these tragic events have been the cause of distress and disappointment. Throughout these last two and a quarter years, my aim has been to bring back democracy in the country and to ensure justice for every region of Pakistan. In particular I have been conscious of the legitimate demands of the East Pakistanis. Many steps have been taken and planned towards meeting them.

I have every reason to believe that my scheme to revive the democratic way of life was fully supported by the people and their political leaders in both wings of the country. They all took part in the elections on the basis of the Legal Framework Order 1970 which provided for maximum autonomy to the provinces within the concept of one Pakistan and adequate strength to the Centre to carry out its functions.

The defunct Awami League also participated in the elections on the basis of the Legal Framework Order and therefore at that time it was felt that they too subscribed to the concept of one Pakistan. However, later their leadership gradually moved away from the principles of the Legal Framework Order and based their electioneering on hatred of West Pakistan and tried to cause tension and misunderstanding between the two wings.

When I questioned Mujibur Rehman on the Awami League Six Points during some of our talks he confirmed to me that these were negotiable. He also clearly indicated that all the major provisions of the constitution would be settled by the political parties in parleys outside the Assembly. This lobbying, he affirmed, was usual practice with politicians. After the elections when I wanted the parties to get together and come to some consensus on the future Constitution of Pakistan, it became quite clear that Mujib was not going to budge from his position which, to put it bluntly, was tantamount to secession. Another indication of his evil design is that he refused to visit West Pakistan and have talks in this wing despite repeated invitations. He had no intention of acting in a responsible and a patriotic manner as leader of the majority party in the country as a whole. He had already made up his mind that he was going to break the country into two, preferably by trickery, and if this did not succeed, by physical violence.

As I told you in my address of 26 March, I had a series of meetings with Sheikh Mujib and his advisers during my stay in Dacca from 15 March onwards. Whilst he was having these talks with us, he and his followers were secretly preparing for a final break, through physical violence. Towards the concluding sessions of the talks, it became quite evident that the

APPENDIXES

intention of Sheikh Mujib and his advisers was not to come to an understanding on the basis of one Pakistan but was somehow to extract from me proclamation which would in effect divide the National Assembly into two separate Constituent Assemblies, give birth to a confederation rather than a federation and, by the removal of the authority of Martial Law, create complete chaos in the country. Through this plan they expected to establish a separate State of Bangla Desh. That, needless to say, would have been the end of Pakistan as created by the Father of the Nation.

The unscrupulous and secessionist elements of the defunct Awami League had brought the country to the brink of disintegration. Our dear homeland, which symbolizes the fulfilment of the aspirations and the culmination of the relentless struggle of the Muslims of the subcontinent, was in very grave danger of breaking up. The violent non-co-operation movement of Sheikh Mujibur Rehman and his clique for over three weeks had let loose widespread loot, arson and killing.

The people of East Pakistan had voted for provincial autonomy and not for the disintegration of the country. Instead of settling the controversial political and constitutional issues with mutual understanding and in a spirit of give and take for the sake of national solidarity, some of the leading elements of the defunct Awami League chose the path of defiance, disruption and secession. All my efforts to help political parties to arrive at a consensus over an acceptable and lasting constitutional framework were frustrated by certain leaders of the defunct Awami League. On the one hand they brought the negotiations to an *impasse* by their persistent intransigence and obduracy and on the other, intensified their nefarious activities of open defiance of the Government. The very existence of the country, for the creation of which thousands of our brethren laid down their lives and millions suffered untold miseries, was at stake. It was in these circumstances that I ordered the Armed Forces to restore the authority of the Government. No Government worth its name could allow the country to be destroyed by open and armed rebellion against the State.

The valiant Armed Forces of Pakistan, who have always served the nation with devotion, moved out with firm determination to put an end to the activities of the miscreants. They had a difficult task to perform. It is unfortunate that our neighbour, which has never missed an opportunity to weaken or cripple our country, rushed to help the secessionists with men and material to inflame the situation further. This was all preplanned. As the troops moved forward and fanned out, the whole dark plan of collusion between the Awami League extremists, rebels and our hostile neighbour gradually unfolded itself.

It became obvious that the secessionists, miscreants, rebels and intruders from across the border had planned their whole operation carefully and over a considerable period of time. The aim was to destroy integrity of Pakistan and force the Eastern Zone to secede from the rest of the country. Whilst the miscreants, rebels and intruders were putting up

SOUTH ASIAN CRISIS

physical resistance to the Pakistan Army, the Indian radio and press launched a malicious campaign of falsehood against Pakistan and tried to mislead the world about happenings in East Pakistan.

The Indian Government began to utilise every coercive measure including diplomatic offensives, armed infiltration and actual threats of invasion. This open interference in our internal affairs could have had very grave consequences but by the Grace of Allah our Armed Forces soon brought the situation under control, destroying the anti-national elements. The nation is proud of the Armed Forces who deserve all its admiration and appreciation. Let us on this occasion bow down our heads in gratitude to Almighty Allah that the country has been saved from disintegration.

In my last address to the nation I had assured you that my main aim remained the transfer of power and I had further stated that I would take fresh steps towards the achievement of this aim. Let me at the outset say categorically that there is no question of holding fresh elections. The mischief of some misguided persons should not be allowed to nullify the entire results of the first ever elections held in the country at enormous cost in terms of money, time and energy. I have banned the Awami League as a political party. However, the MNAs and MPAs-elect of this defunct party retain their status as such in their individual capacities. I may, however, add that those elected members who have taken part in anti-State activities or have committed criminal acts or have indulged in anti-social activities will be disqualified from membership of the National and Provincial Assemblies. I have not finally assessed the exact number of those who would be disqualified. After a thorough investigation a list of such persons will be published. Once this is done, the vacancies caused would be filled in through the usual method of by-elections.

In the meanwhile, I would ask those MNAs and MPAs-elect of the defunct Awami League, who had nothing to do with the secessionist policies of the ruling clique of that party and who are not guilty of any criminal acts in pursuance of such policies or who have not committed atrocities against their fellow Pakistanis, to come forward and play their part in re-building the political structure in East Pakistan.

After a close and careful study of the situation, particularly of the recent happenings, I have come to the conclusion that the task of framing a constitution by an Assembly is not feasible. In fact, the history of constitution-making in our country is not a very encouraging or a happy one. The two Constituent Assemblies took nine years to produce a constitution, that is from 1947 to 1956. The leaders of the country spent an inordinately long period of time on the floor of the Legislature in trying to produce a constitution while urgent social and economic problems remained unattended and neglected.

But the most regrettable phenomenon of constitution-making in Pakistan was that it gave vent to all sorts of regional and parochial sentiments. In fact, constitution-making gave rise to the worst type of political bickering and intrigue which threatened the very existence of our country. And when in the end they at last produced a constitution in 1956

APPENDIXES

it was a product of all sorts of conflicting compromises and expediencies. The result was that the constitution was short-lived and the country came under Martial Law from October 1958 to June 1962. After that, the country was governed under a constitution which, for well-known reasons, was unpopular right from the start. There was great resentment and political upheaval in 1969 against this constitution.

I, therefore, thought that the people's representatives should frame a constitution of their own but in order to eliminate the unhappy aspects of the previous attempts at constitution-making in Pakistan, I put a limit of one hundred and twenty days for this exercise. And I also laid down some basic principles for the constitution in my Legal Framework Order. When I fixed the time limit of 120 days it was done in consultation with political leaders, including Mujibur Rehman and it was expected that they would devote their full attention to the framing of the constitution and that a general agreement on the broad aspects of the constitution would be arrived at outside the Assembly so as to facilitate the task of constitution-making within the stipulated period. But unfortunately my hopes and plans were frustrated by the uncompromising and unpatriotic attitude of the defunct Awami League.

Against this background and in view of the present circumstances I find that there is no other alternative for me but to have a constitution prepared by a group of experts. This constitution will be subject to amendments by the National Assembly on the basis of the amending procedure as will be laid down in the constitution itself. The constitution will be based on a careful study of a number of constitutions and also based on the aspirations of the people of various regions of Pakistan as assessed by me over the last two years. I have already set up a Constitution Committee and a draft is being prepared by them. Once the draft is ready I will consult various leaders of the Assembly regarding the provisions of the draft. Final shape will be given to the constitution in the light of my discussions and consultations with various experts and leaders.

I may add that certain guidelines with regard to the future constitution have already been spelt out in the Legal Framework Order of 1970, which were generally welcomed by the people. First, the Constitution of Pakistan must be based on Islamic ideology, on the basis of which Pakistan was created and on the basis of which it is still preserved. It must be the Constitution of the Islamic Republic of Pakistan in the true sense.

The constitution shall also provide for full social and economic justice to various sections of our society. The constitution should be a federal one and it must have all the characteristics of a Federal Constitution. As stated in the Legal Framework Order, the provinces shall have maximum autonomy including legislative, administrative and financial but the Federal Government shall also have adequate powers, including legislative, administrative and financial, to discharge its responsibilities in relation to external and internal affairs and to preserve the independence and territorial integrity of the country.

SOUTH ASIAN CRISIS

I have also indicated to the Committee that, in the interest of the integrity of the country, it would be a good thing if we ban any party which is confined to a specific region and is not national in the practical sense. Then again we must eschew this business of having 2, 3 or 4 sub-parties within a party. In short, it is my hope that this constitution will ensure that everything which tends to make our political life cumbersome, shaky, insecure and unpatriotic is eradicated and that it helps to infuse the right spirit in the people and the politicians. The constitution must serve Pakistan as a whole and not any individual or group. It must allow each province to develop itself along the right lines without in any way detracting from the strength of the Centre and the integrity of the nation as a whole. I might clarify here that this constitution will come into force with effect from the first session of the National Assembly. The by-elections to be held before this will, however, be on the same basis as the general elections already held, namely, the Legal Framework Order.

So much for the future constitution of Pakistan. Now to continue with my plan of transfer of power. As I said earlier, by-elections will be held to fill in the vacant seats in the National as well as in Provincial Assemblies. Considering the mood of the people, I feel sure that the campaign for these by-elections will be based on the principles contained in the Legal Framework Order. No one will tolerate the propagation of views which tend to militate against the integrity of Pakistan. I also feel that the campaign should be a brief one. After these elections are completed, the National and Provincial Assemblies will be duly summoned and Governments will be formed at the National as well as Provincial levels throughout the country. The National Assembly will not have to function as a Constituent Assembly but will become our Central Legislature as soon as it is sworn in.

Since the nation has recently been subjected to a very severe jolt, I have decided that the National and the Provincial Governments will have at their disposal the cover of Martial Law for a period of time. In actual practice Martial Law will not be operative in its present form but we cannot allow chaos in any part of the country and the hands of the Governments need to be strengthened until things settle down. In order to meet the requirements of this new plan, the Legal Framework Order 1970, will be duly amended. Let me now say a word about the time frame of this plan. It is obvious that the plan, in its entirety, cannot be launched immediately because it is important that a reasonable amount of normalcy returns to the country before we think in terms of transferring power. But, on the other hand, the launching of the plan must not be delayed unduly. When we speak of normalcy, the main considerations are the restoration of law and order, rehabilitation of the administrative structure, which was badly disrupted, and a degree of economic rehabilitation.

As regards law and order, I am glad to be able to tell you that the Army is in full control of the situation in East Pakistan. It has crushed the mischief-mongers, saboteurs and infiltrators. But it will take some time

APPENDIXES

before the law and order situation becomes completely normal. The process is in full swing with the active co-operation of the people and their patriotic leaders. The people of East Pakistan have manifested a great sense of patriotism and national unity in helping the Armed Forces in routing out the miscreants and infiltrators.

As a result of the non-co-operation movement the economy of East Pakistan had come to a standstill. The widespread arson, loot and intimidation resorted to by the Awami League secessionists, anti-social elements and infiltrators brought untold sufferings to the innocent people. A large number of them were terrorised and uprooted and their properties were mercilessly destroyed. They have my fullest sympathy as also the sympathy of the entire nation. It would be inhuman if their speedy rehabilitation is not given the priority and attention it deserves. I would like to repeat once again that all citizens of Pakistan of any religion, caste or creed who crossed the border and went into India because of panic created due to false propaganda by rebels, miscreants and others must return to their homes and hearths. The Government of East Pakistan have made all necessary arrangements for their reception and transportation. I would ask the Indian Government not to put impediments in the way of these unfortunate people who want to resume their normal lives in their own homes and who want to be reunited with their near and dear ones. We shall gladly and gratefully accept any assistance that the United Nations can extend in facilitating the move of these displaced persons back to Pakistan.

I have heard a view being expressed that power should not be transferred to the elected representatives of the people until complete normalcy has returned in every sphere. I am afraid I do not agree with this view because it is utterly unrealistic and impracticable. It also ignores one very important aspect of national life which is that normalcy in its accepted meaning can never return to a country without full participation of the people in its administration. The very process of bringing back normalcy requires active interest of the people in the process and this can happen only when the representatives of the people assume responsibility for the administration of the country. I firmly believe that as soon as we have acquired a basic infrastructure of law and order and various echelons of administration gather full strength, it will be possible for me to put my plan of transfer of power into operation.

Appreciating the situation as it exists today and as it is likely to develop in the near future, it is my hope and belief that I would be able to achieve my goal in a matter of four months or so. The precise timing will naturally depend on the internal and external situation at the time. I am absolutely convinced that the country's integrity and well-being lie in the fulfilment of the plan that I have just outlined to you and in the achievement of the final objective.

Let me now turn to the vital subject of economy. Recent events have cast their shadow on the general economic situation. The economy had been subjected to serious strains during the long period of political

SOUTH ASIAN CRISIS

uncertainty before and after the elections. In March, the economy of East Pakistan was brought to a virtual standstill. With the success of army action, the situation is generally returning to normal and economic activity is reviving in the province. I am sure that all patriotic elements in the province would rally round the forces of law and order to achieve complete normalcy and to restart the process of building up the economy of Pakistan. The rehabilitation of the economy will demand both short-term measures and long-term strategy to rehabilitate it and revive it to its full vigour. For this purpose, we have taken many initiatives which will soon begin to produce the results we desire. Our exports have sharply declined in recent months in East Pakistan causing a drain on our foreign exchange reserves which were already under severe strain. Collection of taxes had also suffered at a time when we need all the resources at our command to preserve our national integrity and maintain the tempo of economic activity. The Government is taking various steps to meet the present difficult economic situation. These are not always pleasant decisions. We have to use our resources with much greater restraint. This involves hardship and sacrifices. But there is no alternative. This is the only realistic way for a nation to solve its economic problems. Some weeks ago I ordered a thorough revision of the import policy. All inessential items or those without which we could do for some time were banned even under bonus scheme. Bonus vouchers thus released are to be used under the revised import policy for raw materials and other essential imports.

In domestic spending also, maximum economy is being exercised. For the next year, we have prepared a modest development programme which would meet our immediate and unavoidable needs. The emphasis would be on rehabilitation of the economy particularly in East Pakistan. I want the country to make early progress towards self-reliance. We must look increasingly towards our own resources for meeting our national objectives. This requires maximum austerity in both public and private spending. The Government is making all necessary adjustments in economic policies with the objective. But these can succeed only with the enthusiastic support of the people. Let us as a nation adopt a more austere way of life suited to our own stage of economic development and eschew every form of ostentatious consumption.

For many years now we have been receiving aid for our development programme from a number of aid-giving countries. This we thankfully acknowledge. I regret to have to say, however, that lately there have been indications that the foreign aid is acquiring certain political overtones and the people of Pakistan are getting the impression that strings are being sought to be attached to such aid. If this be the case, let me say quite categorically that aid which seeks to make in-roads into our sovereignty is not acceptable to us. We shall be fully prepared to do without it.

I am confident that the private sector would come forward to play an active role in developing Pakistan's own resources. Private investment

APPENDIXES

financed from its own savings can play a major role in reviving the economy at this stage. This is an hour of crisis for the nation. We need the same determination and resolute will which we showed on a number of previous occasions to safeguard the integrity of Pakistan against internal upheavals and external aggression. Each one of us has a duty to work hard and to rebuild the momentum of economic activity. This is necessary to generate resources for economic development. Each worker in the factory and the peasant in his farm can contribute to this national effort by taking part in the overall effort to maximize production and make his contribution to the integrity and solidarity of Pakistan. Let us resolve today, individually and collectively, to maximize production and exports. We must work hard and learn to reduce our dependence on others in every field in the shortest possible time. The sacrifice which this will entail must be borne with patriotic fervour and national solidarity. I appeal to both labour and management to maintain the best of relations. Let there be understanding and accommodation rather than bickering and strife. Strikes and lock-outs should be avoided at all costs. Such a wastage of the country's productive capacity would be totally unpatriotic at this critical juncture in our national life. I cannot afford to let such unpatriotic activities go unchallenged. Stringent measures shall be taken to curb such tendencies.

Our agriculturists have done a remarkable job in recent years. Food production has increased rapidly since 1965 bringing the country to the threshold of food self-sufficiency. Let them consolidate and improve on their performance in foodgrains and at the same time turn their attention to the production of export crops which present great opportunities for increased output. Government would be willing to provide all necessary facilities and incentives for this purpose.

I have candidly presented before you the difficulties we face today. But let this not give rise to despondency. A large part of the problem we face today is of a temporary nature. It has not affected the basic strength of the economy. We have a large potential for increasing production both in agriculture and industry. We have today a sizeable class of progressive agriculturists, industrial entrepreneurs and middle-class investors. These are the assets on which the foundation of a rapidly developing economy are laid. The nation has faced difficult challenges before in its short history. I have no doubt that *Inshallah* we would be able to overcome present difficulties with our united efforts and resume our endeavour to build for a prosperous and just society.

Now a word about foreign reactions to our internal trouble. It is a matter of satisfaction that in the difficult situation that the country has faced in the past few months the reaction and response from an overwhelming number of countries has been one of sympathy and understanding of the problem we are facing and trying to resolve. Our friends abroad have given complete support to the action taken by the Government to maintain the unity and integrity of Pakistan. They have at the same time warned those who have attempted to interfere in our internal affairs to desist from such actions, I should like to take this opportunity to express, on behalf of the Government and the people of Pakistan and on my own behalf, appreciation and gratitude to them. We are also heartened by the favourable response of the international community, particularly the United Nations Organization and its Agencies, to the need for co-operative assistance in repairing the damage to the economic life of East Pakistan. At present, we are engaged in consultations with friendly governments and the UN Secretary-General for securing necessary help for relief work in different fields.

Our plans for the reconstruction of economy and the early resumption of political activity in East Pakistan are threatened by India's continued interference in our internal affairs. Armed infiltration and open encouragement and assistance to secessionists have heightened tension between the two countries. There has also been a spate of unfriendly statements from responsible sources in India, threatening unilateral action against Pakistan if we did not yield to arbitrary demands. The need of the hour is to desist from such actions and statements as they would further inflame the situation. It is through discussions and not through conflict that problems can be resolved. Statesmanship demands exercise of caution and restraint so that our problems are not further complicated. As I have said before, armed conflict would solve nothing. On our part, we want to live in peace and harmony with all our neighbours. We do not interfere in the affairs of other people and we will not allow any one else to interfere in ours. If, however, a situation is forced upon us, we are fully prepared to defend our territorial integrity and sovereignty. Let there be no misunderstanding or miscalculation about our resolve to maintain the independence and solidarity of Pakistan.

My dear countrymen, in the end I would again like to impress upon you that it is an hour of trial for the nation. Each one of us has to do his utmost honestly and sincerely so that our homeland, which is so dear to us, continue its march on the path of progress. No sacrifice would be too great to bring back economic stability and to ensure unity of Pakistan. What we need to meet this challenge is the revival of the spirit and enthusiasm with which we succeeded in establishing Pakistan and the firm determination and resolute will which we have on many occasions shown in defending our country from internal and external threats. Our enemies are gloating on false hopes of disunity amongst our ranks. They have tried their level best to undo our dear country but they forget that they are dealing with a people whose life is pulsating with the love of the Holy Prophet, whose hearts are illuminated with the light of *Iman* and who have an unshakable reliance on the help of Almighty Allah.

Let us rise to the occasion, let us come up to the expectations of the Father of the Nation and once again prove it to the enemies that we are a united nation always ready to frustrate their designs and foil their evil intentions. Each one of us is a Mujahid and any effort to harm will spell their own disaster. I have full faith in the patriotism of our people and I am sure that every single Pakistani will cooperate with me whole-heartedly

APPENDIXES

in the achievement of our common goal, namely, the restoration of democracy in the country, preservation of its integrity and solidarity and the betterment of the lot of the common man. May Allah grant us success in our efforts. God be with you. God bless you all.
PAKISTAN PAINDABAD.

Source: *Pakistan Horizon*, XXIV, No. 3, pp. 111–12.

SOUTH ASIAN CRISIS

7. U Thant's Memorandum to the President of the Security Council, 19 July 1971

For some months now members of the Security Council and many other members of the United Nations have been deeply preoccupied with developments in East Pakistan and adjacent Indian States and their consequences or possible consequences. I, myself, expressed my concern over the situation to President Yahya Khan shortly after the events of March 1971 and have been in continuous touch with the Governments of Pakistan and India, both through their Permanent Representatives at the United Nations and through other contacts. In these exchanges I have been acutely aware of the dual responsibility of the United Nations, including the Secretary-General under the Charter, both to observe the provisions of article 2, paragraph 7 and to work within the framework of international economic and social cooperation to help promote and ensure human well-being and humanitarian principles.

It was with this latter responsibility in mind that I appealed for assistance both for refugees from East Pakistan now in India and for the population of East Pakistan. In order to channel assistance given in response to those appeals, I designated the United Nations High Commissioner for Refugees as focal point for assistance to refugees in India and appointed with the agreement of the Government of Pakistan, a Representative in Dacca in order to make as effective use as possible of international assistance made available for relief of the population of East Pakistan. Both of these humanitarian efforts have been reported upon in detail elsewhere and the Economic and Social Council held a full discussion on both operations on 16 July 1971. Based on statements to the Council by the United Nations High Commissioner for Refugees and the Assistant Secretary-General for Inter-Agency Affairs, I take this opportunity to express my warm gratitude to the Governments, United Nations Agencies and programmes and to the voluntary organizations which have responded generously to my appeals. I also wish to express my appreciation to the Governments of India and Pakistan for their co-ordination with my representatives in the field.

As weeks have passed since last March, I have become increasingly uneasy and apprehensive at the steady deterioration of the situation in the region in almost all its aspects. In spite of the generous response of the international community to my appeals for assistance for refugees from East Pakistan now in India, the money and supplies made available are still nowhere near sufficient and the Indian Government still faces the appalling and disruptive problem of caring for an unforeseeable period of time for millions of refugees whose number is still increasing. In East Pakistan international and governmental efforts to cope with results of

APPENDIXES

two successive disasters, one of them natural, are increasingly hampered by the lack of substantial progress towards a political reconciliation and the consequent effect on law, order and public administration in East Pakistan. There is a danger that serious food shortages and even famine could soon add to the suffering of the population unless conditions can be improved to the point where a large scale relief programme can be effective. Equally serious is the undoubted fact that reconciliation, an improved political atmosphere and success of relief efforts are indispensable prerequisites for the return of any large proportion of the refugees now in India. The situation is one in which political, economic and social factors have produced a series of vicious circles which largely frustrate efforts of the authorities concerned and of international community to deal with the vast humanitarian problems involved.

These human tragedies have consequences in a far wider sphere. Violent emotions aroused could have repercussions on the relations of religious and ethnic groups in the subcontinent as a whole and relationship of the Government of India and Pakistan is also a major component of the problem. Conflict between principles of the territorial integrity of States and of self-determination has often before in history given rise to fratricidal strife and has provoked in recent years highly emotional reactions in the international community. In the present case there is an additional element of danger, for the crisis is unfolding in the context of long standing and unresolved differences between India and Pakistan, differences which gave rise to open warfare only six years ago. Although there can be no question of deep desire of both Governments for peace, tension between them shows no sign of subsiding. The situation on the borders of East Pakistan is particularly disturbing. Border clashes, clandestine raids and acts of sabotage appear to be becoming more frequent and this is all the more serious since refugees must cross this disturbed border, if repatriation is to become a reality. Nor can any of us here in the United Nations afford to forget that a major conflict in the subcontinent could all too easily expand.

In the tragic circumstances such as those prevailing in the sub-continent, it is all too easy to make moral judgements. It is far more difficult to face up to political and human realities of the situation and to help the peoples concerned to find a way out of their enormous difficulties. It is this latter course which in my view the United Nations must follow.

I do not think I have painted too dark a picture of the present situation and of its possible consequences. In the light of information available to me I have reluctantly come to the conclusion that the time is past when the international community can continue to stand by watching the situation deteriorate and hoping that relief programmes, humanitarian efforts and good intentions will be enough to turn the tide of human misery and potential disaster. I am deeply concerned about the possible consequences of the present situation not only in the humanitarian sense but also as a potential threat to peace and security and for its bearing on the future of the United Nations as an effective instrument for international co-operation and action. It seems to me that the present tragic situation, in which humanitarian, economic and political problems are mixed in such a way as almost to defy any distinction between them, presents a challenge to the United Nations as a whole which must be met. Other situations of this kind may well occur in the future. If the Organization faces up to such a situation now it may be able to develop new skill and new strength required to face future situations of this kind.

It is for these reasons that I am taking the unusual step of reporting to the President of the Council on a question which has not been inscribed on the Council's agenda. The political aspects of this matter are of such far-reaching importance that the Secretary-General is not in a position to suggest precise courses of action before members of the Security Council have taken note of the problem. I believe, however, that the United Nations with its long experience in peace-keeping and with its varied resources for conciliation and persuasion, must and should now play a more forthright role in attempting both to mitigate human tragedy which has already taken place and to avert further deterioration of the situation.

The Security Council, the world's highest body for the maintenance of international peace and security, is in a position to consider with the utmost attention and concern, the present situation and to reach some agreed conclusions as to the measures which might be taken. Naturally it is for members of the Council themselves to decide whether such consideration should take place formally or informally, in public or in private. My primary purpose at this stage is to provide a basis and an opportunity for such discussions to take place and to express my grave concern that all possible ways and means should be explored which might help to resolve this tragic situation.

The suggestion is simply that a small number of representatives of the High Commissioner might take to field with strictly limited terms of reference and on an experimental basis. The area in which these representatives might operate would be decided upon by the Governments concerned in consultation with the United Nations High Commissioner for Refugees. This suggestion was made with the sole aim of facilitating, if possible, repatriation of refugees.

The other document (the memorandum by U Thant to the President of the Security Council) deals with a far-reaching political matter relating to international peace and security and is primarily within the competence of the Security Council, apart from the Secretary-General's competence under the Charter in such matters. I recall that at its 1329th meeting on 2 December 1966, members of the Security Council unanimously endorsed a statement that 'they fully respect his – the Secretary-General's – position and his action in bringing basic issues confronting the Organisation and disturbing developments in many parts of the world to their notice'.

The memorandum is not an official document of the Security Council and was intended to record my own deep concern with the wider potential

APPENDIXES

dangers of the situation in the region and to provide an opportunity for an exchange of views among members of the Security Council on the potentially very grave situation.

Source: *Pakistan Horizon*, XXIV, No. 3, pp. 127–30.

SOUTH ASIAN CRISIS

8. The Indo-Soviet Treaty of Peace, Friendship and Co-operation, 9 August 1971

Desirous of expanding and consolidating the existing relations of sincere friendship between them,
Believing that the further development of friendship and co-operation meets the basic national interests of lasting peace in Asia and the world,
Determined to promote the consolidation of universal peace and security and to make steadfast efforts for the relaxation of international tensions and the final eliminations of the remnants of colonialism,
Upholding their firm faith in the principles of peaceful co-existence and co-operation between States with different political and social systems,
Convinced that in the world today international problems can only be solved by co-operation and not by conflict,
Reaffirming their determination to abide by the purposes and principles of the United Nations Charter,
The Republic of India on the one side, and the Union of Soviet Socialist Republics on the other side,
Have decided to conclude the present treaty, for which purposes the following plenipotentiaries have been appointed:
On behalf of the Republic of India: Sardar Swaran Singh, Minister of External Affairs.
On behalf of the Union of Soviet Socialist Republics: Mr A. A. Gromyko, Minister of Foreign Affairs.
Who, having each presented their credentials, which are found to be in proper form and due order, have agreed as follows:

(ARTICLE I)

The High Contracting Parties solemnly declare that enduring peace and friendship shall prevail between the two countries and their peoples. Each party shall respect the independence, sovereignty and territorial integrity of the other party and refrain from interfering in the other's internal affairs. The High Contracting Parties shall continue to develop and consolidate the relations of sincere friendship, good neighbourliness and comprehensive co-operation existing between them on the basis of the aforesaid principles as well as those of equality and mutual benefit.

(ARTICLE II)

Guided by the desire to contribute in every possible way to ensure enduring peace and security of their people, the High Contracting Parties declare their determination to continue their efforts to preserve and to strengthen peace in Asia and throughout the world, to halt the arms race and to achieve general and complete disarmament, including both nuclear and conventional, under effective international control.

APPENDIXES

(ARTICLE III)

Guided by their loyalty to the lofty ideal of equality of all peoples and nations, irrespective of race or creed, the High Contracting Parties condemn colonialism and racialism in all forms and manifestations, and reaffirm their determination to strive for their final and complete elimination.

The High Contracting Parties shall cooperate with other States to achieve these aims and to support the just aspirations of the peoples in their struggle against colonialism and racial domination.

(ARTICLE IV)

The Repubic of India respects the peace-loving policy of the Union of Soviet Socialist Republics aimed at strengthening friendship and co-operation with all nations.

The Union of Soviet Socialist Republics respects India's policy of non-alignment and reaffirms that this policy constitutes an important factor in the maintenance of universal peace and international security and in the lessening of tensions in the world.

(ARTICLE V)

Deeply interested in ensuring universal peace and security, attaching great importance to their mutual co-operation in the international field for achieving these aims, the High Contracting Parties will maintain regular contacts with each other on major international problems affecting the interests of both the States by means of meetings, and exchanges of views between their leading statesmen, visits by official delegations and special envoys of the two Governments, and through diplomatic channels.

(ARTICLE VI)

Attaching great importance to economic, scientific and technological co-operation between them, the High Contracting Parties will continue to consolidate and expand mutually advantageous and comprehensive co-operation in these fields as well as expand trade, transport and communications between them on the basis of the principles of equality, mutual benefit and most-favoured nation treatment, subject to the existing agreements and the special arrangements with contiguous countries as specified in the Indo–Soviet trade agreement of 26 December 1970.

(ARTICLE VII)

The High Contracting Parties shall promote further development of ties and contacts between them in the fields of science, art, literature, education, public health, press, radio, television, cinema, tourism and sports.

(ARTICLE VIII)

In accordance with the traditional friendship established between the two countries, each of the High Contracting Parties solemnly declares that it shall not enter into or participate in any military alliance directed against the other Party.

Each High Contracting Party undertakes to abstain from any aggression against the other Party and to prevent the use of its territory for the commission of any act which might inflict military damage on the other High Contracting Party.

(ARTICLE IX)

Each High Contracting Party undertakes to abstain from providing any assistance to any third country that engages in armed conflict with the other Party. In the event of either being subjected to an attack or a threat thereof, the High Contracting Parties shall immediately enter into mutual consultations in order to remove such threat and to take appropriate effective measures to ensure peace and the security of their countries.

(ARTICLE X)

Each High Contracting Party solemnly declares that it shall not enter into any obligation, secret or public, with one or more States, which is incompatible with this Treaty. Each High Contracting Party further declares that no obligation be entered into, between itself and any other State or States, which might cause military damage to the other Party.

(ARTICLE XI)

This Treaty is concluded for the duration of twenty years and will be automatically extended for each successive period of five years unless either High Contracting Party declares its desire to terminate it by giving notice to the other High Contracting Party twelve months prior to the expiration of the Treaty. The Treaty will be subject to ratification and will come into force on the date of the exchange of Instruments of Ratification which will take place in Moscow within one month of the signing of this Treaty.

(ARTICLE XII)

Any difference of interpretation of any Article or Articles of this Treaty which may arise between the High Contracting Parties will be settled bilaterally by peaceful means in a spirit of mutual respect and understanding.

The said Plenipotentiaries have signed the present Treaty in Hindi, Russian and English, all text being equally authentic and have affixed thereto their seals.

Done in New Delhi on the Ninth day of August in the year One Thousand Nine Hundred and Seventy One.

APPENDIXES

ON BEHALF of the UNION OF SOVIET SOCIALIST REPUBLICS.
(Sd.) A. A. Gromyko,
Minister of External Affairs,
ON BEHALF of the REPUBLIC OF INDIA,
(Sd.) Swaran Singh,
Minister of External Affairs.

Source: *Survival*, XIII, October 1971, pp. 351–3.

SOUTH ASIAN CRISIS

9. Joint Statement by Mr Andrei Gromyko and Mr Swaran Singh in New Delhi, 12 August 1971

On the invitation of the Government of India, the Minister of Foreign Affairs of the USSR, His Excellency Mr A. A. Gromyko, paid an official visit to India from 8 to 12 August 1971.

During his stay in New Delhi the Minister of Foreign Affairs of the USSR called on the President of India, Mr V. V. Giri, and was received by the Prime Minister of India, Mrs Indira Gandhi. He also met the Food and Agriculture Minister, Mr Fakhruddin Ali Ahmed, the Finance Minister, Mr Y. B. Chavan, and the Defence Minister, Mr Jagjivan Ram. He had several meetings and talks with Mr Swaran Singh, Minister of External Affairs of India.

The meetings and talks were held in an atmosphere of warm friendship and cordiality. It was noted with deep satisfaction that the friendly relations and fruitful co-operation between the Soviet Union and India in the political, economic, cultural, technical and scientific fields are developing successfully and hold great promise for further expansion. The political and legal basis for this co-operation is further strengthened by the Treaty of Peace, Friendship and Co-operation between the USSR and India, which was signed in New Delhi by Mr Swaran Singh, Minister of External Affairs of India, and Mr A. A. Gromyko, Minister of Foreign Affairs of the USSR.

Both sides consider that the conclusion of the treaty is an outstanding historic event for their two countries. The treaty is a logical outcome of the relations of sincere friendship, respect, mutual trust and the varied ties which have been established between the Soviet Union and India in the course of many years and have stood the test of time. It corresponds to the basic interests of the Indian and Soviet peoples and opens up wide prospects for raising the fruitful co-operation between the USSR and India to a higher level. Alongside other provisions concerning bilateral Soviet–Indian relations the treaty provides for the two sides maintaining regular contacts with each other on major international problems and holding mutual consultations with a view to taking appropriate effective measures to safeguard the peace and security of their countries.

The treaty between the USSR and India is a real act of peace expressing the community of policy and aspirations of the USSR and India in the struggle to strengthen peace in Asia and throughout the world and for safeguarding international security. All provisions of the treaty serve these purposes.

The treaty is not directed against anyone; it is meant to be a factor in developing friendship and good neighbourliness, in keeping with the principles of the UN Charter.

APPENDIXES

The Government of India and the USSR are confident that the conclusion of the Treaty of Peace, Friendship and Co-operation will meet with complete approval on the part of all those who are really interested in the preservation of peace in Asia and throughout the world and on the part of the Governments of all peace-loving States.

In the course of the meetings and talks, both sides noted with satisfaction that their positions on various problems discussed were identical or very close. The Minister of External Affairs of India explained the heavy burden placed on India's resources due to over 7 million refugees who had entered India. Both sides, after a detailed discussion, reiterated their firm conviction that there can be no military solution and considered it necessary that urgent steps be taken in East Pakistan for the achievement of a political solution and for the creation of conditions of safety for the return of the refugees to their homes which alone would answer the interests of the entire people of Pakistan and the cause of the preservation of peace in the area.

The Indian side expressed its gratitude for the understanding of the problem shown by the Soviet Union as was evident from the appeal addressed on 2 April 1971, to the President by the Chairman of the Supreme Soviet of the USSR, Mr N. V. Podgorny.

Both sides held the view that outside interference in the affairs of Indo-China should immediately cease. They consider that it will be futile to attempt to impose any settlement not acceptable to the peoples of the area. They welcomed the recent seven-point proposal of the Provisional Revolutionary Government of South Vietnam as a concrete step forward which could form the basis of a peaceful political settlement.

On West Asia, both sides were convinced of the urgent need for the implementation of the resolution of the Security Council of 22 November 1967, so that the consequences of aggression are liquidated.

Both sides considered that all international problems, including border disputes, must be settled by peaceful negotiations and the use of force or the threat of use of force is impermissible for their settlement.

Both sides declare that they are strongly in favour of an early agreement on general and complete disarmament, including both nuclear and conventional weapons, under effective international control.

The Minister of Foreign Affairs of the USSR expressed his gratitude for the cordial reception given to him by the Government of India.

Source: Naik, pp. 147–48.

SOUTH ASIAN CRISIS

10. *Joint Statement on the Occasion of Mrs Indira Gandhi's Visit to Moscow, 29 September 1971*

(This is the text released by the Indian side. In the Soviet text 'East Bengal' is replaced by 'East Pakistan'.)

At the invitation of the Government of the Union of Soviet Socialist Republics, Mrs Indira Gandhi, Prime Minister of the Republic of India, paid a visit to the USSR from 27 to 29 September 1971.

The head of the Government of friendly India and her party were accorded a warm welcome testifying to the profound feelings of sincere friendship and respect of the Soviet people towards the great Indian people and India's leaders.

During her visit in Moscow, the Prime Minister laid wreaths on the mausoleum of V. I. Lenin and the Tomb of the Unknown Soldier.

At a solemn meeting of the Indo–Soviet friendship, the Soviet public warmly greeted the head of the Indian Government. The Lomonosov State University of Moscow conferred on Mrs Indira Gandhi the degree of Doctor of Science, *honoris causa*.

The Prime Minister of India, Mrs Indira Gandhi, had talks and discussions with the General Secretary of the Central Committee of the Communist Party of the Soviet Union, Mr L. I. Brezhnev; the Chairman of the Supreme Soviet of the USSR, Mr N. V. Podgorny; and the Chairman of the Council of Ministers, Mr A. N. Kosygin.

Taking part in the talks were, on the Soviet side: Mr N. S. Potolichev, Mr S. A. Skatchkov, Mr V. V. Kuznetsov, Mr N. P. Firyubin, Mr N. M. Pegov, and Mr A. A. Fomin.

On the Indian side, Mr D. P. Dhar, Mr T. N. Kaul, Mr K. S. Shelvankar, Mr D. R. Sathe, Mr N. P. S. Menon, Mr A. P. Venkateswaran, Mr A. K. Damodharan, Mr K. K. Bhargava, Mr S. V. Purushottam and Mr N. M. Malhotra.

The talks, which were held in an atmosphere of cordiality and mutual understanding, covered a wide range of subjects of Soviet–Indian bilateral relations as well as important current international problems of mutual interest.

Both sides expressed their profound satisfaction at the successful development of relations of friendship and fruitful co-operation between the Soviet Union and India in the political, economic, trade, scientific, technical, cultural and other fields.

They declared their conviction that this co-operation acquires still more firm political and legal basis in the Treaty of Peace, Friendship and Co-operation between the USSR and India, signed in New Delhi on 9 August 1971.

APPENDIXES

The two sides fully agreed that the conclusion of the treaty is an event of outstanding and historic importance for both countries and has further strengthened the relations of sincere friendship, respect, mutual confidence and good-neighbourly co-operation existing between the Soviet Union and India.

The conclusion of the treaty reaffirms the Soviet Union–Indian friendship is based not on any transient factor but on long-term vital interests of the peoples of both countries and their desire to develop to the utmost many-sided co-operation with each other for the purpose of economic and social progress for safeguarding peace as well as security of both countries.

Both sides declared their firm determination to be guided by the letter and spirit of the treaty in regard to the further development of Soviet–Indian relations.

They expressed their satisfaction at the fact that the treaty has met with the full and unreserved support of the peoples of the Soviet Union and India and has been widely welcomed throughout the world.

They noted with satisfaction the successful development of mutually beneficial economic and technical co-operation between the two countries and emphasized the fact that there are favourable prospects for the further expansion and deepening of such co-operation, particularly in the fields of iron and steel industry, including special steel, alloys and nonferrous metallurgy, survey, exploration and refining of oil and natural gas and in the field of petro-chemical industry.

The two sides expressed satisfaction at the recent steps taken by them to identify new forms of mutual co-operation in the economic and technical fields, including such spheres as space research, utilisation of nuclear energy for peaceful purposes, productive co-operation between industrial enterprises of both countries, etc. They consider it necessary to identify additional new fields in which such mutual co-operation could be expanded.

In this connection, agreement was reached that experts of both countries would meet and work out specific proposals on the above-mentioned questions.

The two sides decided to set up an inter-Government commission on economic, scientific, and technical co-operation. Both sides recognized the need, in accordance with the treaty, to develop contacts and ties at different levels, to enlarge and to make more comprehensive the exchange of views between the Governments of the USSR and India on major international problems.

NON-ALIGNMENT

The Soviet side expressed its respect for India's policy of non-alignment aimed at lessening tensions in Asia and throughout the world, for strengthening peace and international co-operation.

The Indian side expressed its respect for the Soviet Union's peaceful foreign policy aimed at strengthening peace, friendship and international co-operation.

SOUTH ASIAN CRISIS

The two sides paid primary attention to the development of the situation in Asia, to the hotbeds of tensions and military conflicts existing there, to the discussion of ways to stop and prevent the acts of aggression and to consolidate the foundations of peace on the Asian continent.

The two sides expressed their concern over the grave situation which has arisen on the Indian sub-continent as a result of the recent events in East Bengal and declared their determination to continue efforts aimed at the preservation of peace in that region.

The Prime Minister of India informed the Soviet side that the presence in India of over nine million refugees from East Bengal has engendered serious social and political tensions and economic strains in India.

This has caused a serious set-back to the socio-economic programmes of India.

The Soviet side highly appreciated India's humane approach to the problem created by the influx of these refugees from East Bengal and expressed its understanding of difficulties confronting friendly India in connection with the mass inflow of refugees.

The Soviet side took into account the statement by the Prime Minister that the Government of India is fully determined to take all necessary measures to stop the inflow of refugees from East Bengal to India and to ensure that those refugees who are already in India return to their homeland without delay.

The Soviet side reaffirmed its position regarding the problem of refugees and other questions which have arisen as a result of the events in East Bengal as laid down in the appeal of the Chairman of the Presidium of the USSR Supreme Soviet, Mr N. V. Podgorny, to the President of Pakistan, General Yahya Khan, on 2 April 1971.

Taking note of the developments in East Bengal since 25 March 1971, both sides consider that the interests of the preservation of peace demand that urgent measures should be taken to reach a political solution of the problems which have arisen there paying regard to the wishes, the inalienable rights and lawful interests of the people of East Bengal as well as the speediest and safe return of the refugees to their homeland in conditions safeguarding their honour and dignity.

Taking into account the seriousness of the situation which has developed in the Indian sub-continent, the two sides agreed to maintain further mutual contacts and to continue to exchange views on the questions arising in this connection.

The two sides expressed their profound concern over the situation in South-East Asia and pronounced themselves in favour of the necessity to withdraw all foreign troops from Indo-China in order to ensure peace and security for the people of that region, the realization of their legitimate rights to shape their own future in accordance with their national interests and without any foreign interference.

They welcomed the recent seven-point proposal by the Provisional Revolutionary Government of South Vietnam as an important step

APPENDIXES

towards the creation of a basis for a peaceful political settlement, and declared their support for these proposals.

The two sides expressed their serious concern over the situation in the Middle East. They stressed the need for all States concerned to make efforts with a view to achieve a lasting, stable and just peace on the basis of the full implementation of the UN Security Council resolution of 22 November 1967.

Desirous of contributing to the improvement of the international situation, the Government of India highly appreciates the proposal to convene an all-European conference on the questions of security and co-operation as an important step aimed at the relaxation of tensions not only on the European continent but throughout the world.

Both sides believe that the cessation of the arms race and the achievement of general and complete disarmament, covering both nuclear and conventional types of weapons under strict and effective international control, are of primary importance for the preservation and strengthening of peace and security.

In the opinion of the two sides the convening of a world disarmament conference with the participation of all countries for achieving practicable and generally acceptable ways of solving pressing disarmament problems could be of great importance. The two sides consider it important to achieve in the near future an agreement on the prohibition of the development, production and stockpiling of biological weapons and toxins and on their destruction as the step on the way to the complete prohibition of chemical and biological methods of warfare.

The Prime Minister of India reaffirmed that the Indian Ocean area should be made a zone of peace. The Soviet side expressed its readiness to study this question and to solve it together with other powers on an equal basis.

The Soviet Union and India call for the speedy and complete elimination of the vestiges of colonialism and unqualified implementation of the UN declaration on the granting of independence to colonial countries and peoples. They unequivocally condemn racism and apartheid in all forms and manifestations.

The two sides reaffirmed their adherence to the principles of peaceful coexistence among States with different social systems and pronounced themselves in favour of all questions at issue in relations between countries being solved by peaceful means.

The Soviet Union and India attach great importance to the United Nations. Both sides confirmed their determination to seek the strengthening of the UN and the enhancing of its effectiveness in maintaining universal peace and security in accordance with the UN Charter.

Both sides expressed their confidence that the visit of the Prime Minister of India to the Soviet Union and the talks and discussions which were held with Soviet leaders during the visit will promote the further development of friendly co-operation between the two countries and the strengthening of peace and international security.

SOUTH ASIAN CRISIS

The Prime Minister of India extended a cordial invitation to the General Secretary of the Central Committee of the CPSU, Mr L. I. Brezhnev, and the Chairman of the Council of Ministers of the USSR, Mr A. N. Kosygin, to visit India. The invitations were accepted with thanks.

Source: Naik, *op. cit.*, pp. 150–54.

APPENDIXES

11. President Yahya Khan's Broadcast of 12 October 1971

My dear countrymen,
Assalam-o-Alaikum,
I am addressing you today on a matter of grave concern to all of us. As you are aware, the hostile forces which opposed the establishment of Pakistan have never accepted its existence and have constantly been on the look-out to weaken us and to ultimately destroy this country. In spite of our sincere endeavours towards amity and friendship over the past 24 years I regret to say that India has never missed any opportunity to bring harm to Pakistan. Her hostile designs towards us have been evident from a number of actions that she has taken and continues to take against us.

The forcible occupation of Kashmir, the attack on Pakistan in 1965 and the construction of Farraka Barrage despite our persistent efforts to point out the terrible misery that it would cause the people of East Pakistan, are some of the major examples of India's efforts to weaken us and to harm us in every possible way. There are innumerable instances of their ill-will towards Pakistan.

India's latest efforts to disintegrate Pakistan are well-known to all of you. She has tried to cut away East Pakistan from the rest of the country in collusion with certain secessionists in that wing by assisting the miscreants with arms, ammunition and funds and sending infiltrators to cause damage to life and property of the patriotic East Pakistanis. She has shelled and continues to shell a number of areas in that wing with her artillery and mortars.

The world is gradually coming to know that all major sabotage activities like the blowing up of bridges and disruption of communications in East Pakistan are being conducted by the Indian infiltrators in the name of the secessionists. Frogmen and saboteurs trained and sent by India attempted to damage food-ships in and around our ports in the Eastern Wing, but have been dealt with by our Armed Forces. By such acts India's aim cannot be anything else but to create famine conditions and to starve the people in East Pakistan. So much for their claims of sympathy for the people of our Eastern Wing.

In addition to these hostile activities, India has moved forward army formations of all types including infantry, armour and artillery all round the borders of East Pakistan. Similarly, Indian Air Force units have been located in positions from where they can pose a direct threat to that wing. In the West also, a large number of units and formations have been moved out of their peace stations and brought forward towards our borders.

It is obvious from these moves and the posture adopted by her armed forces that there is a serious possibility of aggression by India against

SOUTH ASIAN CRISIS

Pakistan. These feverish military preparations can lead to but one conclusion, namely that she can launch a war of aggression against Pakistan at short notice.

While there is no reason for undue alarm I have described to you the hostile moves of India, as the Nation must know and realize the dangerous situation the country is facing today.

However let me assure you that the Government and the armed services are fully alive to the situation and are aware of the imminent danger of aggression against this country by India in both wings. Your valiant armed forces are fully prepared to defend and protect every inch of the sacred soil of Pakistan. With complete faith in the righteousness of their cause and trust in the help of Allah our armed forces will successfully meet the challenge of aggression as they have done in the past.

But let me remind you that in the event of war, or equally grave emergencies, it is not enough that only the Government and the armed forces should be ready to meet the challenge. Each one of you has a responsibility and duty to perform. In the present critical situation everyone must work hard with the spirit of a true Mujahid in his own particular sphere. With the aggressive forces at our doorstep we must sink all our differences, eschew parochial and provincial prejudices and eliminate suspicion and mistrust. People in every walk of life must make positive efforts to bring about harmony and promote unity so that the whole nation stands up like a solid rock in defence of the country. I have no doubt that the people will rise to the occasion and join hands with their Armed Forces to meet the challenge to our security and integrity with patriotism and courage.

Indian leaders by their bellicose statements have left no doubt in anybody's mind about their intentions. They have been openly talking about unilateral action against Pakistan and some of them have deliberately sought to whip up war frenzy. A number of important Indian leaders have been visiting foreign capitals to vilify and malign Pakistan and to solicit support for the cause of secessionist elements who have crossed over to India. The world, however, can see through the Indian game and cannot be hoodwinked by her propaganda. All peace-loving countries of the world have understood with sympathy the problem that we are facing and striving to resolve. A number of friendly countries have given us assistance directly and through the United Nations, for the relief and rehabilitation of displaced persons and for the reconstruction of East Pakistan's economy. I would like to express my thanks to them.

We have been gratified by the reassuring attitude of a very large number of countries who have fully supported the stand that the events in East Pakistan are our internal matter and that no one has any right to tell us how to conduct our affairs. Recently, I sent special envoys to call on the leaders of some African and Latin American countries who were most forthright in upholding our action in suppressing internal rebellion and disorder.

Heart-warming messages expressing solidarity with our cause have been

APPENDIXES

received from friends in the Muslim World and a number of Asian and African countries. We deeply appreciate the friendship and support by the Government of the People's Republic of China in our just stand. The understanding shown by the United States Government in the present situation is an important contribution to the principle that every nation has a right to find a solution to its own problems.

I have noted with interest the keen desire of Premier Kosygin expressed during a recent speech at Moscow for the maintenance of peace in the sub-continent and that the Soviet Union would do everything possible to prevent a breach of peace. I welcome this and sincerely hope that the Soviet Union would use its influence to persuade India to refrain from indulging in acts which could lead to an armed conflict. I however regret that Premier Kosygin made no mention of the various positive steps taken by me to transfer power to the elected representatives of the people as well as to facilitate the return and rehabilitation of displaced persons. Many proposals of the United Nations like posting of UN observers to facilitate the return of displaced persons and defusing the explosive situation on the borders have been welcomed by us but spurned by the Indians. This is not the way towards peace.

As a result of general amnesty granted by the Government and the adequate arrangements for their rehabilitation about two hundred thousand displaced persons have come back to Pakistan, but India [is] still holding back a large proportion, although their number is grossly exaggerated by her. In this regard, we would welcome any international agency to assess the correct number of displaced persons. This proposal has also been turned down by the Indians.

The obvious conclusion one can draw from this is that the bloated figures, as given out by India can only be for one purpose and that is to attract maximum external aid under false pretences. She is forcibly keeping displaced persons in a pitiable state in stinking slums and camps and does not allow them to return. We would be grateful to all friendly countries if they would influence India to regard the issue of displaced persons as a human problem and instead of making political and financial capital out of it, let them return to their homes. International community should also impress upon India the need to desist from interfering in our internal affairs and withdraw her forces from our borders. This is the only solution for reducing tension in this area and saving it from a disastrous war which would result in colossal damage to life and property in both countries.

It is our sincere belief that whether it be for the creation of a climate conducive to the return of the displaced persons or for the normalisation of the situation, it is essential that India and Pakistan should work out ways and means to reduce tension and allow normalcy to return at the earliest. Having this in mind we have accepted in the past and will always be prepared to reconsider any positive initiative from any quarter which would help to realize these objectives.

Here, I would like to address a word to my countrymen who are living

SOUTH ASIAN CRISIS

abroad and who were misled by the horrifying tales born in the imagination of Indian propagandists and their foreign protagonists. I am glad that facts are now becoming known to them. I wish it were possible for them to come home to see things for themselves and to discover how the Indian propagandists have distorted the truth.

I have repeatedly said, and I say it again, that we are a peace-loving country and want to live in peace with all nations of the world, particularly with our neighbours. We have no desire to interfere in the affairs of other people, nor shall we allow others to interfere in ours. Undisturbed and lasting peace is essential for the prosperity and well-being of our people. We have throughout done our utmost to avoid conflict and exercised every restraint in the interest of peace. However, unilateral efforts by us alone in such a situation are not enough and there has to be response and reciprocity from India. We know and I hope that our neighbour also realizes, that armed conflicts do not solve any problem. In fact such conflicts create more problems and hamper the pace of progress. We firmly believe that all outstanding issues between the two countries, including those of Kashmir and Farraka Barrage, should be settled peacefully in a just and equitable manner. While we desire peace, we are fully prepared to defend and protect our territorial integrity and sovereignty. Let there be no misunderstanding or miscalculation on that account.

I would like to apprise you of the details of my plan of transfer of power which I had announced on the 18th of June this year and which was followed by a statement by me on 18 September. I might mention here that the plan was fully discussed with the political leaders and they were informed in clear terms of what I was going to announce.

As you are aware, I have already taken certain steps towards the fulfilment of the plan. Arrangements have been made by the Chief Election Commissioner to hold by-elections to fill in the vacancies in the National Assembly as well as the Provincial Assembly in East Pakistan.

The Constitution will be published by 20th of December and the National Assembly will be summoned on 27th of December 1971.

You are also aware that the National Assembly will have every opportunity of suggesting amendments to the Constitution and a special easier procedure for facilitating this task has been evolved for the initial period of 90 days. This procedure would be that the Assembly may propose an amendment to the Constitution by a simple majority of the total number of seats of the Assembly and a consensus of the Provinces, that is to say by a minimum of 25% of the total seats of each Province. For purposes of arriving at these figures, a fraction will be taken as a whole. I might add that this period of 90 days includes the time taken for consideration or reconsideration of proposed amendments by me.

I thus visualize that proposed amendments will continue to be submitted to me throughout this period from its commencement. Last amendments, however, may be submitted to me by the House not later than 80 days from the commencement of the three months period in

APPENDIXES

order to give me at least 10 days for their reconsiderations. Thus the completion of the whole of this process will not exceed a total period of 90 days.

The polls for the National Assembly will be completed on the 23rd of December, 1971. The National Assembly will be summoned to meet on the 27th of December under the chairmanship of the oldest member of the House who will be nominated by me. This will be followed by oath-taking by the members and the election of the Speaker and the Deputy Speaker.

In order to accelerate the process of transfer of power, the Central Government will be formed soon after the inaugural session of the National Assembly. The 90 days period for submission and consideration of amendments will commence after the Central Government has been formed.

The Provincial Assemblies in West Pakistan can be summoned at short notice after completing the elections for women's seats and a few by-elections. As regards East Pakistan the election schedule for the by-elections of that Provincial Assembly has already been announced by the Chief Election Commissioner. That is to say by-elections for 105 seats are being held along with the 78 seats of the National Assembly from the 12th to the 23rd of December 1971 and the polls for 88 seats of the Provincial Assembly will be held from the 18th of December 1971 to the 7th of January 1972.

The way for the functioning of Provincial Assemblies in the Provinces will thus have been cleared and the stage for the formation of Governments in the Provinces would have been set.

My dear countrymen, I have explained my plan for the transfer of power in detail. As I said earlier, this plan was made fully known to the political leaders and now I have explained it to the nation. There should be no longer any cause for speculation. While I would expect all political parties to sincerely devote their attention towards the fulfilment of the plan, I would appeal to the leaders and the nation not to forget the grave danger of the external and internal threats to the solidarity and integrity of our country.

The stakes are so high and the danger so grave that on no account should we be diverted from our main objectives of the defence of the country and the achievement of the democratic way of life. Any actions or statements by any one in the country which would divert the nation from these aims cannot be patriotic. I would appeal to my nation particularly to the national Press and political leaders to desist from causing or giving ear to the speculations and rumours, which if not curbed, can only seriously hamper the process that I have spelt out earlier and would only gladden the hearts of our enemies.

Let the nation stand up as one man and march ahead towards the achievement of our goal. Let us show to the world what stuff we Pakistanis are made of. I have no doubt in my mind that the people of Pakistan whose patriotic fervour is unmatched, whose hearts are pulsating with the love of the Holy Prophet (may peace be upon him) and whose greatest strength

SOUTH ASIAN CRISIS

is that of their Imam and who rely on the help of Allah, will rise to the occasion and meet any challenge from any direction.

In the end, I would again like to impress upon you that there is no cause for undue alarm, but there certainly is no room for complacency. The situation must be faced in a calm and cool manner. We must be vigilant and make full preparations to meet any threat to our integrity and sovereignty. Let us sink all our differences and once again prove it to those who have designs against us that we are a united nation firmly resolved to frustrate their plans. No power on earth can cow down a nation of 120 million Mujahids of Islam determined to guard their independence and fulfil their destiny. Let us demonstrate it once again that every single citizen of Pakistan is capable of making supreme sacrifices for the noble cause of the defence of their country.

May Allah help us and grant us success in protecting Pakistan, restoring democracy and raising the standard of living of our people. God be with you, God bless you all.

PAKISTAN PAINDABAD

Source: *Dawn*, 13 October 1971.

12. Mr Chi Peng-fei's Statement of 7 November 1971

A Pakistan delegation, under the leadership of Z. A. Bhutto, visited China from 5 to 8 November. China's Acting Foreign Minister, Chi Peng-fei, gave a banquet in honour of the visiting Pakistani delegation on 7 November 1971. In his welcome speech, Mr Chi Peng-fei said: 'The friendly relations and co-operation between our two countries and the friendship between our two peoples have been consolidated and developed continuously.'

He spoke highly of the Pakistan people who had a glorious tradition of opposing imperialism and expansionism. He said: 'In order to defend their state sovereignty, territorial integrity and national independence, they have waged unremitting struggles against foreign aggressors, interventionists and domestic secessionists. The Pakistan Government has adhered to its foreign policy of independence and contributed to the defence of peace in Asia and the promotion of Afro–Asian solidarity.'

Chi Peng-fei continued: 'Of late, the Indian Government has crudely interfered in Pakistan's internal affairs, carried out subversive activities and military threats against Pakistan by continuing to exploit the East Pakistan question. The Chinese Government and people are greatly concerned over the present tension in the sub-continent. We maintain that the internal affairs of any country must be handled by its own people. The East Pakistan question is the internal affair of Pakistan and a reasonable settlement should be sought by the Pakistan people themselves, and it is absolutely impermissible for any foreign country to carry out interference and subversion under any pretext. Consistently abiding by the Five Principles of peaceful co-existence, the Chinese Government never interferes in the internal affairs of other countries and firmly opposes any country interfering in the internal affairs of other countries. This is our firm and unshakable stand. We believe that the broad masses of the Pakistan people are patriotic and they want to safeguard national unity and unification of the country, oppose internal split and outside interference. It is our hope that the Pakistan people will strengthen their unity and make joint efforts to overcome difficulties and solve their own problems. We have noted that certain persons are truculently exerting pressure on Pakistan by exploiting tension in the sub-continent, in a wild attempt to realize their ulterior motives. The Chinese Government and people have always held that disputes between states should be settled by the two sides concerned through consultations and not by resorting to force. The reasonable proposal put forward recently by President Yahya Khan for the armed forces of India and Pakistan to withdraw from the border respectively and disengage is helpful to easing tension in the sub-continent and should be received with welcome. Our Pakistan friends may rest assured that should Pakistan be subjected to foreign aggression, the Chinese Government and people will, as always, resolutely support the Pakistan Government and people in their just struggle to defend their state sovereignty and national independence.'

Source: Naik, *op cit.*, pp. 155–6.

APPENDIXES

13. Dr Henry Kissinger's Press Briefing of 7 December 1971 and Mr Kenneth Keating's comments

(**A**) Excerpts from a background briefing for a news conference given on 7 December by Henry A. Kissinger, President Nixon's adviser on national security. Senator Barry Goldwater of Arizona obtained the transcript from the White House and inserted it in *The Congressional Record* on 9 December. It constitutes a Nixon Administration summary of American policy at the time of the meeting discussed in the documents made public on 5 January.

OPENING STATEMENT

There have been some comments that the Administration is anti-Indian. This is totally inaccurate. India is a great country. It is the most populous free country. It is governed by democratic procedures.

Americans through all administrations in the postwar period have felt a commitment to the progress and development of India, and the American people have contributed to this to the extent of $10-billion.

Therefore, when we have differed with India, as we have in recent weeks, we do so with great sadness and with great disappointment.

Now let me describe the situation as we saw it, going back to 25 March. 25 March is, of course, the day when the central Government of Pakistan decided to established military rule in East Bengal and started the process which has led to the present situation.

The United States has never supported the particular action that led to this tragic series of events, and the United States has always recognized that this action has consequences which had a considerable impact on India. We have always recognized that the influx of refugees into India produced the danger of communal strife in a country always precariously poised on the edge of communal strife. We have known that it is a strain on the already scarce economic resources of a country in the process of development.

The United States position has been to attempt two efforts simultaneously: one, to ease the human suffering and to bring about the return of the refugees; and secondly, we have attempted to bring about a political resolution of the conflict which generated the refugees in the first place.

Now the United States did not condone what happened in March 1971; on the contrary, the United States has made no new development loans to Pakistan since March 1971.

Secondly, there has been a great deal of talk about military supplies to Pakistan. The fact of the matter is that immediately after the actions in East Pakistan at the end of March of this past year, the United States suspended any new licenses. It stopped the shipment of all military supplies

207

SOUTH ASIAN CRISIS

out of American depots or that were under American Governmental control. The only arms that continued to be shipped to Pakistan were arms on old licenses in commercial channels, and these were spare parts. There were no lethal and end-items involved.

To give you a sense of the magnitude, the United States cut off $35-million worth of arms at the end of March of this year, or early April of this year, immediately after the actions in East Bengal, and continued to ship something less than $5-million worth; whereupon, all the remainder of the pipeline was cut off.

It is true the United States did not make any public declarations on its views of the evolution, because the United States wanted to use its influence with both Delhi and Islamabad to bring about a political settlement that would enable the refugees to return.

We attempted to promote a political settlement, and if I can sum up the difference that may have existed between us and the Government of India, it was this:

We told the Government of India on many occasions – the Secretary of State saw the Indian Ambassador 18 times; I saw him seven times since the end of August on behalf of the President. We all said that political autonomy for East Bengal was the inevitable outcome of political evolution and that we favored it. The difference may have been that the Government of India wanted things so rapidly that it was no longer talking about political evolution, but about political collapse.

We told the Indian Prime Minister when she was here of the Pakistan offer to withdraw their troops unilaterally from the border. There was no response.

We told the Indian Prime Minister when she was here that we would try to arrange negotiations between the Pakistanis and members of the Awami League, specifically approved by Mujibur, who is in prison. We told the Indian Ambassador shortly before his return to India that we were prepared even to discuss with them a political timetable, a precise timetable for the establishment of political autonomy in East Bengal.

When we say that there was no need for military action, we do not say that India did not suffer. We do not say that we are unsympathetic to India's problems or that we do not value India.

This country, which in many respects has had a love affair with India, can only, with enormous pain, accept the fact that military action was taken in our view without adequate cause, and if we express this opinion in the United Nations, we do not do so because we want to support one particular point of view on the subcontinent, or because we want to forego our friendship with what will always be one of the great countries of the world; but because we believe that if, as some of the phrases go, the right of military attack is determined by arithmetic, if political wisdom consists of saying the attacker has 500 million, and, therefore, the United States must always be on the side of the numerically stronger, then we are creating a situation where, in the foreseeable future, we will have international anarchy, and where the period of peace, which is the greatest

APPENDIXES

desire for the President to establish, will be jeopardized; not at first for Americans, necessarily, but for peoples all over the world.

QUESTIONS AND ANSWERS

Q. Why was the first semi-public explanation of the American position one of condemning India, and why this belated explanation that you are now giving? The perception of the world is that the United States regards India as an aggressor; that it is anti-India, and you make a fairly persuasive case here that that is not the case. So why this late date?

A. We were reluctant to believe for a long time that the matter had come down to a naked recourse to force, and we were attempting for the first two weeks of the military operations to see what could be done to quiet it through personal diplomacy conducted by the Department of State.

We made two appeals to the Indian Prime Minister. We appealed also to the Pakistan President, and we appealed also to the Soviet Union.

Now, then, on Friday the situation burst into full-blown war and it was decided to put the facts before the public. Now, I cannot, of course, accept the characterization that you made of the way these facts were put forward: that they were put forward as anti-Indian.

Q. I said the perception of the world public was that the United States was anti-Indian because of the nature of that first background briefing at the State Department on Friday.

A. We are opposed to the use of military force in this crisis, and we do not believe that it was necessary to engage in military action. We believe that what started as a tragedy in East Bengal is now becoming an attempt to dismember a sovereign state and a member of the United Nations.

So the view that was expressed on Saturday is not inconsistent with the view that is expressed today. What was done today is an explanation of the background that led to the statement on Saturday, and it might have been better if we had put the whole case forward.

Source: *New York Herald Tribune*, Paris edition, 6 January 1972.

(B) A slightly paraphrased form of the text of a secret cablegram from Kenneth B. Keating, United States Ambassador to India, to William P. Rogers, the Secretary of State, on 8 December 1971, made available to *The New York Times* by the columnist Jack Anderson:

Mr Keating said he was very interested to read an article by The International Press Service [U.S.I.A.] correspondent in the morning's wireless file reporting 'White House officials'' explanation of development of present conflict and United States role in seeking to avert it. While he appreciated the tactical necessity of justifying the Administration's position publicly, he felt constrained to state that elements of this particular story do not coincide with his knowledge of the events of the past eight months.

SOUTH ASIAN CRISIS

Specifically, the I.P.S. account states that the United States Government's $155-million relief program in East Pakistan was initiated 'at the specific request of the Indian Government'. His recollection, and he referred the State Department to his conversation with Foreign Minister Swaran Singh in New Delhi on 25 May, is that the Government of India was reluctant to see the relief program started in East Pakistan prior to a political settlement on grounds that such an effort might serve to 'bail out Yahya'. [General Mohammad Agha Yahya Khan was the President of Pakistan at the time.]

In noting offer of amnesty for all refugees, story fails to mention qualification in Yahya's 5 September proclamation that amnesty applies to those 'not already charged with specific criminal acts', which Ambassador Keating took to be more than a minor bureaucratic caveat in East Pakistan circumstances.

Story indicates that both the Secretary [Mr Rogers] and Dr Kissinger informed Ambassador Jha [Lakshmi Kant Jha, Indian Ambassador to the United States] that Washington favored autonomy for East Pakistan. Mr Keating said he was aware of our repeated statements that we had no formula for a solution, and our relief that the outcome of negotiations would probably be autonomy if not independence, but he regretted that he was uninformed of any specific statement favoring autonomy.

Also according to story, Jha was informed by department on 19 November that 'Washington and Islamabad [capital of Pakistan] were prepared to discuss a precise timetable for establishing political autonomy for East Pakistan'. Ambassador Keating said the only message he had on record of this conversation [a department message to him on 21 November] makes no reference to this critical fact.

With vast and voluminous efforts of the intelligence community, reporting from both Delhi and Islamabad, and with his own discussions in Washington, Ambassador Keating said he did not understand the statement that 'Washington was not given the slightest inkling that any military operation was in any way imminent'. See [for] example DIAIB, 219–71 of 12 November [Defense Intelligence Agency Intelligence Bulletin No. 219–71, of 12 November] stating specifically that war is 'imminent'.

Statement that Pakistan had authorized U.S. to contact Mujibur through his attorney seems an overstatement, since according to Islamabad 11760 [message from American Embassy in Pakistan] Yahya on 29 November told Ambassador Farland [Joseph Farland, United States Ambassador to Pakistan] nothing more than that a Farland–Brohi meeting would be a good idea since Ambassador Farland would be able to obtain from Brohi at least his general impressions as to the state of the trial and its conduct'. Mr Keating said he was unaware of any specific authorization from Yahya 'to contact Mujibur' through Brohi. [Mr Brohi was apparently the defense attorney for Sheik Mujib, leader of the East Pakistani autonomy movement, then imprisoned and on trial in West Pakistan.] In any case, as we are all only too unhappily aware, Yahya

APPENDIXES

told Ambassador Farland on 2 December [Islamabad 11555] that Brohi allegedly was not interested in seeing him.

The statement on G.O.P. [Government of Pakistan] agreement on distribution by U.N. of relief supplies in East Pakistan obscures the fact that the U.N. never had nor intended to have sufficient personnel in East Pakistan to handle actual distribution, which was always in Pakistani Government hands.

Mr Keating said he made the foregoing comments in the full knowledge that they may not have been privy to all the important facts of this tragedy. On the basis of what he did know, he did not believe those elements of the story [reporting the backgrounder] either add to our position or, perhaps more importantly, to American credibility.

KEATING.

Source: *New York Herald Tribune*, Paris edition, 6 January 1972.

SOUTH ASIAN CRISIS

14. Minutes of the Washington Special Action Group (WSAG) Meetings of 3, 4, 6 and 8 December 1971 and Mr Jack Anderson's article of 10 January 1972*

(A) Memo on 3 December Meeting
Secret Sensitive
ASSISTANT SECRETARY OF DEFENSE
WASHINGTON, D.C. 20301
International Security Affairs Refer to: 1-29643/71

MEMORANDUM FOR RECORD
SUBJECT
WSAG meeting on India/Pakistan

PARTICIPANTS
Assistant to the President for national security affairs — Henry A. Kissinger
Under Secretary of State — John N. Irwin
Deputy Secretary of Defense — David Packard
Director, Central Intelligence Agency — Richard M. Helms
Deputy Administrator (A.I.D.) — Maurice J. Williams
Chairman, Joint Chiefs of Staff — Adm. Thomas H. Moorer
Assistant Secretary of State (N.E.E.A.R.) — Joseph J. Sisco
Assistant Secretary of Defense (I.S.A.) — G. Warren Nutter
Assistant Secretary of State (I.O.) — Samuel De Palma
Principal Deputy Assistant Secretary of Defense (I.S.A.) — Armistead I. Selden Jr.
Assistant Administrator (A.I.D./N.E.S.A.) — Donald G. MacDonald

TIME AND PLACE
3 December 1971, 1100 hours, Situation Room, White House.

SUMMARY
Reviewed conflicting reports about major actions in the west wing. C.I.A. agreed to produce map showing areas of East Pakistan occupied by India. The President orders hold on issuance of additional irrevocable letters of credit involving $99 million, and a hold on further action implementing the $72-million P.L. 480 credit. Convening of Security Council meeting planned contingent on discussion with Pak Ambassador this afternoon plus further clarification of actual situation in West Pakistan. Kissinger asked for clarification of secret/special interpretation of March 1959, bilateral U.S. agreement with Pakistan.

*For terms used in text see p. 228.

APPENDIXES

KISSINGER: I am getting hell every half-hour from the President that we are not being tough enough on India. He has just called me again. He does not believe we are carrying out his wishes. He wants to tilt in favor of Pakistan. He feels everything we do comes out otherwise.

HELMS: Concerning the reported action in the West Wing, there are conflicting reports from both sides and the only common ground is the Pak attacks on the Amritsar, Pathankat and Srinagar airports. The Paks say the Indians are attacking all along the border; but the Indian officials say this is a lie. In the East Wing the action is becoming larger and the Paks claim there are now seven separate fronts involved.

KISSINGER: Are the Indians seizing territory?

HELMS: Yes; small bits of territory, definitely.

SISCO: It would help if you could provide a map with a shading of the areas occupied by India. What is happening in the West—is a full-scale attack likely?

MOORER: The present pattern is puzzling in that the Paks have only struck at three small airfields which do not house significant numbers of Indian combat aircraft.

HELMS: Mrs Gandhi's speech at 1:30 may well announce recognition of Bangladesh.

MOORER: The Pak attack is not credible. It has been made during late afternoon, which doesn't make sense. We do not seem to have sufficient facts on this yet.

KISSINGER: It is possible that the Indians attacked first and the Paks simply did what they could before dark in response?

MOORER: This is certainly possible.

KISSINGER: The President wants no more irrevocable letters of credit issued under the $99-million credit. He wants the $72-million P.L. 480 credit also held.

WILLIAMS: Word will soon get around when we do this. Does the President understand that?

KISSINGER: That is his order, but I will check with the President again. If asked, we can say we are reviewing our whole economic program and that the granting of fresh aid is being suspended in view of conditions on the subcontinent. The next issue is the U.N.

IRWIN: The Secretary is calling in the Pak Ambassador this afternoon, and the Secretary leans toward making a U.S. move in the U.N. soon.

KISSINGER: The President is in favor of this as soon as we have some confirmation of this large-scale new action. If the U.N. can't operate in this kind of situation effectively, its utility has come to an end and it is useless to think of U.N. guarantees in the Middle East.

SISCO: We will have a recommendation for you this afternoon, after the meeting with the Ambassador. In order to give the Ambassador time to wire home, we could tentatively plan to convene the Security Council tomorrow.

KISSINGER: We have to take action. The President is blaming me, but you people are in the clear.

SOUTH ASIAN CRISIS

SISCO: That's ideal!

KISSINGER: The earlier draft for Bush is too even-handed.

SISCO: To recapitulate, after we have seen the Pak Ambassador, the Secretary will report to you. We will update the draft speech for Bush.

KISSINGER: We can say we favor political accommodation but the real job of the Security Council is to prevent military action.

SISCO: We have never had a reply either from Kosygin or Mrs Gandhi.

WILLIAMS: Are we to take economic steps with Pakistan also?

KISSINGER: Wait until I talk with the President. He hasn't addressed this problem in connection with Pakistan yet.

SISCO: If we act on the Indian side, we can say we are keeping the Pakistan situation 'under review'.

KISSINGER: It's hard to tilt toward Pakistan if we have to match every Indian step with a Pakistan step. If you wait until Monday, I can get a Presidential decision.

PACKARD: It should be easy for us to inform the banks involved to defer action inasmuch as we are so near the weekend.

KISSINGER: We need a WSAG in the morning. We need to think about our treaty obligations. I remember a letter or memo interpreting our existing treaty with a special India tilt. When I visited Pakistan in January 1962, I was briefed on a secret document or oral understanding about contingencies arising in other than the SEATO context. Perhaps it was a Presidential letter. This was a special interpretation of the March 1959, bilateral agreement.

Prepared by:
/S/ initials
JAMES M. NOYES
Deputy Assistant Secretary for Near Eastern, African and South Asian Affairs
Approved:
(illegible signature)
For G. Warren Nutter, Assistant Secretary of Defense for International Security Affairs.

Distribution: Secdef, Depsecdef, CJCS, ASD(ISA), PDASD(ISA), DASD: NEASA & PPNSCA, Dep Dir: NSCC & PPNSCA, CSD files, R&C files, NESA.

Source: *New York Herald Tribune*, Paris edition, 6 January 1972.

APPENDIXES

(B) Account of December 4th Meeting
Covering Memorandum
THE JOINT CHIEFS OF STAFF
WASHINGTON, D.C. 20301
Secret-Sensitive
Memorandum for: Chief of Staff, U.S. Army
Chief of Staff, U.S. Air Force
Chief of Naval Operations
Commandant of the Marine Corps

SUBJECT
Washington Special Action Group meeting on Indo–Pakistan hostilities; 4 December 1971.
1. Attached for your information is a memorandum for record concerning subject meeting.
2. In view of the sensitivity of information in the N.S.C. system and the detailed nature of this memorandum, it is requested that access to it be limited to a strict need-to-know basis.
For the chairman, J.C.S.:
A. K. KNOIZEN
Captain, U.S. Navy
Executive assistant to the Chairman, Joint Chiefs of Staff

Report on the Meeting
Secret Sensitive
THE JOINT CHIEFS OF STAFF
WASHINGTON, D.C. 20301
5 December 1971
MEMORANDUM FOR RECORD
SUBJECT
Washington Special Action Group meeting on Indo–Pakistan hostilities; 4 December 1971.
1. The N.S.C. Washington Special Action Group met in the Situation Room, the White House, at 1100, Saturday, 4 December, to consider the Indo–Pakistan situation. The meeting was chaired by Dr Kissinger.
2. Attendees
A. Principals:
Dr Henry Kissinger
Dr John Hannah, A.I.D.
Mr Richard Helms, C.I.A.
Dr G. Warren Nutter, Defense
Admiral Elmo Zumwalt, J.C.S.
Mr Christopher Van Hollen, State
B. Others
Mr James Noyes, Defense

SOUTH ASIAN CRISIS

Mr Armistead Selden, Defense
Rear Adm. Robert Welander, O.J.C.S.
Capt. Howard Kay, O.J.C.S.
Mr Harold Saunders, N.S.C.
Col. Richard Kennedy, N.S.C.
Mr Samuel Hoskanson, N.S.C.
Mr Donald MacDonald, A.I.D.
Mr Maurice Williams, A.I.D.
Mr John Waller, C.I.A.
Mr Samuel De Palma, State
Mr Bruce Lanigen, State
Mr David Schnelder, State

3. Summary. It was decided that the U.S. would request an immediate meeting of the Security Council. The U.S. resolution would be introduced in a speech by Ambassador Bush as soon as possible. The U.S.G.–U.N. approach would be tilted toward the Paks. Economic aid for Pakistan currently in effect will not be terminated. No requirements were levied on the J.C.S.

4. Mr Helms opened the meeting by indicating that the Indians were currently engaged in a no-holds-barred attack of East Pakistan and that they had crossed the border on all sides this morning. While India had attacked eight Pak airfields there were still no indications of any ground attacks in the West. Although not decreeing a formal declaration of war, President Yahya has stated that 'the final war with India is upon us', to which Mrs Gandhi had responded that the Pak announcement of war constituted the ultimate folly. The Indians, however, had made it a point not to declare war. The Indian attacks have hit a major P.O.L. area in Karachi resulting in a major fire which will likely be blazing for a considerable length of time, thus providing a fine target for the India air force. Mr Helms indicated that the Soviet assessment is that there is not much chance of a great power confrontation in the current crisis.

5. Dr Kissinger remarked that if the Indians have announced a full scale invasion, this fact must be reflected in our U.N. statement.

6. Mr Helms indicated that we do not know who started the current action, nor do we know why the Paks hit the four small airfields yesterday.

7. Dr Kissinger requested that by Monday the C.I.A. prepare an account of who did what to whom and when.

8. Mr De Palma suggested that if we refer to the India declaration in our discussion in the U.N., that we almost certainly will have to refer to remarks by Yahya.

9. Dr Kissinger replied that he was under specific instructions from the President, and either someone in the bureaucracy would have to prepare this statement along the lines indicated or that it would be done in the White House.

10. Mr Helms referred to the 'no holds barred' remark in the official India statement and similar remarks that were being made from the Pak side.

APPENDIXES

11. Dr Kissinger asked whether the Indians have stated anything to the effect that they were in an all-out war.

12. Mr Helms said that the terminology was 'no holds barred'.

13. Dr Kissinger asked what the Paks have said. Mr Helms said the terminology was 'final war with India'. Dr Kissinger suggested this was not an objectionable term. It did not seem outrageous to say that they (the Paks) were trying to defend themselves.

14. Dr Kissinger then asked what was happening in the U.N., to which Mr De Palma responded that the U.K., Belgium, Japan and possibly France were joining for a call for a Security Council meeting. The Japanese had detected some slight tilt in our letter requesting the meeting. The Japanese preferred a blander formulation. We have not, however, reacted to the Japanese.

15. Dr Kissinger asked to see the letter and requested that it be promulgated in announcing our move in the U.N., to which Mr De Palma responded affirmatively.

16. Dr Kissinger stated that while he had no strong view on the letter, our position must be clearly stated in the announcement.

17. Dr Kissinger stated he did not care how third parties might react, so long as Ambassador Bush understands what he should say.

18. Dr Kissinger said that whoever was putting out background information relative to the current situation is provoking Presidential wrath. The President is under the 'illusion' that he is giving instructions; not that he is merely being kept apprised of affairs as they progress. Dr Kissinger asked that this be kept in mind.

19. Mr De Palma indicated that he did not yet know whether the Security Council would be convened in the afternoon or evening (this date). However, the first statements at the meeting would likely be those by the Indians and Paks. He suggested that Ambassador Bush should be one of the first speakers immediately following the presentation by the two contesting nations. He felt that the impact of our statement would be clearer if it were made early. Dr Kissinger voiced no objections.

20. Mr De Palma asked whether we wanted to get others lined up with our resolution before we introduced it. This, however, would take time. Dr Kissinger suggested rather than follow this course, we had better submit the resolution as quickly as possible, alone if necessary. According to Dr Kissinger the only move left for us at the present time is to make clear our position relative to our greater strategy. Everyone knows how all this will come out and everyone knows that India will ultimately occupy East Pakistan. We must, therefore, make clear our position, table our resolution. We want a resolution which will be introduced with a speech by Ambassador Bush. If others desire to come along with us, fine; but in any event we will table the resolution with a speech by Ambassador Bush.

21. Dr Kissinger continued that it was important that we register our position. The exercise in the U.N. is likely to be an exercise in futility, inasmuch as the Soviets can be expected to veto. The U.N., itself, will in

all probability do little to terminate the war. He summarized the foregoing by saying that he assumed that our resolution in the U.N. will be introduced by a speech and there will be no delay. We will go along in general terms with reference to political accommodation in East Pakistan but we will certainly not imply or suggest any specifics, such as the release of Mujib.

22. Dr Kissinger asked how long the Indians could delay action in the Council. Mr De Palma said they could make long speeches or question our purpose. Mr Van Hollen said that they would draw out as long as possible which would allow them to concentrate on the situation in East Pakistan. Mr De Palma said that they could shilly-shally for three or four days which, Mr Helms stated, would be long enough for them to occupy East Pakistan. Mr De Palma stated that we could always try to force a vote. Dr Kissinger reiterated that there was no chance in getting anything useful in the U.N.

23. Mr De Palma suggested that in all likelihood one side or the other will veto.

24. Concerning the matter of economic aid, Dr Kissinger stated that the President had directed that cutoff was to be directed at India only. He indicated, however, that he wanted to read the announcement to the President so that the latter would know exactly what he might be getting into. At this point Mr Williams asked whether some mention should be made in the statement explaining why aid for Pakistan is not being cut off. Dr Kissinger said that information would be kept for background only.

25. Mr Williams said that the Department of Agriculture indicated that the price of vegetable oil was weakening in the United States; thus cutting off this P.L. 480 commodity to India could have repercussions on the domestic market. He asked, therefore, whether oil could be shipped in place of wheat. Dr Kissinger said that he will have the answer to that by the opening of business Monday.

26. Dr Kissinger then asked for a brief rundown on the military situation. Admiral Zumwalt responded that he thought the Paks could hold the line in East Pakistan for approximately one or two weeks before the logistic problems became overriding. He expected the Soviets to cement their position in India and to push for permanent usage of the naval base at Visag. He anticipated that the Soviets' immediate short range objective would be to gain military advantages through their current relationship with India.

27. Dr Kissinger indicated that the next meeting will convene Monday morning (6 December).

/S/ H. N. Kay
H. N. KAY
Captain, U.S.N.
South Asia/M.A.P. Branch, J5
Extension 72400

Source: *Ibid.*

APPENDIXES

(C) Memo on December 6th meeting

THE JOINT CHIEFS OF STAFF
WASHINGTON, D.C. 20301
6 December 1971
MEMORANDUM FOR RECORD
SUBJECT

Washington Special Action Group meeting on Indo–Pakistan hostilities; 6 December 1971.

1. The N.S.C. Washington Special Action Group met in the Situation Room, the White House, at 1100, Monday, 6 December, to consider the Indo–Pakistan situation. The meeting was chaired by Dr Kissinger.

2. Attendees

A. Principals:
Dr Henry Kissinger
Mr David Packard, Defense
Ambassador U. Alexis Johnson, State
Gen. William Westmoreland, J.C.S.
Mr Richard Helms, C.I.A.
Mr Donald MacDonald, A.I.D.

B. Others
Mr Christopher Van Hollen, State
Mr Samuel De Palma, State
Mr Bruce Lanigen, State
Mr Joseph Sisco, State
Mr Armistead Selden, Defense
Mr James Noyes, Defense
Mr John Waller, C.I.A.
Mr Samuel Hoskanson, N.S.C.
Col. Richard Kennedy, N.S.C.
Mr Harold Saunders, N.S.C.
Rear Adm. Robert Welander, O.J.C.S.
Capt. Howard Kay, O.J.C.S.
Mr Maurice Williams, A.I.D.

3. Summary. Discussion was devoted to the massive problems facing Bangladesh as a nation. Dr Kissinger indicated that the problem should be studied now. The subject of possible military aid to Pakistan is also to be examined, but on a very close hold basis. The matter of Indian redeployment from East to West was considered, as was the legality of the current sea 'blockade' by India.

4. Mr Helms opened the meeting by briefing the current situation. He stated that the Indians had recognized Bangladesh and the Paks had broken diplomatic ties with India. Major fighting continued in the East but India is engaged in a holding action in the West. Mr Helms felt that the Indians will attempt to force a decision in the East within the next 10 days. The Indians have almost total air superiority now in the East,

SOUTH ASIAN CRISIS

where they can employ approximately a hundred of their aircraft against Pak ground forces and logistic areas. The Indians, however, have not yet broken through on the ground in East Pakistan. Major thrust of the Indian effort in East Pakistan is in the north-west corner of the province. The airfield at Dacca is all but closed. The Indians are registering only minor gains in the Jessore area, but they claim to have taken Kamalpur. In the West, Indian activity is essentially limited to air attacks. The Paks appear to be on the offensive on the ground and have launched air strikes in Punjab. Overall, the Paks claim 61 Indian aircraft destroyed; the Indians claim 47 Pak planes. In naval action one Pak destroyer has been sunk by the Indians and another claimed sunked [sic]. The Indians also claim the sinking of one Pak submarine in eastern waters. Moscow is increasingly vocal in its support of India and is not supporting any U.N. moves to halt the fighting. The Chinese press made its strongest attack on India this morning.

5. Dr Kissinger then asked for a military assessment, questioning how long the Paks might be able to hold out in the East. General Westmoreland responded that it might be as much as three weeks.

6. Dr Kissinger asked what is to be done with Bangladesh. Mr Helms stated that for all practical purposes it is now an independent country, recognized by India.

7. Ambassador Johnson suggested that the Pak armed forces now in East Pakistan could be held hostage. General Westmoreland reinforced this by noting there was no means of evacuating West Pak forces from the East Wing, particularly in view of Indian naval superiority.

8. Dr Kissinger stated that the next state of play will involve determining our attitude toward the state of Bangladesh.

9. Mr Williams referred to the one and a half million Urdu-speaking (Bihari) people in East Pakistan who could also be held hostage.

10. Dr Kissinger asked if there had already been some massacre of these people. Mr Williams said that he certainly thinks there will be. Dr Kissinger asked if we could do anything, to which Mr Williams stated that perhaps an international humanitarian effort could be launched on their behalf. Dr Kissinger asked whether we should be calling attention to the plight of these people now. Mr Williams said that most of these people were, in fact, centered around the rail centers; that they are urban dwellers and that some efforts on their behalf might well be started through the U.N. Dr Kissinger suggested that this be done quickly in order to prevent a bloodbath. Mr Sisco stated that while the U.N. cannot do anything on the ground at this time, public attention could be focused on this situation through the General Assembly.

11. Mr Williams referred to the 300,000 Bengalis in West Pakistan, and that they too were in some jeopardy. Mr Sisco said that this humanitarian issue could be a very attractive one for the General Assembly and that we would begin to focus on Assembly action. Mr MacDonald cited as a possible precedent the mass movement of population from North Vietnam in 1954.

APPENDIXES

12. Returning to the military picture, Mr Williams stated that he felt that the primary thrust of the Indian Army would be to interdict Chittagong and cut off any supply capability still existing for the Paks in the East. He said that he felt that the major thrust of the Indian Army in the East would be to destroy the Pak regular forces. He felt that a major job would be to restore order within the East, inasmuch as it will be faced with a massacre as great as any we have faced in the 20th century.

13. General Westmoreland suggested that the Indians would probably need three or four divisions to continue to work with the Mukti Bahini; the remainder could be pulled out to assist the Indian forces in the West.

14. Mr Sisco opined that the Indians would pull out most of their troops once the Pak forces are disarmed, inasmuch as the Indians will be working with a very friendly population; thus, they will turn the military efforts over to the Mukti Bahini as quickly as possible. He felt that the extent and timing of Indian withdrawal from East Pakistan would depend to a large degree on developments in the West.

15. In response to a question, General Westmoreland stated that Indian transportation capabilities were limited from West to East, and that it would probably take at least a week to move one infantry division. It might take as much as a month to move all or most of the Indian forces from the East to the West.

16. Mr Sisco said that the long-term presence of Indian forces in Bangladesh would have to be addressed. Mr Van Hollen remarked that should the Indian Army remain more than two or three weeks after the situation in East Pakistan is wrapped up they would, in fact, become a Hindu army of occupation in the eyes of the Bengalis.

17. Mr Van Hollen raised the problem of the return of the refugees from India. Inasmuch as Bangladesh is predominantly Moslem, the return of 10 million refugees, most of whom are Hindu, would present another critical problem.

18. General Westmoreland suggested that the Indian position in the West was not unadvantageous. He briefly discussed the order of battle in West Pakistan and suggested that the Indians were in relatively good shape. He said that he expected the major Pak effort to be toward Kashmir and the Punjab. The Indians, he felt, will be striking toward Hyderabad so as to cut the main L.O.C. to Karachi. He did not think that the Indians necessarily plan to drive all the way to Karachi. He also suggested that the current Indian move in that direction could very well be diversionary, in order to force the Paks to pull reserves back from the Kashmir area.

19. Mr Packard asked about the P.O.L. supply situation for Pakistan. Mr Helms said that at the present time it looked very bad. The overland L.O.C.'s from Iran, for example, were very tenuous.

20. Mr Williams suggested that the reason for the Indian thrust to the south was essentially political. Inasmuch as the Indians do not want to fight on the border they will have to give ground in Kashmir. In order to

SOUTH ASIAN CRISIS

ward off parliamentary criticism, Mrs Gandhi may be going for some Pak real estate in the south.

21. Dr Kissinger then asked about U.N. initiatives. Mr Sisco said that we are now reviewing the situation with Ambassador Bush. Two Security Council resolutions have been vetoed by the Soviets. However, there is a ground-swell building in New York for an emergency session by the General Assembly to be convened under the provisions of the 'threat to peace' mechanism. The crisis could be moved into the Assembly through a simple majority vote.

22. Dr Kissinger and Mr Sisco agreed that any resolution introduced into the General Assembly must retain two key elements: Cease fire and withdrawal of military forces. Dr Kissinger agreed that our U.N. delegation has handled the situation extremely well to date. Mr Sisco said that although it is very likely that the crisis will be introduced in the General Assembly, we must remember that there are 136 countries represented therein, and we can expect all sorts of pressure to be generated. Mr De Palma suggested that when the resolution is introduced in the Assembly there will be a new twist, i.e.: the Indians will be no longer terribly interested in political accommodation. By that time that issue will have ceased to be a problem.

23. Mr De Palma said that a Council meeting was scheduled for 3:30 today and at that time we could try to get the Council to let go of the issue in order to transfer it to the Assembly, it being quite obvious that we are not going to get a cease-fire through the Security Council.

24. Dr Kissinger asked if we could expect the General Assembly to get the issue by the end of the day, to which Mr De Palma replied that hopefully this will be the case.

25. Dr Kissinger said that we will go with essentially the same speech in the General Assembly as was made in the Security Council, but he would like something put in about refugees and the text of our resolution.

26. Dr Kissinger also directed that henceforth we show a certain coolness to the Indians; the Indian Ambassador is not to be treated at too high a level.

27. Dr Kissinger then asked about a legal position concerning the current Indian naval 'blockade'. Mr Sisco stated that we have protested both incidents in which American ships have been involved. However, no formal proclamation apparently has been made in terms of a declaration of a war, that it is essentially still an undeclared war, with the Indians claiming power to exercise their rights of belligerency. State would, how- however, prepare a paper on the legal aspects of the issue. Ambassador Johnson said that so far as he was concerned the Indians had no legal position to assert a blockade.

28. Dr Kissinger asked that a draft protest be drawn up. If we considered it illegal, we will make a formal diplomatic protest. Mr Sisco said that he would prepare such a protest.

29. Dr Kissinger then asked whether we have the right to authorize Jordan or Saudi Arabia to transfer military equipment to Pakistan. Mr

APPENDIXES

Van Hollen stated the United States cannot permit a third country to transfer arms which we have provided them when we, ourselves, do not authorize sale direct to the ultimate recipient, such as Pakistan. As of last January we made a legislative decision not to sell to Pakistan. Mr Sisco said that the Jordanians would be weakening their own position by such a transfer and would probably be grateful if we could get them off the hook. Mr Sisco went on to say that as the Paks increasingly feel the heat we will be getting emergency requests from them.

30. Dr Kissinger said that the President may want to honor those requests. The matter has not been brought to Presidential attention but it is quite obvious that the President is not inclined to let the Paks be defeated. Mr Packard then said that we should look at what could be done. Mr Sisco agreed but said it should be done very quietly. Dr Kissinger indicated he would like a paper by tomorrow (7 December).

31. Mr Sisco suggested that what we are really interested in are what supplies and equipment could be made available, and the modes of delivery of this equipment. He stated that from a political point of view our efforts would have to be directed at keeping the Indians from 'extinguishing' West Pakistan.

32. Dr Kissinger turned to the matter of aid and requested that henceforth letters of credit not be made irrevocable. Mr Williams stated that we have suspended general economic aid, not formally committed, to India, which reduces the level to $10 million. He suggested that what we have done for Pakistan in the same category does not become contentious inasmuch as the Indians are now mobilizing all development aid for use in the war effort, whereas remaining aid for East Pakistan is essentially earmarked for fertilizer and humanitarian relief. A case can be made technically, politically and legally that there is a difference between the aid given India and that given to Pakistan.

33. Dr Kissinger said to make sure that when talking about cutoff of aid for India to emphasize what is cut off and not on what is being continued.

34. Dr Kissinger then asked about evacuation. Mr Sisco said that the Dacca evacuation had been aborted.

35. Dr Kissinger inquired about a possible famine in East Pakistan. Mr Williams said that we will not have a massive problem at this time, but by next spring this will quite likely be the case. Dr Kissinger asked whether we will be appealed to bail out Bangladesh. Mr Williams said that the problem would not be terribly great if we could continue to funnel 140 tons of food a month through Chittagong, but at this time nothing is moving. He further suggested that Bangladesh will need all kinds of help in the future, to which Ambassador Johnson added that Bangladesh will be an 'international basket case'. Dr Kissinger said, however, it will not necessarily be our basket case. Mr Williams said there is going to be need of massive assistance and resettling of refugees, transfers of population and feeding the population. Dr Kissinger suggested that we ought to start studying this problem right now.

SOUTH ASIAN CRISIS

36. Mr Williams suggested that the Indians had consistently requested refugee aid in cash. The Indians in turn will provide the food and support for the refugees. This has provided India with a reservoir of foreign currency. Dr Kissinger also asked that this problem be looked at by tomorrow to determine whether we could provide commodities in lieu of cash. We do not want to cut off humanitarian aid. We would like to provide material rather than cash.

37. The meeting was then adjourned.

/S/ H. N. KAY
H. N. KAY
CAPTAIN, U.S.N.
South Asia/M.A.P. Branch, J5
Extension 72400.

Source: *Ibid.*

(D) Memo on 8 December Meeting
Secret Sensitive
THE JOINT STAFF
THE JOINT CHIEFS OF STAFF
WASHINGTON, D.C. 20301
8 December 1971
MEMORANDUM FOR RECORD

SUBJECT: Washington Special Action Group meeting on Indo–Pakistan hostilities; 8 December 1971.

1. The N.S.C. Washington Special Action Group met in the Situation Room, the White House, at 1100, Wednesday, 8 December to consider the Indo–Pakistan situation. The meeting was chaired by Dr Kissinger.

2. Attendees

A. Principals: Dr Henry Kissinger, Mr Richard Helms, C.I.A., Gen. John Ryan, J.C.S., Mr Donald MacDonald, A.I.D, Mr David Packard, Defense, Ambassador U. Alexis Johnson, State.

B. Others: Mr Maurice Williams, A.I.D., Mr John Waller, C.I.A., Col. Richard Kennedy, N.S.C., Mr Samuel Hoskanson, N.S.C., Mr Harold Saunders, N.S.C., Mr Armistead Selden, Defense, Mr James Noyes, Defense, Mr Christopher Van Hollen, State, Mr Samuel De Palma, State, Mr Bruce Lanigen, State, Mr David Schneider, State, Mr Joseph Sisco, State, Rear Adm. Robert Welander, O.J.C.S., Capt. Howard Kay, O.J.C.S.

3. Summary. Dr Kissinger suggested that India might be attempting, through calculated destruction of Pak armored and air forces, to render Pakistan impotent. He requested that the Jordanian interest in assisting Pakistan not be turned off, but rather kept in a holding pattern. He asked that Pak capabilities in Kashmir be assessed.

224

APPENDIXES

4. Mr Helms opened the meeting by briefing the current situation. In the East, the Indians have broken the line at Comilla. Only major river crossings prevent them from investing Dacca. The Indians are advancing rapidly throughout East Pakistan. All major Pak L.O.C.'s in the East are now vulnerable. In the West, the Paks are now claiming Poonch, inside the Indian border. However, the Paks are admitting fairly heavy casualties in the fighting. Tank battles are apparently taking place in the Sind/Rajasthan area. Mrs Gandhi has indicated that before heeding a U.N. call for cease-fire, she intends to straighten out the southern border of Azad Kashmir. It is reported that, prior to terminating present hostilities, Mrs Gandhi intends to attempt to eliminate Pakistan's armor and air force capabilities. Thus far only India and Bhutan have recognized Bangladesh. It is believed that the Soviets have held off recognition primarily so as not to rupture relations with the Paks. Soviet action on the matter of recognition, however, may be forthcoming in the near future.

5. Mr Sisco inquired how long the Paks might be expected to hold out in East Pakistan, to which Mr Helms replied 48 to 72 hours. The time to reach the ultimate climax is probably a function of the difficulties encountered in river crossings.

6. Assessing the situation in the West, General Ryan indicated that he did not see the Indians pushing too hard at this time, rather they seem content with a holding action.

7. Dr Kissinger asked how long it would take to shift Indian forces from East to West. General Ryan said it might take a reasonably long time to move all the forces, but that the airborne brigade could be moved quickly, probably within a matter of five or six days.

8. Dr Kissinger inquired about refugee aid. After a discussion with Mr Williams it was determined that only a very small number of U.S. dollars earmarked for refugee relief was actually entering the Indian economy. Contrary to the sense of the last meeting, the Indians have actually lost foreign exchange in the process of caring for refugees. In any event, the entire relief effort is currently suspended in both India and Pakistan.

9. Dr Kissinger then emphasized that the President has made it clear that no further foreign exchange, PL-480 commodities, or development loans could be assigned to India without approval of the White House. Mr Williams stated there was no problem of anything sliding through.

10. Dr Kissinger inquired what the next turn of the screw might be. Mr Williams said that the only other possible option was taking a position concerning aid material currently under contract. This however would be a very messy problem inasmuch as we would be dealing with irrevocable letters of credit. Mr Williams further stated that we would have to take possession of material that was being consigned to the Indians by U.S. contractors and thus would be compelled to pay U.S. suppliers, resulting in claims against the U.S.G.

11. Mr Packard said that all of this could be done, but agreed that it would be a very laborious and difficult problem. He further elaborated that all the items involved would have to be located, the United States,

would have to take ownership, settle with suppliers, locate warehousing, etc. Nevertheless, if such was desired it could be done. Mr Williams said that in a very limited way this type of action had been taken against some Mid-East countries, but that it had taken years to settle the claims.

12. Dr Kissinger asked how India was handling next year's development loan program, to which Mr Williams responded that nothing was under negotiation at the present time.

13. Dr Kissinger inquired about next year's [A.I.D.] budget. Mr Williams stated that what goes into the budget did not represent a commitment. Dr Kissinger stated that current orders are not to put anything into the budget for A.I.D. to India. It was not to be leaked that A.I.D. had put money in the budget for India, only to have the 'wicked' White House take it out.

14. Dr Kissinger suggested that the key issue if the Indians turn on West Pakistan is Azad Kashmir. If the Indians smash the Pak air force and the armored forces we would have a deliberate Indian attempt to force the disintegration of Pakistan. The elimination of the Pak armored and air forces would make the Paks defenseless. It would turn West Pakistan into a client state. The possibility elicits a number of questions. Can we allow a U.S. ally to go down completely while we participate in a blockade? Can we allow the Indians to scare us off, believing that if U.S. supplies are needed they will not be provided?

15. Mr Sisco stated that if the situation were to evolve as Dr Kissinger had indicated then, of course, there was a serious risk to the viability of West Pakistan. Mr Sisco doubted, however, that the Indians had this as their objective. He indicated that Foreign Minister Singh told Ambassador Keating that India had no intention of taking any Pak territory. Mr Sisco said it must also be kept in mind that Kashmir is really disputed territory.

16. Mr Helms then stated that earlier he had omitted mentioning that Madame Gandhi, when referring to China, expressed the hope that there would be no Chinese intervention in the West. She said that the Soviets had cautioned her that the Chinese might rattle the sword in Ladakh but that the Soviets have promised to take appropriate counter-action if this should occur. Mr Helms indicated that there was no Chinese build-up at this time but, nevertheless, even without a build-up they could 'make motions and rattle the sword'.

17. Turning then to the question of military support of Pakistan, Dr Kissinger referred to an expression of interest by King Hussein relative to the provision of F-104s to Pakistan, and asked how we could get Jordan into a holding pattern to allow the President time to consider the issue. Dr Kissinger also asked whether we should attempt to convey to the Indians and the press that a major attack on West Pakistan would be considered in a very serious light by this country.

18. Mr Packard explained that we could not authorize the Jordanians to do anything that the U.S.G. could not do. If the U.S.G. could not give the 104's to Pakistan, we could not allow Jordan to do so. If a third country had material that the U.S.G. did not have, that was one thing, but we

APPENDIXES

could not allow Jordan to transfer the 104's unless we make a finding that the Paks, themselves, were eligible to purchase them from us directly.

19. Dr Kissinger suggested that if we had not cut the sale of arms to Pakistan the current problem would not exist. Mr Packard agreed.

20. Dr Kissinger suggested that perhaps we never really analysed what the real danger was when we were turning off the arms to Pakistan.

21. Mr Packard suggested that another consideration in the Jordan issue is that if Jordan delivers this equipment we would be expected to replace it. Ambassador Johnson stated we do not have any more M.A.P. left.

22. Dr Kissinger states that what we may be witnessing is a situation wherein a country equipped and supported by the Soviets may be turning half of Pakistan into an impotent state and the other half into a vassal. We must consider what other countries may be thinking of our action.

23. Mr Helms asked about our CENTO relationships with Pakistan. Ambassador Johnson stated we had no legal obligations towards Pakistan in the CENTO context. Dr Kissinger agreed but added that neither did we have legal obligations toward India in 1962 when we formulated the air defense agreement. We must consider what would be the impact of the current situation in the larger complex of world affairs.

24. Dr Kissinger said that we must look at the problem in terms of Security Council guarantees in the Mid-East and the impact on other areas. We must look at the military supply situation. One could make a case, he argued, that we have done everything two weeks too late in the current situation.

25. Mr Packard stated that perhaps the only satisfactory outcome would be for us to stand fast, with the expectation that the West Paks could hold their own.

26. Ambassador Johnson said that we must examine the possible effects that additional supplies for Pakistan might have. It could be that eight F-104's might not make any difference once the real war in the West starts. They could be considered only as a token. If, in fact, we were to move in West Pakistan we would be in a new ball game.

27. Ambassador Johnson said that one possibility would be our reply to Foreign Minister Singh, in which we could acknowledge the Indian pledge that they do not have territorial designs. He also stated we must also consider the fact that the Paks may themselves be trying to take Kashmir.

28. After discussing various possible commitments to both Pakistan and India, Mr Packard stated that the overriding consideration is the practical problem of either doing something effective or doing nothing. If you don't win, don't get involved. If we were to attempt something it would have to be with a certainty that it would affect the outcome. Let's not get in if we know we are going to lose. Find some way to stay out.

29. Mr Williams suggested that we might now focus efforts for a cease-fire in West Pakistan. Ambassador Johnson stated this might, however, stop the Paks from moving into Kashmir.

SOUTH ASIAN CRISIS

30. Dr Kissinger asked for an assessment of the Pak capabilities and prospects in Kashmir. He asked C.I.A. to prepare an assessment of the international implications of Mrs Gandhi's current moves. He indicated that we should develop an initial stand on the military supply question. He reiterated that he desired to keep Hussein in a 'holding pattern' relative to the latter's expression of support for Pakistan and that he should not be turned off. The U.S.G. should indicate to Hussein that we do not consider trivial his feelings in this matter.

31. Turning to the question of the blockade, Ambassador Johnson said that both India and Pakistan have taken blockade action, even though the Pak blockade is essentially a paper blockade. Dr Kissinger said that we should also protest to the Paks. Ambassador Johnson indicated we do not have a legal case to protest the blockade. The belligerent nations have a right to blockade when a state of war exists. We may think it unwise and we may question how it is carried out. We have, in fact, normally expressed our concern. On the other hand we have no problem in protesting the incident of the S.S. *Buckeye State*.

32. Dr Kissinger said that we are not trying to be even-handed. There can be no doubt what the President wants. The President does not want to be even-handed. The President believes that India is the attacker. We are trying to get across the idea that India has jeopardized relations with the United States. Dr Kissinger said that we cannot afford to ease India's state of mind. 'The Lady' is cold-blooded and tough and will not turn into a Soviet satellite merely because of pique. We should not ease her mind. He invited anyone who objected to this approach to take his case to the President. Ambassador Keating, he suggested, is offering enough reassurance on his own.

33. Addressing briefly the question of communal strife in East Pakistan, Dr Kissinger asked whether anyone would be in a position to know that massacres were occurring at the time when they took place. Mr Helms indicated that we might not know immediately, but we certainly would know after a massacre occurred.

34. The meeting was adjourned at 12:10.

/S/ H. N. KAY
H. N. KAY
Captain, U.S.N.
South Asia/M.A.P. Branch, J5
Extension 72400

Source: *ibid.*, 15 January 1972.

Note

Terms used in the Text

A.I.D.   Agency for International Development.
A.S.D. (I.S.A.)   Assistant Secretary of Defense, International Security Affairs.

APPENDIXES

Azad Kashmir   Free Kashmir, name of the Pakistani-held parts of Kashmir.
CENTO   Central Treaty Organization.
C.I.A.   Central Intelligence Agency.
C.J.C.S.   Chairman, Joint Chiefs of Staff.
D.A.S.D., N.E.A.S.A. & P.P.N.S.C.A.   Deputy Assistant Secretary of Defense, Near Eastern, African and South Asian Affairs; Deputy Assistant Secretary of Defense, Policy Plans and National Security Council Affairs.
Dep. Dir., N.S.C.C. & P.P.N.S.C.A.   Deputy Director, Policy Plans and National Security Council Affairs.
Depsecdef   Deputy Secretary of Defense.
F-104   *Starfighter* jet aircraft.
I.S.A.   International Security Affairs of Defense Department.
J.C.S.   Joint Chiefs of Staff.
L.O.C.   Line(s) of communication.
M.A.P.   Military Assistance Program.
N.E.A.   Near Eastern Affairs, Section of State Department.
N.E.S.A.   Near East and South Asia.
N.S.C.   National Security Council.
O.J.C.S.   Office of Joint Chiefs of Staff.
Paks   Pakistanis.
PL480   Public Law 480, governing surplus sent abroad as aid.
P.D.A.S.D. (I.S.A.)   Principal Deputy Assistant of Defense, International Security Affairs.
P.O.L.   petroleum, oil, and lubricants.
P.L.   Public Law.
R & C Files   Records and Control Files.
Secdef   Secretary of Defense.
S.S. *Buckeye State*   American vessel strafed in a Pakistani port.
U.S.G.   United States Government.
W.S.A.G.   Washington Special Action Group, arm of National Security Council.

(E) Article by Mr Jack Anderson, 10 January 1972

The secret White House papers reveal some ominous similarities between the Bay of Bengal and the Gulf of Tonkin. The Gulf of Tonkin incident on 4 August 1964, led to America's deep involvement in the Vietnam war.

The American public was told that North Vietnamese torpedo boats had staged an unprovoked attack upon a United States destroyer, although later evidence indicated that the attack was actually provoked.

The risk of a similar naval incident in the Bay of Bengal caused grave apprehensions inside the State Department as a United States task force

SOUTH ASIAN CRISIS

steamed toward a Soviet task force at the height of the Indian–Pakistan fighting.

On 7 December a top secret warning was flashed to Washington that 'three Soviet naval ships, a seagoing minesweeper and a tanker have begun to move northeastward into the Bay of Bengal.

'The units entered the Indian ocean from the Malacca Strait on 5 December and were located approximately 500 nautical miles east of Ceylon on 7 December.'

Urgent huddles in the White House led to a decision on 10 December to assemble in Malacca Strait a United States task force, spearheaded by the aircraft carrier *Enterprise*, the Navy's most powerful ship.

The primary purpose was to make a 'show of force' and to divert Indian planes and ships from Pakistan.

As the task force moved into position, Adml John McCain, our Pacific commander, inquired on 11 December about 'the feasibility of . . . aerial surveillance of Soviet task group located approximately 180 NM [nautical miles] south-west of Ceylon'.

Authorization was flashed back the same day 'in the event task force 74 is directed to transmit [to go through] the Strait of Malacca. At that time appropriate . . . screening-surveillance flights are authorized.'

As the American warships moved through the Strait and headed into the Bay of Bengal, even more ominous reports reached Washington from the defence intelligence agency.

'Recent indicators have been received which suggest the People's Republic of China may be planning actions regarding the Indo–Pakistan conflict.'

A top secret message reported tersely: 'According to a reliable clandestine source, [Pakistan's] President Yahya Khan claimed . . . today that the Chinese Ambassador in Islamabad has assured him that within 72 hours the Chinese Army will move towards the border.

'President Yahya's claim cannot be confirmed. However, recent Peking propaganda statements have become more critical of India's involvement in East Pakistan'.

From Kathmandu in the Himalayas, meanwhile, came word that both the Soviet and Indian military attachés had asked Col. Melvin Holst, the American attaché, what he knew about Chinese troop movements and United States fleet movements.

'USSR attaché Loginov,' said the secret dispatch, called upon the Chinese military attaché Chao Kuang Chih in Kathmandu advising Chao that China 'should not get too serious about intervention, because USSR react, had many missiles, etc.'

Holst concluded, the dispatch added that 'both the USSR and India embassies have a growing concern that China might intervene.'

Simultaneously, the Central Intelligence Agency rushed out a top secret report that 'the Chinese have been passing weather data for locations in Tibet and along the Sino–Indian border since 8 December. The

APPENDIXES

continued passing of weather data for these locations is considered unusual and may indicate some form of alert posture.'

And from New Delhi, the CIA reported: 'According to a reliable clandestine source, Prime Minister Gandhi told a leader of her Congress party that she had some indications that the Chinese intend to intervene along India's northern border. ... Mrs Gandhi said that the Chinese action might be in the Ladakh area.'

Russia's Ambassador to India, Nikolai M. Pegov, however, promised on 13 December that the Soviets 'would open a diversionary action' against the Chinese and 'will not allow the Seventh Fleet to intervene.'

Here are the highlights of this ominous Soviet pledge, which the CIA claimed to have picked up from a 'reliable source'.

'Pegov stated that Pakistan is trying to draw both the United States and China into the present conflict. The Soviet Union, however, does not believe that either country will intervene.

'According to Pegov, the movement of the Seventh Fleet is an effort by the U.S. to bully India, to discourage it from striking against West Pakistan, and at the same time to boost the morale of the Pakistani forces.

'Pegov noted that a Soviet fleet is now in the Indian Ocean and that the Soviet Union will not allow the Seventh Fleet to intervene.

'If China should decide to intervene in Ladakh, said Pegov, the Soviet Union would open a diversionary action in Sinkiang.

'Pegov also commented that after Dacca is liberated and the Bangla Desh Government is installed both the United States and China will be unable to act and will change their current attitude toward the crisis.'

This is how the big powers danced precariously on the edge of the brink just before Christmas as people sang about peace on earth and good will toward men.

Source: *Daily Telegraph* (London), 10 January 1972.

SOUTH ASIAN CRISIS

15. Diplomatic Cables showing American Attitudes to India as revealed by Mr Jack Anderson 12 January 1972

Secret diplomatic cables demonstrate graphically how America used the threat of large-scale military aid to Pakistan as a psychological weapon against India during their recent war.

While direct arms shipments were ruled out from the start, America came within an ace of providing back-door weapons assistance through several of Pakistan's Arab allies.

The back-door scheme was never adopted, but the cables show that America wanted India to continue to think the possibility was imminent, thus strengthening Pakistan's position.

The most revealing of the cables was addressed to the American Embassies in Saudi Arabia and New Delhi:

'In view of intelligence reports spelling out Indian military objectives in West Pakistan, we do not want in any way to ease Indian Government concern re help Pakistan might receive from outside sources.

Consequently, the Embassy should give India no assurances re third country transfers.'

The secret cable was signed by Mr John Irwin, Under-Secretary of State.

Another cable to the American Embassy in Jordan shows that King Hussein was under heavy pressure from Pakistan for arms aid and that he, in turn, was putting the heat on America to help to furnish it.

'You should tell King Hussein we fully appreciate heavy pressure he feels himself under by virtue of request from Pakistan.

We are nevertheless not yet in a position to give him definite response, while subject remains under intensive review at very high level of US Government.

We are fully alive to your delicate situation in not being able to give definite answer to King's urgent pleas. But we ask you to bear with us and put situation to Hussein in best light possible.'

The cable, addressed to Mr L. Dean Brown, the American Ambassador, was again signed by Mr Irwin.

Source: *Daily Telegraph* (London), 12 January 1972.

APPENDIXES

16. *The Instrument of Surrender of Pakistan Eastern Command, 16 December 1971*

The Pakistan Eastern Command agree to Surrender all Pakistan Armed Forces in Bangla Desh to Lieutenant-General Jagjit Singh Aurora, General Officer Commanding in Chief of the Indian and Bangla Desh forces in the Eastern Theatre. This surrender includes all Pakistan land, air and naval forces as also all para-military forces and civil armed forces. These forces will lay down their arms and surrender at the places where they are currently located to the nearest regular troops under command of Lieutenant-General Jagjit Singh Aurora.

The Pakistan Eastern Command shall come under the orders of Lieutenant-General Jagjit Singh Aurora as soon as this instrument has been signed. Disobedience of orders will be regarded as breach of the surrender terms and will be dealt with in accordance with the accepted laws and usages of war. The decision of Lieutenant-General Jagjit Singh Aurora will be final, should any doubt arise as to the meaning or interpretation of the surrender terms.

Lieutenant-General Jagjit Singh Aurora gives a solemn assurance that personnel who surrender shall be treated with dignity and respect that soldiers are entitled to in accordance with the provisions of the Geneva Convention and guarantees the safety and well-being of all Pakistan military and para-military forces who surrender. Protection will be provided to foreign nationals, ethnic minorities and personnel of East Pakistan origin by the forces under the command of Lieutenant-General Jagit Singh Aurora.

Sd/- Jagjit Singh	Sd/- A. A. K. Niazi
Lieutenant-General	(Amir Abdullah Khan Niazi)
General Officer Commanding in Chief	Lieutenant-General
Indian and Bangla Desh Forces	*Marshal Law Administrator Zone B*
in the Eastern Theatre	*and Commander Eastern Command*
16th December 1971	*(Pakistan).*
	16th December 1971.

INDEX

NOTE: The following frequently recurring topics are not indexed; Bangla Desh; Bengal; India; Pakistan. Newpapers referred to in footnotes are also not indexed.

Afghanistan, 48, 128 151, 152
Agartala: 'conspiracy' trial, 21, 109 (map), 130, 133
Agra, 116
Ahmad Khan, Lieutenant-Genera Irshad, 115
Ahmed Khan, Sir Syed, 10
Ahmed, M. M., 50
Ahmed, Tajuddin, 37, 45, 56, 57, 59, 77, 87, 89, 104, 136; see also Awami League
Ahsan, Admiral 26, 28
Akbar, Major-General, 26
Akhaura, 110 (map), 134, 135
Akhnur, 43, 118 (map), 119
Ali, Hossain, 67
Ali Khan, Liaquat, 36
Ali Khan, Major-General Rao Farman, 81, 108, 112, 113, 141, 142, 143
Ali, Mahmud, 81
Amin, Nurul, 52, 144
Amritsar, 115, 116, 117
Anderson, Jack, 97, 98, 125n, 138n, 139, 209, 229–31, 233
Ansari, Major-General, 134
Anupgarh, 115, 120
Arabia, 39
Argentina, 126, 127, 129
Ashuganj, 110 (map), 130, 133, 135, 142
Assam, 13, 46, 109 (map)
Aurora, Lieutenant-General Jagjit Singh, 136, 144, 232
Avantipur, 116, 118 (map)
Awami League: and Bengali nationalism, 17, 18, 21, 26, 29–32; six-point manifesto, 21, 24–5, 26, 27, 30, 31, 147, (text) 166–7; and 1970 election, 24; homes of supporters raided, 33; charges against, 34; proscribed, 34; and concept of

Pakistan, 51, 52; leadership denounced by Yahya, 53; Bangla Desh Awami League provisional government, 56–7, 59, 76–9, 136; and India, 73, 98; Yahya and moderate elements in, 75, 96–9, 104–5; right-wing elements, 78; radical elements, 148; see also Mujibur Rahman; National Awami Party
Ayub Khan, 18, 19, 20,21, 22, 25, 39, 48, 107, 108, 147

Baghdad, 15
Baluchistan, 13, 24, 29
Balurghat, 109 (map), 110 (map)
Bandung (conference), 40
Bangkok, 142
Bangla Desh National Congress, 79
Bangla Desh National Liberation Struggle Co-ordination Committee, 78, 89
Barisal, 109 (map), 110 (map), 134
Barmer, 117 (map), 121
Bashani, Maulana, 18, 24, 57, 79; see also National Awami Party
'Basic Democrats', 18
Bay of Bengal, 109 (map), 137, 138, 139, 158, 160
Belgium, 116, 127n
Belonia, 35, 101, 130, 135
Boumédienne, President Houari, 85
Bengal United Front, 30
Bewoor, Lieutenant-General G. G., 115
Bhairab Bazar, 109 (map), 110 (map), 134, 142
Bhurungamari, 35
Bhutan, 109 (map)
Bhutto, Zulfikar Ali: leader of Pakistan People's Party, 21, 24, 26, 27;

234

INDEX

threatens landed estates in Punjab, 23; post-election negotiations of, 27–8; speech at Karachi, 31, 32; hijacking incident, 37; advocate of pro-China policy, 41; calls for civilian government, 52; threatened by Yahya, 53–4; obliged to accept constitutional advance in E. Pakistan, 79–80; gains ground in Islamabad, 95; visits Peking, 95–6; Deputy Premier and Foreign Minister, 128, 144; statement at United Nations, 129, 144; representative of West Wing, 148; pressure of internal forces on, 149; *see also* Pakistan People's Party
Bihar, 109 (map); Biharis, 34, 76, 132, 137
Bogra, 110 (map), 130, 133, 135
Boyra, 102, 104, 109 (map), 112, 132, 134
Brahmanbaria, 35, 43, 110 (map), 133, 135
Brahmaputra R., 109 (map), 110 (map), 133
Brar, Major-General M. S., 134
Brazil, 161
Brèzhnev, L. I., 71
Britain: British Raj, 10, 13, 16, 18, 20, 151; first major power to express view of crisis, 38, 150; and United Nations, 43, 126–9; aid to Pakistan, 49; and Mrs Gandhi, 93, 141; evacuation of nationals, 142
Brohi, A. K., 98, 99
Burma, 15
Burundi, 126, 127n
Bush, George, 125, 126, 129

Calcutta, 13, 17, 19, 44, 45, 57, 66, 77, 97, 109 (map), 130, 133, 142
Canada, 161
Candeth, Lieutenant-General K. P., 115
Cargill, P. M., 48, 62, 64, 75, 79
CENTO, 138
Central Intelligence Agency, 136, 140
Ceylon, 15, 37, 139
Chachro, 117 (map), 121
Chalna, 30, 109 (map), 130, 134
Chander, 116
Chandigarh, 96
Chandpur, 110 (map), 133, 134, 135
Changa Manga, 120
Chaugacha, 102
Chandpur, 133
Chenab R., 118 (map), 119
Chhad Bet, 117 (map), 121
Chhamb, 114, 116, 118 (map), 119, 122, 123

Chi Peng-fei, 42, 95, 205–6
Chile, 128
China: view of situation in Pakistan, 40–43, 150; and United States, 42–3, 65, 68, 83, 153–7, 159; aid to Pakistan, 49, 54, 94; relations with Pakistan, 71, 94–6, 104–5, 106, 112, 140, 144, 153–4; entry into United Nations, 94; frontier with India, 111, 130; relations with India, 139–40, 152–4; risk of intervention from, 113, 160; and UN Security Council, 124, 126–9; and Soviet Union, 151–3, 155
Chittagong, 30, 33, 34, 35, 51, 58, 77, 109 (map), 110 (map), 130, 133, 135
Chou En-lai, 41, 95, 150, 154, 173
Chuadanga, 35, 44, 109 (map), 134
Comilla, 34, 51, 109 (map), 110 (map), 130, 133, 134, 135
Communist Parties, World Congress of, 71
Communist Party of Bangla Desh, 79
Cooch Behar, 110 (map), 135
Cornwallis' Permanent Settlement of 1793, 10
Council Muslim League, 81, 90n
Crowe, Sir Colin, 127
Curzon, Marquess, 10, 13

Dacca, 10, 15, 27, 28, 30, 31, 33, 34, 35, 36, 52, 80, 109 (map), 110 (map), 114, 130, 131, 132, 133, 134, 135, 139, 141, 142, 143, 144, 145,
Daily Telegraph (London), 229–31
Darsana, 109 (map), 134
Daudkandi, 110 (map), 135
Delhi, 13, 40, 41, 45, 51, 57, 61, 65, 66, 71, 77, 85, 87, 95, 97, 98, 101, 138n, 157, 160
Denmark, 128
Dera, 110 (map)
Dera Baba Nanak, 115, 117 (map), 118 (map), 120
Dhar, D. P., 78, 139
Dharamnagar, 130
Dinajpur, 51, 109 (map), 110 (map), 130, 133, 135

East India Company, 9
Egypt, 39, 72
Enterprise task-force, 137, 139, 141, 158, 160

Faridkot, 116
Faridpur, 109 (map), 110 (map), 133, 134, 135
Farland, Joseph, 98, 99
Fatehpur-Burj, 117 (map), 120
Fazilka, 115, 117 (map), 121, 123
Feni, 35, 58, 109 (map), 133

235

SOUTH ASIAN CRISIS 1971

Ferozepore, 115, 117 (map)
Firyubin, Nikolai, 91, 95, 99, 103
Formosa, 157
France, 38, 126, 127, 128, 129, 141, 144

Gaibanda, 110 (map), 135
Gandhi, Indira: moves resolution in Parliament, 36 (text), 171; speaks on situation in E. Pakistan, 44, 45n; and refugees, 46, 47; receives letter from Nixon, 50; suggests political solution, 60; and Yahya, 66, 73; and U Thant, 69; India's international alignment, 70; and Soviet Union, 71; visits Moscow, 84–5, statement 194–8; desires to avert war, 88, 125; rejects mutual withdrawal of forces, 90; tours Western capitals, 91–3, 101; and China, 94; visits Washington, 96; aware of American moves, 97; writes to Nixon, 99n, 141; reports engagement with Pakistani forces, 102; refuses to withdraw troops from E. Pakistan, 128; announces recognition of Bangla Desh, 136; views as reported by CIA, 137; orders unilateral cease-fire, 144; pressure of domestic politics on, 149
Ganga R. (Ganges), 109 (map), 110 (map), 130
Garibpur, 109 (map), 134
Garo hills, 130
Gilgit, 49
Government of India Acts, 1919 and 1935, 16
Gromyko, A. A., 71, 83, 191, 192–3
Gubbar, 117 (map), 121
Gujarat, 117 (map), 122
Gurdaspur, 115, 117 (map), 118 (map)

Hamid Khan, General, 108
Haq, A. K. Falzlul, 11, 12, 13, 14, 17, 21
Hardinge bridge, 109 (map), 130, 133, 134
Hasan, Vice-Admiral Muzaffar, 108
Hassan, General Gul, 108
Haveli, 117 (map), 120
Henri, M. Paul-Marc, 67n, 141
Hilli, 102, 109 (map), 110 (map), 132, 134, 135
Himalayas, 111, 133
Hindu culture, 9, 10, 11, 12, 14, 75–6, 146
Home, Sir Alec Douglas-, 38, 63, 97n
Hua, Huang, 126
Human Rights, Universal Declaration of, 40
Hussain, Dr Kamal, 65
Hussainiwala, 115, 117 (map), 120

Hyderabad, 115, 117 (map), 121, 137

Indochina, 157
Indo-Soviet Treaty of Peace, Friendship and Co-operation (9 August 1971), 71–3, 78, 153, 159, (text) 188–91
Iran, 38
Irwin, John, 138n
Ishurdi, 109 (map), 110 (map)
Islam, 9, 10, 11, 14, 16, 18, 76n, 146–7, 149
Islam, Syed Nazrul, 70, 136
Islamabad, 23, 24, 30, 37, 38, 40, 47, 49, 50, 51, 52, 54, 61, 65, 66, 71, 73, 79, 80, 81, 82, 94, 95, 98, 100, 103, 105, 111, 118 (map), 141, 146, 150, 153, 154, 158, 160
Islamgarh, 117 (map), 121
Itthwal, 119
Izvestia, 70

Jacob, General J. F. R., 143
Jaisalmer, 117 (map), 121
Jalpaiguri, 110 (map), 135
Jamaat-i-Islami, 52, 81, 76n, 90n
Jamalpur, 110 (map), 133, 143
Jammu, 114, 118 (map), 119
Jamshed, Major-General, 132
Jamuna R., 109 (map), 110 (map), 130, 135
Janjua, Major-General Iftikhar Khan, 114
Japan, 126, 127n, 152, 154
Jessore, 34, 35, 51, 102, 104, 109 (map), 130, 133, 134, 135
Jhenida, 109 (map), 132, 133, 134
Jiddah, conference of Muslim countries in, 38
Jinnah, Mohammed Ali, 12
Jordan, 137, 138
Joydebpur, 109 (map), 110 (map), 143
Jullundur, 115 (map)

Kahuta, 116, 118 (map)
Kaliganj, 109 (map), 110 (map), 134
Kalni R., 116
Kamalpur, 101, 109 (map)
Kamurazzaman, A. H. M., 59, 89n, 97
Karachi, 15, 18, 39, 40, 48, 116, 122, 137
Karakoram highway, 49, 96, 114, 151
Karimganj, 135
Kargil, 114, 118 (map)
Kashgar, 49
Kashmir, hijacking incident, 37; December fighting, 112, 113, 114, 115, 116, 118 (map), 119, 129, 137, 149, 151
Kasuri, Mian Mahmoud Ali, 90n

236

INDEX

Kathua, 117 (map), 118 (map)
Keating, Kenneth, 98, 125, 207, 209-11
Kelly, John, 67
Khadilkar, R. K., 46
Khan, Khan Wali, 24, 25
Khem Karan, 117 (map), 120
Khulna, 34, 49, 109 (map), 110 (map), 130, 133, 134
Khruschev, Nikita, 152
Kilgit, 49
Kissinger, Dr Henry, 65, 97, 98, 125, 137, 138, 207-9; *see also* Washington Special Action Group
Kittani, Ismat T., 51, 66
Korea, 157
Kosciusko-Morizet, M., 128
Kosygin, A. N., 21, 39, 40, 69, 70, 85, 87, 89, 153
Kotchandpur, 109 (map), 134
Kotli, 114, 118 (map)
Krishak Praja Samiti (peasants' and tenants' party), 11
Krishak Shramik party, 81
Krishnagar, 109 (map), 133
Kumarkhalighat, 109 (map), 110 (map)
Kurshid, Mohammed, 30
Kurivilla, Admiral E. C., 122
Kushtia, 35, 43, 51, 62, 109 (map), 130, 134
Kusnetsov, Vasily, 139, 160
Kutch, 115, 117 (map), 121

Lahore, 37, 115, 117 (map), 118 (map)
Laird, Melvin, 139
Lakhya R., 109 (map), 110 (map), 142
Laksham, 110 (map), 135
Lal, Air Marshal P. C., 108
Libya, 48
Lok Sabha, 36, 46
London, 54, 93
Longewala, 117 (map), 121
Lahore, 11
Legal Framework Order, 28 March 1970, 23

Madaripur, 109 (map), 110 (map)
Madhumati R., 109 (map), 133, 134
Magura, 109 (map), 133, 134, 135
Malaysia, 38
Malawi, 128
Malik, Dr A. M., 80, 81, 90n
Malik, Adam, 82
Malik, Jacob, 126, 127
Manekshaw, Generals, 108, 143
Masrur, 116
Maulvi Bazar, 109 (map), 110 (map), 133, 134, 135
Maxwell, Neville, 66

Meghalaya, 46, 109 (map), 130, 131, 133, 142
Meghna R., 109 (map), 110 (map), 123, 130, 132, 135, 136, 142
Mendhar, 116, 118 (map)
Menon, K. P. S., 140n
Mianwali, 116
military forces: *ansars*, 34; Bangla Desh forces 94; Bengali Police, 34, 55; East Bengal Rifles, 35, 55; East Pakistan Civil Armed Forces, 132; East Pakistan Rifles, 33, 34, 55; *'Gono' Bahini* (irregulars), 133; Indian Border Security Force, 35, 56, 121; Indian army, 94, 101, 106-11, 131; Indian Eastern Command, 133-4; *Mukti Fauj* (people's army), 56, 57, 67, 75, 76, 78, renamed *Mukti Bahini*, 76; Pakistani army, 35, 94, 103, 106-11, 131; Pakistani Eastern Command, 132-3, 232; Pakistan Special Services Group, 116; *razakars* (East Pakistan), 76, 132; Soviet naval force, 139; *see also Enterprise* taskforce; *Mukti Bahini*
Mirza, Iskander, 18
Monem Khan, Abdul, 90
Montgomery, 117 (map), 120
Mountbatten plan, 13
Moscow, 39, 54, 70, 71, 73, 83, 84-5, 87, 99, 101, 157, 194
Mughal empire, 9
Muhuri, 35, 58
Mujib-ur Rahman, Sheikh: General Secretary of Awami League, 17, 18, 21, 24-31; alleged conspiracy with Indian agents, 21; complaints about rule from Islamabad, 24; and Yahya Khan, 26, 34, 51, 53, 59, 77, 88, 98-9, 148; and Admiral Ahsan, 26; denounces 'reign of terror' at Chittagong and Rangpur, 33; arrest, 33; 'treason', 34-5; reaction to airliner hi-jacking, 37; friend of Begum Aktar Suleman, 52; rumour of death, 57, 77; 'President of Bangla Desh', 59, 78; and Dr Kamal Hussain, 65; announcement of trial, 77, 78, 80, 86, 87; release, 86, 89 93, 96, 103, 124, 160; leader of moderate elements in Awami League, 96, 97, 98-9; and internal forces in Pakistan, 149; *see also* Awami League
Mukti Bahini, 64, 76, 77, 82, 89, 100, 101, 102, 103, 104, 111, 129, 130, 131, 132, 133, 135, 136, 159; *see also* military forces
Multan, 115, 120
Munnewar Tawi R., 118 (map), 119
Murid, 116, 118 (map)

SOUTH ASIAN CRISIS 1971

Musharraff, Khalid, 35
Muslim League, 10, 11, 12, 13, 14, 16, 17, 52, 90, 147; *see also* Council Muslim League, Pakistan Muslim League, Pakistan Convention Muslim League
Muslims, *see* Islam
Muzaffar, Professor 57, 79
Mymensingh, 51, 101, 109 (map), 110 (map), 132, 133, 143

Nagaland, 133
Nagar Parkar, 117 (map), 121
Nagra, Major-General G. S., 143
Nanda, Admiral, 108
Narowal, 117 (map), 118 (map)
Narsingdi, 110 (map), 142
National Awami Party, 18, 24, 25, 57, 79; 'pro-Moscow' Muzaffar group, 57
Natore, 109 (map), 110 (map), 132, 134
Naushera, 118 (map), 119
'Naxalite' (revolutionary peasant) movement, 55
Nazimuddin, Sir Kwajha, 11, 14
Nehru, Jawarhalal, 36
Nepal, 109 (map), 110 (map), 128
Netherlands, 63
New York, 43, 143
Newsweek, 95
Nezam-i-Islami, 52
New York Herald Tribune, 125n, 207–29
New York Times, 125n, 209
Niamatpur, 110 (map)
Niazi, Lieutenant-General Amir Abdullah Khan, 81, 108, 111, 131, 132, 134, 141, 143, 144, 232
Nicaragua, 126
Nixon, Richard M., 42, 43n, 50, 65, 71, 83, 84, 89n, 93, 99n, 125, 140, 141, 153, 154–7
Nizami-i-Islami party, 90n
Noakhali, 55, 109 (map), 130
North-West Frontier Province, 13, 24
Nyachor, 121

Okha, 122
Oman, 128
Osmani, Colonel A. G., 56, 102

Pabna, 35, 109 (map)
Pachagarsh, 35
Padma R., 109 (map), 110 (map), 130, 132, 134, 135
Pakistan Convention Muslim League, 90n
Pakistan Muslim League, 90n
Pakistan People's Party, 21, 23, 24, 90n, 95; *see also* Bhutto, Z. A.
Parbat Ali, 117 (map)

Patgra, 35
Pathankot, 115, 116, 117 (map), 118 (map), 119
Patuakhali, 109 (map), 110 (map)
Peking, 39, 65n, 83, 95, 104, 153, 154, 157
People's Democratic Party, 51, 81, 90n
Persepolis, 88
Peshawar, 108
Pielkhana, 33
Pirganj, 110 (map), 135
Pirzada, General, 25, 108
Podgorny, N. V., 40, 69, 84, 85, 88, 89, 153, 172
Poland, 126, 127, 129
Pompidou, Georges, 38
Poonch, 114, 116, 118 (map)
Pravda, 87, 88
Punjab, 13, 22–3, 24, 114, 115, 116, 117 (map), 118 (map), 121

Radio Bangla Desh, 58
Rahim Khan, Air Marshal, 108
Rahimyar Khan, 117 (map), 121
Raina, Lieutenant-General, 133
Rajasthan, 115, 116, 117 (map), 121, 123
Rajshahi, 34, 35, 51, 109 (map), 110 (map), 130
Rajya Sabha, 36, 45n
Ram, Jagjivan, 59n, 90, 102
Ranian, 117 (map), 120
Rangpur, 33, 51, 109 (map), 110 (map), 130, 132, 133, 134, 135
Rann of Kutch, 115, 121
Ravi R., 114, 115, 117 (map), 118 (map), 120
Rawalpindi, 52, 108
Rawlley, Lieutenant-General, 115, 120
Red Cross, 50
Risalwala, 116
Rodionov, A. A., 73
Rogers, William P., 50, 83, 209
Rumania, 65n, 128
Ryan, General John, 137

Sadat, President, 39
Sadruddin Aga Khan, Prince (UN High Commissioner for Refugees), 51, 61
Saidpur, 34, 35, 110 (map)
Salimullah, Nawab, 10
Samba, 117 (map), 118 (map)
Sargodha, 116
Saudi Arabia, 48, 138n
SEATO, 138
Sehjra, 115, 117 (map), 120
Sen, Samar, 86, 126
Senegal, 128
Shaffiullah, Major, 35

238

INDEX

Shahi, Agha, 67, 73, 86, 126, 128
Shakargarh, 114, 115, 117 (map), 118 (map), 119, 120, 123, 144
Sher, Lieutenant-General Bahadur, 115
Shikarpur, 101, 117 (map)
Shorkot, 116
Sialkot, 114, 117 (map), 118 (map), 119
Sierra Leone, 126, 127n
Sikkim, 130, 140
Siliguri, 109 (map), 130, 133, 134
Simla agreement of 1905, 16
Sind, 13, 24, 115, 117 (map), 121, 123, 137, 144
Singapore, 15, 128
Singh, Major-General Dalbir, 134
Singh, Lieutenant-General K. K., 115
Singh, Lieutenant-General Sagat, 135
Singh, Lieutenant-General Sartaj, 114
Singh, Swaran, 36, 45n, 54, 60, 62, 63, 64n, 70, 71, 86, 87, 88, 96, 124, 128, 129, 141, 191, 192–3
Singkiang, 140
Sisco, Joseph, 137
Somalia, 126, 127
South Vietnam, 139
Soviet Union: Tashkent policy, 39; appeal to Yahya, 40, 88–9, 150; trade agreement with Pakistan, 48–9; and India, 54, 82, 84–5, 87, 103, 106, 111, 113, 124, 139–40, 152–4, 159, 160; influence in India and Pakistan, 54, 69–74, 75, 82–6, 103, 150–7, 159–60, 152; *see also* Indo–Soviet Treaty; and Egypt, 72; and United States, 71, 83–4, 86, 155–6, 159, 160; and United Nations, 83, 99, 103, 123, 124, 126–9, 141; naval forces, 139; and China, 151–3, 155
Spivack, Herbert, 143
Srinagar, 116, 118 (map)
Suadhi, 134
Suez Canal, 152
Suhrawardy, H. S., 11, 13, 14, 17, 18, 21, 52
Suleman, Begum Akhtar, 52, 59
Sulemanke (bridge), 115, 117 (map), 120
Sundarbans, 55
Surma R., 130
surrender, instrument of, 134, (text) 233
Sutlej R., 115, 117 (map), 120
Sweden, 63
Sylhet, 19, 51, 109 (map), 130, 133, 134, 135
Syria, 126

Tangail, 109 (map), 110 (map), 131, 143
Tashkent, 21, 39, 70, 85, 153

Taxila, 49, 96
Thapan, Lieutenant-General M. L., 134
Tikka Khan, Lieutenant-General, 29, 51, 52, 75, 76, 80, 81, 114, 115, 119
Tithwal, 114, 118 (map)
Tripura, 46, 47, 109 (map), 110 (map), 133
Tungi, 110 (map), 143
Tura, 143
Turkey, 38

U Thant, 43, 51, 66, 67, 68, 69, 73, 80, 82, 91, 93, 99, 104, 159, 184–7
Ulster, 161
Umar, Major-General, 25
United Arab Republic, *see* Egypt
United Nations Organization: Charter, 40, 43, 127, 155; and Russia, 40, 73; relief efforts in E. Pakistan, 43, 49, 50, 51, 54, 65, 66–8, 100, 158; High Commission for Refugees, 51, 61; Economic and Social Council (ECOSOC), 60, 61, 63n, 66, 67, 159; Security Council, 65, 68, 73, 74, 82, 104, 116n, 123, 124, 126–9, 141, 159; and India, 71, 103, 125–6, 141, 159; 26th Session, 75, 81; observers, 77, 87, 104; General Assembly, 83, 86; forces, 94; prevention of war, 112–13, 114; reactions to deadlock, 139, 160; evacuation effort, 142; supervision of neutral zone, 143
United States: first statement on crisis, 42, 150; and China, 42–3, 65, 68, 83, 153–7; and United Nations, 43, 67, 126–9, 155; aid to Pakistan, 49–50, 54; arms sales to Pakistan, 50, 61, 63, 106; economic and technical assistance to Pakistan, 63–5; concern for constitutional advance, 79; and Soviet Union, 83–4, 86, 155–6, 159, 160; and Awami League exiles, 97; suspends arms exports to India, 105; supports Pakistan in United Nations, 124–5, 144, 157–9; evacuation of nationals from E. Pakistan, 139; deterioration in relations with India, 159
Urdu language, 9, 14, 17, 18, 34
Uri, 118 (map), 119 (map)
USSR, *see* Soviet Union

Virawah, 117 (map), 121
Vizakhapatnam (harbour), 122

Wakhan strip, 151
Washington, 42, 54, 61, 93, 96, 98, 103, 105, 139, 157

Washington Post, 112
Washington Special Action Group (WSAG), 125n, 136–8, 140, 212–29
West Germany, 63
Westmoreland, General William, 136
Wood, Richard, 49
World Bank, 48, 62, 63, 158

Yahya Khan: policy similar to that of 1954 government, 17; Ayub Khan resigns power to, 22; first decisions as President announced 22–4; head of civil and military powers, 25, 108; 'centre' political views, 26–8; visits Dacca, 27, 30, 32; calls session of National Assembly, 29; visit to E. Pakistan, 30–2; broadcast of 26 March, 34, (text) 168–70; purpose of diplomacy, 37–8; and France, 38; and Russia, 39, 40, 69, 73, 87–9, 97; and China, 39, 40, 41, 65, 95; and U Thant, 43, 47; and United States, 50, 65, 84, 93, 97, 98–9, 104, 159; conciliatory declarations, 51–4, 57, 58, 59, 62, 75, 76; broadcast of 28 June, 52–3, (text) 174–83; position in June, 65–6; and United Nations, 47, 61, 67, 73, 79, 93–4, 127; consultations with political leaders, 77, 79–80; constitutional statements, 81, 144; seeks discussions with India, 82; possible negotiations with Bengali leaders, 83, 84, 93; broadcast of 12 October, 87–8, 90, 91, 100, 101, 159 (text) 199–204; closes Karakoram highway to foreigners, 104–5; declares state of emergency, 104; and 'final war', 112; refusal to release Sheikh Mujib, 124; and Security Council, 141; proposals for new constitution, 144; broadcasts of 16 and 17 December, 144–5; attempt to restore principle of consent, 147; use of military force, 148; pressure of internal forces on, 149; letter from Nikolai Podgorny to, 172; letter from Chou En-lai to, 173
Yaqub, Major-General, 28, 29
Yugoslavia, 128, 161

Zafarwal, 118 (map), 120
Zia, Major, 35, 58